D0857157

ROBERT KENNEDY: THE FINAL YEARS

THIS BOOK IS DEDICATED TO MY PARENTS,
JOSEPH AND ELIZABETH DOOLEY

ROBERT KENNEDY: THE FINAL YEARS

Brian Dooley

St. Martin's Press
New York

ROBERT KENNEDY

St. Martin's Press, Scholarly and Reference Division,
175 Fifth Avenue, New York, N.Y. 10010

First published in the United States of America in 1996

Printed in the United Kingdom

ISBN: 0-312-16130-1
ISBN:

Library of Congress Cataloging-in-Publication Data

Dooley, Brian.
  Robert Kennedy, the final years / Brian Dooley.
    p. cm.
  Includes bibliographical references and index.
  ISBN 0-312-16130-1
  1. Kennedy, Robert F., 1925–1968. 2. Legislators – United States
– Biography. 3. Presidential candidates – United States – Biography.
4. United States. Congress. Senate – Biography. I. Title.
E840.8.K4D66 1996
973.922'092—dc20   96-6489
[B]   CIP

Contents

Preface

If Robert Kennedy had decided to retire from politics in 1964, and not to stand in the New York Senate election that year, he might still be alive. Without his Senate years, Robert Kennedy would probably not have bid for the presidency in 1968, run in the California primary election, or been assassinated in Los Angeles.

It was in the Senate that Robert Kennedy's political development took shape, as he changed from a conservative Democrat in favour of US involvement in Vietnam to a champion of the anti-war movement. Yet despite the importance of this period, his Senate career has been strangely ignored, with studies concentrating on his years as Attorney General (1961–1964) and his 85 days as presidential candidate (16 March–6 June 1968).

What follows is an attempt to fill this gap in a modest way, and to trace Kennedy's political development in the Senate.

It is not intended to be a definitive biography of Robert Kennedy, nor the last word on his career as Senator, but rather an accessible study of a relatively unexplored area of his political development aimed at undergraduates studying the period, and the general reader interested in American politics in the 1960s. It does not, for instance, draw on the RFK Archive held at the John F. Kennedy Library in Massachusetts, and is essentially a synthesis of secondary work, supported by some primary material, including interviews with former Kennedy colleagues. The oral history interviews taped with Robert Kennedy are not fully open, and the vast majority of his papers remain unavailable for research (of the 1,541 linear feet of RFK papers in the JFK Library, over 70 per cent are not available for study). Moreover, many oral history interviews conducted with key Robert Kennedy aides and colleagues remain either fully or partially closed, including those with Senator Eugene McCarthy, Kennedy's Senate colleague and rival for the 1968 Democratic nomination, Kennedy's 1968 presidential campaign manager, Fred Dutton, and

Robert Kennedy aide and biographer Arthur Schlesinger. Where possible, I have conducted interviews with former Kennedy aides and colleagues, including McCarthy, Dutton and Schlesinger. Others interviewed include the late John Bartlow Martin, US Ambassador to the Dominican Republic in the Kennedy Administration, and later advisor to Robert Kennedy; Peter Edelman, a key Kennedy aide in the Senate; Walter Fauntroy, an aide to Martin Luther King and later Representative from Washington DC in Congress; Frank Mankiewicz, Kennedy's press secretary in the Senate; Jules Witcover, political journalist and author of a book on Kennedy's presidential campaign; and Senator George McGovern, Kennedy's Senate colleague and the 1972 Democratic Party nominee.

The book focuses on Kennedy's attempts to forge a new coalition during the mid-60s out of the debris of the old New Deal coalition, and concentrates on his bid to build a new power-base primarily made up of blacks, the poor, the young, those disillusioned with the Vietnam war, and those workers outside the traditional labour union structures. The division of chapters reflects these elements, and the book is divided into sections on Kennedy's involvement with civil rights, industry, the New Left and foreign policy. There are also chapters on his 1968 presidential campaign and his assassination.

The chapter on civil rights, for example, traces Kennedy's ideas on ghetto renewal through private enterprise schemes, his charismatic appeal and his recognition – in some quarters – as a hero of the civil rights movement. The chapters on the New Left and on industry deal with his overtures to American youth, and to workers not part of the American Federation of Labor/Congress of Industrial Organisations (AFL-CIO), notably migrant workers, and his relations with elements of the American business community.

Foreign policy issues were paramount to Kennedy during his Senate years, and Kennedy had said he wanted to become a Senator so he could criticise Lyndon Johnson on foreign policy. He made the initial break with the President eleven weeks after entering Congress (over the Dominican Republic), and foreign policy would shape what was to become the foundation for Kennedy's assault on the Johnson White House. Understanding Kennedy's earlier involvement with foreign policy issues in the John Kennedy administration is crucial to the appreciation of his later opposition to the Vietnam War, as it became the central issue of his Senate career.

The first part of the foreign policy chapter concentrates on those important formative years in the JFK White House. It deals with the roots of his stance on Vietnam, his part in the Cuban missile crisis (to which he referred so often during the 1968 primaries), and his attitude to the Third World. The second part of the chapter traces the progression of these foreign policy ideas during his Senate years, particularly his proposals for Latin American and African development, his ideas on the spread of communism, and, of course, his about-turn on Vietnam.

The chapter on the presidential election cannot hope to offer any definitive answer as to whether Kennedy would have won the nomination, or the November election, but focuses on the appeal Kennedy made to the various strands of his new coalition. The final chapter, on Kennedy's assassination, summarises the latest theories and evidence on Kennedy's death but it, too, does not pretend to present any solution to the question of whether Sirhan Sirhan acted alone, or as part of a conspiracy.

There are several people I would like to thank for their contributions to this book. Richard Maidment and Anthony McGrew of the Open University offered invaluable help with the manuscript. Richard Maidment helped at every stage of the project when it was a thesis, and I am extremely grateful for his advice and encouragement over several years.

Brian Ward at the University of Newcastle upon Tyne also suggested important amendments, especially in the sections dealing with civil rights and Robert Kennedy's charismatic appeal.

I am grateful to Chris Bailey of the University of Keele and John Dumbrell, who acted as Editorial Consultant, for the many important amendments they suggested to the manuscript.

Thanks are also due to Tanya Thorpe for explaining the intricacies of word processing to me, and to Maggie Sadler for help at the LSE Library in London. Also to Oumar Watt in Dakar, Senegal, for assistance with the technical side of the text, and to Thomas Hodges and Mark Toner at the US Cultural Centre in Dakar for help in locating historical references. Thanks too to Alison Dooley for her patient assistance with the index.

Several people have offered advice on the manuscript, and improved it significantly; any errors remaining are entirely my own.

Brian Dooley
October 1994

Introduction

Just before the nomination of Bill Clinton at the 1992 Democratic Convention in New York, a documentary film about Robert Kennedy was shown to delegates in the hall. For twenty minutes the Convention stood silent as Kennedy's image appeared on the giant screen, his words echoing across the decades to a new generation of Democrats hoping for a presidential victory.

The symbolism was clear: Clinton wanted to be associated with Democrats who could win elections. The film portrayed Kennedy as the last great radical, the last legendary Democrat. It featured his glorious presidential campaign of spring 1968 and his untimely and tragic death. The film served to rally Democrats to their new leader and projected Robert Kennedy's image as the spirit and soul of a great liberal tradition. In a tribute to Kennedy's political legacy, the 1968 campaign was presented as a romantic and idealistic quest to end the Vietnam War and restore social justice. Despite Lyndon Johnson's Great Society, despite Jimmy Carter's win in 1976, it was Robert Kennedy's 1968 campaign which many liberals of the 1990s hoped would inspire a revival.

Although Robert Kennedy is probably best remembered today for the 1968 presidential campaign and his years as Attorney General in his brother's administration, his real political legacy was forged in the Senate. Much of the American public first heard of Bobby Kennedy during his prosecution of union management corruption in a Senate committee between 1957 and 1959. He served as the chief prosecutor on the committee and through the televised hearings soon established a reputation for ruthlessness, and for fierce interrogations of witnesses. It was as Senator for New York (from 1965 to his death in 1968) that Kennedy held the only elected office of his life.

Although he was a reluctant Senator (he would, at least originally, have preferred to be Vice-President and he was often impatient with the slow, deliberate nature of the legislative body) his personal history ensured that he would always be more than just the junior member for New York. By 1965 he was already a national politician, and during his three and a half years as Senator he embarked on a remarkable transformation of his political ideas which later reverberated throughout the Democratic Party. His sharp move to the left of his party was so extreme that it produced an almost unique strand of liberalism, personal to Kennedy.

His image now is one of a bona-fide radical who could win elections. His former press secretary Frank Mankiewicz describes him as a 'tough liberal', today almost a contradiction in American political terms.[1] One reporter at the 1960 Democratic Convention noted that 'whenever you see Bobby Kennedy in public with his brother, he looks as though he showed up for a rumble', and his reputation as the White House toughie developed throughout the Kennedy administration.[2] It was Bobby Kennedy who stood firm over the Cuban missile crisis (although not as firm as was originally believed), Bobby Kennedy who sent his deputy to stand eyeball to eyeball with George Wallace at the entrance to the University of Alabama, and Bobby Kennedy who championed the Green Beret counter-insurgency force.[3]

Although Kennedy often dismissed his ruthless reputation, at times he really does appear to have moved with remarkable aggression. During problems with the steel companies in 1962, for instance, Kennedy unleashed the full power of his office against individual steel executives who, the Kennedy administration believed, had betrayed an earlier understanding not to raise prices. 'I had the grand jury', he later recalled. 'We looked over all of them as individuals. We were going to go for broke: their expense accounts and where they'd been and what they'd been doing. I picked up all their records and I told the FBI to interview them all – march into their offices the next day. All of them were subpoenaed for their personal records ... If I started an investigation of you in your community, you're ruined. The FBI coming round and asking all the neighbours: "What do you know?" ... You'd never recover.'[4]

The ruthless image began to fade after the assassination in Dallas, as American television viewers saw Kennedy suffering at his brother's funeral. No softening job by public relations experts was needed for Kennedy's 1964 Senate race, as less than a year before the nation had watched him accompany President Kennedy's coffin to Arlington Cemetery, engulfed by grief and burdened by the responsibility of carrying on his brother's political work. A wave of emotion almost took him to the vice-presidency in 1964, but President Johnson managed to avoid offering it to him by skilful stage management of the 1964 Democratic

Convention, arranging that Kennedy's emotional appearance before the delegates came on the last day of the convention, after the vice-presidential spot had already been given to Hubert Humphrey.[5] The Lyndon Johnson–Robert Kennedy feud simmered throughout Kennedy's Senate career. 'The basic fact is that those two men simply didn't like each other. Everybody has seen when two dogs come into a room together … and there's a low growl from each one. That was the situation between Bobby and Lyndon Johnson', remembered George Reedy, Johnson's Press Secretary.[6] Robert Kennedy had not wanted Johnson to be JFK's running-mate in 1960, and in 1964 described him as 'mean, bitter, vicious – an animal in many ways'.[7] In May 1964 Kennedy decided the vice-presidential option was not a good idea. 'As vice-president, I'm not going to have any influence. [Johnson]'s not going to have to pay any attention to me whatsoever any more,' he told an aide.[8]

Kennedy's election to the Senate came less than twelve months after JFK's assassination, and his campaign had relied on his family name and White House experience. As such, he had not been required to outline a clear manifesto for his plans for New York. Barry Goldwater remarked in 1966 that 'there is a religious fervour building up about this guy that is even stronger than they built up around Jack'.[9] Kennedy was the benefactor of a Weberian 'transferral of charisma' from his dead brother, which gave him considerable room for manoeuvre in developing links with almost any political group he chose.[10]

His immediate and obvious need was to stake out a political base for himself, and although he won New York comfortably, he had relied heavily on assistance from Lyndon Johnson. Kennedy won 55% of the vote to incumbent Senator Kenneth Keating's 45%, and although his winning margin was 719,693 votes, Johnson had carried the state in the presidential election by over 2.7 million.[11]

He recognised the need for a separate power base, independent of Johnson, as early as the summer of 1964, and criticised Johnson's new-look Democratic Party to an aide. 'Lyndon Johnson has explained quite clearly that it's not the Democratic Party any more; it's an all-American party. The businessmen like it. All the people who were opposed to the President [JFK] like it. I don't like it much.'[12]

At the beginning of 1965, Kennedy could have moved in several directions, but chose – whether motivated by acute political cunning or personal preference, and probably both – to outflank rivals to the left of the party like Humphrey and Senator Eugene McCarthy of Minnesota, and claim the most radical wing for himself.

This was not a cold decision he took one morning on entering Congress, but rather a series of responses made to political and international events during 1965 and 1966. It soon became clear, however, that Kennedy had the potential to commandeer the radical element in the Democratic Party and use it as his political base. There were many voters, of course, who would have followed Kennedy whatever position he had taken on Vietnam or the ghettos, but some liberals distrusted Kennedy's new-found radicalism.

He started his attacks on the White House early, criticizing the President's handling of the situation in the Dominican Republic, charging that Johnson had been too heavy-handed on the reformers just because some Communists might have been involved.

The leftward shift accelerated when he broke from the administration in early 1966 over Vietnam and, later that year, on the Alliance for Progress. Other Senate liberals remained more cautious and less aware of the potential of the new political forces emerging in the country. Liberal colleagues in the Senate such as Eugene McCarthy and Walter Mondale of Minnesota, Frank Church of Idaho and George McGovern of South Dakota still approached poverty problems with New Deal remedies, whereas Kennedy was proposing radical programmes to lure private investment into the ghettos, such as his programme for the development of Bedford Stuyvesant in New York City.

Arthur Waskow, a contributing editor to the radical magazine *Ramparts*, described Kennedy at this time as 'a new kind of liberal, in the same way the SDS [Students for a Democratic Society] and SNCC [Students' Non-violent Co-ordinating Committee] are new kinds of radicals'.[13] Blacks, the young, the anti-Vietnam War movement and what SDS President Tom Hayden called 'the unorganised poor' were the cornerstones of Kennedy's new coalition.[14] Although Kennedy was never fully cognisant of how far this alternative coalition might go, or even what it would look like, in 1967 and 1968 he was at least aware that it had serious political potential.

The study of Kennedy's Senate career which follows aims to trace his attempt at moulding an alternative power coalition. He responded early to the new political forces of the mid-1960s, notably the black and youth movements. However, the political forces centred around women's issues and those concentrating on health and ecological concerns had yet to take off in a significant way by 1968, and he never enjoyed the support those groups later provided to Democratic candidates.

Although the National Organization for Women (NOW) was formed in 1966, its relations with the rest of the left were strained at this time, as mainstream liberalism initially regarded it as a threat. The New Left, whose radicalism appealed to Kennedy, was also hostile. Women drawing attention to women's liberation issues at an SDS convention in 1966 'were pelted with tomatoes and thrown out of the convention'.[15] The women's liberation movement, however, had not mustered enough political muscle in the mid-1960s for Kennedy to have regarded it as essential to his coalition, and the first feminist activity to obtain front-page coverage (the disruption of a 'Miss America' beauty contest) did not happen until September 1968, four months after Kennedy's death.

Nevertheless, Kennedy reached towards some of the emerging forces before any other national figure realized their significance. He tried to understand how they could be put together to make a powerful national constituency which he could lead. At times, however, he could be ridiculously off target in his search for blocks to build the new framework. In reaching out to the youth movement, he invited 'beat' poet Allen Ginsberg to his Senate office for a political talk in early 1968. Ginsberg described how he treated Kennedy to a monologue on the joys of drugs but was finally interrupted by the Senator. 'He wanted to know the relationship between the flower-power people or the hip-generation people and the Black Power leaders. He wanted to know whether there was any kind of political relationship or any political muscle behind such a coalition. I said I had turned onto grass a number of times in Nashville with Stokely Carmichael. But it didn't extend to any formal political alliance ...'[16]

Kennedy realized there was something in the anti-war demonstrations and the hippie counter-culture, and tried to grasp the dimensions of its political muscle.[17] Occasionally, however, it would appear that hard political considerations were not paramount, and he championed unpopular causes like Indian and Eskimo rights. Kennedy assigned a staff member to work with Indian tribes in New York, and in 1967 persuaded the Senate to establish a subcommittee to conduct a three-year study of Indian education.[18]

'In his first trip to the Fort Hall reservation in Idaho, he asked where the library was,' recalled an aide: 'He was shown a large closet with about 500 books. "Are there any books about Indians here?" he asked. Rustling through, one was found – "Captive of the Delawares." The cover picture showed a blond boy being scalped.'[19] In 1966, there were only about 600,000 Indians left in the whole of the US. 'There were no votes among Indians,' said one of Kennedy's staff, 'but Kennedy had made a commitment [to their cause] and was determined to carry it out.'[20]

Kennedy had planned to take the subcommittee to Alaska in the spring of 1968 to examine the facilities for Eskimo education, but the trip was cancelled because of the assassination of Martin Luther King.[21]

Other forays into 'unpopular' areas (i.e. those without obvious political capital) included siding with Cesar Chavez and the grape-pickers against some West Coast fruit companies. In 1964, Chavez formed the Farm Workers Association, which taught newly-arrived Mexican-American migrants in California to read English, buy goods and manage their money. Chavez organised several strikes on the large grape farms in the following years to demand recognition for his association.[22] 'Noone was taking any notice of what we were doing,' said Chavez. 'Then Robert Kennedy came out to see us. He joined our picket lines. That was unheard of. Once he took an interest, lots of other people started coming, offering help.'[23]

Even so, this identification with politically weak groups can also be seen as a part of Kennedy's effort to break away from the traditional labour power blocks. Kennedy's problems with some organized labour dated back to his prosecution of union leaders in the previous decade.

Nevertheless, he needed to show he was on the workers' side if he were to become the new radical hope, and opportunities such as links with Chavez – whose union was not part of the old-established network – offered the opportunity to identify with strikers while avoiding association with big-time unionism. Kennedy admirer Jack Newfield described Kennedy 'not as anti-union, but un-union', a phrase perfectly inoffensive to all those Kennedy was trying to woo.[24]

However, this is not to suggest that Kennedy's Senate career was simply one long bid for the 1968 presidential election. By identifying himself with the new political forces he was broadening his political base and making himself a more significant national figure. This constituency could not only be used for the presidential campaign, but also would secure his power base in New York, would make him more attractive as a vice-presidential candidate for the extra weight he could bring to the ticket (an outside possibility he considered seriously until early 1967), and would enable him to make more progress on the issues in which he believed.

These considerations motivated the search for a new coalition and dictated the policy directions Kennedy took while in the Senate. Although they were not incompatible, from time to time one consideration would take priority over the others. For example, the decision to enter the 1968 election obviously meant that most of his energies went into the primaries, and not on his New York constituents.

Moreover, Kennedy's search for a new coalition did not mean he burned his bridges with the old. His political training, above all, had been in managing successful campaigns for John Kennedy. He had worked in JFK's 1946 campaign for Congress, managed JFK's bid for the Senate in 1952, and masterminded his brother's 1960 victory over Richard Nixon. He was an expert on the various power blocks which controlled the Democratic Party, and knew better than most what was required to run a successful campaign for the presidency.

Some parts of the old Democratic coalition were still extremely powerful in 1968 and, of course, it would have been virtually impossible for Kennedy to have become the party's nominee without the blessing of dozens of political professionals, the most powerful of whom was Richard Daley, the Mayor of Chicago. Daley controlled the party machine in Illinois and was seen as a barometer for the traditional elements of the Democratic Party nationwide. Throughout 1968, Kennedy was keen to impress Mayor Daley with his electability. If Daley gave his blessing to Kennedy's candidacy, party officials all over the country would follow suit.

Although the old boss structures had partially been undermined by 1968, the new politics had not yet fully taken over. Only fourteen states held presidential primaries, for example, which principally served as 'beauty contests' for powerful party chieftains to see how attractive a candidate was to the electorate. Throughout his Senate career Kennedy was careful to remain in favour with party hacks who represented the remnants of the old order.

Additionally, Kennedy's problem during this time of political flux was that no one knew exactly how powerful any particular movement really was. The Vietnam War remained popular during Kennedy's Senate career, although he did detect that its appeal was fading.[25] Also, there was little way of knowing how the country would react at election time to the rioting which characterized black frustration during the mid-1960s.

To accommodate the variables, Kennedy's approach appears to have been one of 'options open'. No door was shut, no group left behind, no political leader offended unless it was absolutely necessary. This, of course, was basic political sense, but it is remarkable that Kennedy managed to keep so many plates spinning, as it were, while other national figures were forced to identify with one side of an issue or the other.

The best example is his stance on the Vietnam War.[26] Kennedy could oppose US involvement in the war, but – unlike many other politicians – he could at the same time easily evade the charges of being 'soft on Communism' because of his earlier record as Attorney General. Similarly, while Kennedy was regarded as sympathetic to the black struggle, he had also been the chief law-enforcement officer in the country for four years, as he regularly reminded voters during the Indiana primary of 1968.

Kennedy's personal history made his political position highly unusual – he did not enter the Senate with the same problems of issue identification which beset his colleagues, and he had a much freer role in developing his policy than most other senators. 'I'd not just be a Senator,' he said in the summer of 1964, 'I'd be the Senator from New York. And I'm head of the Kennedy wing of the Democratic Party.'[27]

As such, he was able to make huge leaps in policy direction in a very short space of time. In 1956 he had persuaded segregationist Alabama Governor George Wallace to back John Kennedy's bid for the vice-presidential nomination. By 1966 he was trying to identify himself with the emerging black consciousness movement. In 1963 he was publicly an ardent proponent of the war against the Communists in Vietnam, but by 1966 he appeared to be advocating a coalition government there.

In fairness, however, it should be pointed out that he had privately voiced qualms about the war as early as 6 September 1963. Pentagon minutes of a confidential National Security Council (NSC) meeting (published only after Kennedy's death) report him as reasoning that if the war was unwinnable by any foreseeable South Vietnamese regime it was time to get out of Vietnam.[28] During the 6 September meeting, Kennedy also advocated giving US Ambassador to Saigon Henry Cabot Lodge 'the necessary power to sort things out if Diem is the problem' (i.e. replace the Ngo Dinh Diem regime). Kennedy was not alone in rapid policy development during these years, of course, but his personal history, and his capacity to recognize new political movements at an early stage, make his career in the Senate a fascinating case study of a liberal politician.

On Kennedy's funeral train, psychiatrist Dr Leonard Duhl noted that the crowd of Kennedy supporters included 'oddballs ... You really began to see what a floating crap game it was. Bobby essentially began to evolve a form of coalition politics. Now, I don't think he understood all of this verbally, and he couldn't put it together. But yet, he was sensing this; so many people on the train could not understand why everybody else was there; they didn't understand this floating crap game in which he was the centre and connecting link, and that all the other players were not like themselves.'[29]

Whether Kennedy had put enough of this new coalition together in 1968 will never be known. George McGovern laid claim to it in 1972, but without ultimate success. Ted Kennedy could not resurrect it powerfully enough in 1980 either, and perhaps it would never have been strong enough to take Robert Kennedy to the presidency. Newfield believes that Kennedy 'was trying to test a revisionist liberalism before there was a party or coalition to sustain it'.[30] Although the coalition might have been brought together long enough to have propelled Kennedy to the presidency, it would have relied on combining old Democratic Party forces with elements of the new politics. Political commentator Tom Wicker did not believe that Kennedy's coalition was feasible in the long term:

> At one and the same time, he wanted to have Mayor Daley's support and the support of the college students. The two are incompatible in the long run. I'm not trying to say that you could not, by force of personality and personal example – as Robert Kennedy did – have uneasily allied them for a time. I'm trying to say that in the long run, it isn't a feasible alliance, and it isn't an alliance that's going to hold political power.[31]

Quite how much this new liberalism relied on Kennedy's own personality should also be addressed: his brother Ted, for instance, ran for the presidency in 1980 on issues and with an organization very similar to his, but without the same success (although, significantly, Ted Kennedy's bid for the 1980 nomination did prove useful in redefining the party's basic principles, identifying employment as the primary issue, for example).

Robert Kennedy's alternative power base died with him in Los Angeles in June 1968. Although many candidates since have attempted to resurrect the Robert Kennedy coalition, none can properly be regarded as having succeeded.

Chapter One

Kennedy, Poverty and Civil Rights

'Too white to be all right ...' – Eldridge Cleaver of RFK[1]

Race was not the primary issue in the election campaign of 1960. John Kennedy did invoke Abraham Lincoln during a television debate with Richard Nixon, but only to illuminate a point he was making about the Cold War and not to highlight the candidates' differences in racial policies.[2]

Although John Kennedy won a large percentage of the black vote in the election (68%), his identification with the racial issue probably owed as much to the highly publicized intervention he made during the campaign on behalf of the jailed Martin Luther King as to his rather unspectacular voting record on civil rights.[3]

If John Kennedy's political career was not especially identified with the racial issue by 1960, his brother's involvement in the 'negro question' had almost been non-existent. His main political experience had been on various Senate committees, notably during the McCarthy hearings and on the McClellan racketeering committee, where he had earned a reputation as a tough interrogator during investigations into corruption in unions.[4] By the time of his formal appointment as Attorney General in 1961, his political experience was largely confined to these years as a member of the Congressional staff and to managing John Kennedy's bid for the 1956 vice-presidential nomination and the successful run at the presidency in 1960.

Robert Kennedy admitted to Harris Wofford (later White House Special Assistant on Civil Rights) in 1960: 'We really don't know much about this whole thing ... I haven't known many negroes in my life ... It's up to you. Tell us where we are and go to it.'[5] Liberals though they were, at the time of winning power the Kennedys could not even claim that some of their best friends were black. 'I won't say I stayed awake at

21

nights worrying about civil rights before I became Attorney General'
Robert Kennedy later remembered.[6]

During his time in the White House, Robert Kennedy's position as
head of the Justice Department meant that his efforts in the field were
concentrated on enforcing the law on matters such as desegregation and
voting rights rather than analysing social conditions in the inner cities.
Although poverty was a major problem for blacks at the time, it was not
a legal issue and so did not come in for special scrutiny by the Attorney
General's office, except where it overlapped with issues such as drugs or
gun control.

During his years in the Justice Department, Kennedy successfully
petitioned the Interstate Commerce Commission to desegregate bus
terminals in interstate travel facilities in accordance with the Supreme
Court's 1960 Boynton decision.[7] He arranged for the protection of
Freedom Riders at Montgomery, Alabama, where federal marshalls held
back a violent mob surrounding the First Avenue Baptist Church. He
supported the establishment of the Voter Education Project to promote
black voter registration and filed numerous suits to prevent denial of the
franchise on racial grounds. In May 1963, he sent Assistant Attorney
General Burke Marshall to Birmingham to mediate between the city's
white leadership and the civil rights movement, and later that year
dispatched his assistant, Nicholas Katzenbach, to confront Alabama Governor George Wallace in the doorway of the University of Alabama and
secure the safe admittance of two black students to the university.[8]

However, he had also permitted wire taps to be placed on the
telephones of Martin Luther King and King's aide Stanley Levison.[9]
When the existence of the taps became known, Kennedy experienced
considerable animosity from black leaders, although this hostility was
not generally shared by the majority of blacks, who increasingly came to
regard him as a hero.

In the main, Attorney General Kennedy preferred to confine the racial
issue to one of voting and encouraged black leaders to press for voting
rights as it placed them clearly on the side of law enforcement and was
less of an immediate threat to whites than the desegregation of public
amenities. The moves to desegregate the bus terminals came only after
well-organized and highly publicized campaigns by non-governmental
civil rights activists threatened to embarrass the administration. Robert
Kennedy had criticized the Freedom Riders for generating bad publicity
which weakened his brother's hand at a meeting with Khrushchev, and
during the desegregation of the universities at Alabama and Mississippi

he was keen to settle the controversy quickly and without undue embarrassment to local politicians.[10] However, Kennedy did become increasingly aware that the issue was not confined to voting power, partly as a result of his chairing of the administration's committee on delinquents, which included the Secretary of Health, Education and Welfare (HEW). Congress had also passed the Juvenile Delinquency Act, which authorized expenditure of $30 million over three years to test new approaches to delinquency prevention and control.

Delinquency was regarded by Robert Kennedy and others in the White House as a disease which could be cured if sufficient federal resources were made available. In a speech entitled 'Juvenile Delinquency: An Ounce of Prevention', delivered in New York in 1962, the Attorney General noted how one particular delinquent was 'doing well in the prison high school, and making rapid progress ... because of his dramatic response to treatment'.[11]

This type of response, which relied heavily on the animal laboratory approach to urban problems, permeated progressive opinion. Much liberal thinking on civil rights and poverty at this time was influenced by works such as Gunnar Myrdal's *An American Dilemma*, perhaps the standard exposition of post-war liberal orthodoxy.[12] In 1944 Myrdal cited white prejudice and racism as the roots of black disadvantage and defined the issue in moral terms. He proposed that discrimination was something which ought to be fought in the best traditions of American democratic ideals. He suggested that the worst excesses of inequality could be fought by vigorous and committed federal action, and his analysis provided the foundation for liberal reformers through the 1950s and 1960s. Robert Kennedy, through his ideas for private enterprise in urban renewal, would later develop some of Myrdal's earlier assumptions.

By the early 1960s, however, poverty was only beginning to appear on the political agenda as a serious issue. Michael Harrington's 1962 book *The Other America* had a great impact on popular and governmental appreciation of poverty, and urban centres were regarded as valid testing-grounds for many pet theories.[13] An explosion in the popularity of social sciences, coupled with a dramatic increase in available government funds, saw sociologists produce a substantial amount of data on ghettos. By 1966 federal funding for social science research, which had stood at $4 million ten years earlier, had increased to $44 million.[14]

The staff of the delinquency committee (often referred to as the HEW committee after the initials of the relevant government department) included Richard Boone of the Ford Foundation. Boone had worked as a community organiser in Chicago and at the time the Ford Foundation was among those trying out the idea of community partici- pation in poverty programmes. Robert Kennedy's assistant David Hackett sought out the ideas of the institution's experts on urban poverty.[15]

Local involvement in poverty legislation, or Community Action Programmes (CAPs), as it became known, was formally introduced to the federal government through the HEW committee, and to the rest of the country through the War on Poverty legislation. The April 1965 Elementary and Secondary School Act granted $1.3 billion to school districts on the basis of the number of needy children, and the Omnibus Housing Act of October the same year established a new programme of rent supplements to low-income families.[16]

Within the Kennedy administration the notion of CAP remained largely a sociological theory, the reality of which was confined to a moderately successful experiment in the Lower East Side of New York. The New York experiment was funded by the Ford Foundation and the HEW committee and was essentially a pilot project, although the money later made available by the War on Poverty legislation meant that the CAP idea became nationwide in scope.

However, as Daniel Patrick Moynihan (Assistant Secretary of Labor in the Kennedy administration, Assistant for Urban affairs under Richard Nixon and later Senator for New York) pointed out, 'the poor were put on the agenda by reformers, not by themselves'.[17] Moynihan suggested that because of the steady economic growth of the period (GNP grew in constant dollar terms from $503 billion in 1960 to $807 billion in 1967) the economy needed large injections of spending to stay buoyant, and explained the theory of fiscal drag, which stated that unless the revenue increment of the government was immediately returned to the economy it would have a depressing effect. 'This, in a word, was money you had to spend in order to get', noted Moynihan.[18]

There was no shortage of ideas about where the money should be spent, and funds were available for the alleviation of urban poverty if appropriate methods were approved by the government. The HEW committee was enthusiastic about CAPs, and the Bureau of the Budget also believed they offered greater scope to monitor what was happening on the ground and preferred the CAP ideas on spending to those where funds were tumbled about in a massive bureaucracy.[19]

However, the assassination of President Kennedy in November 1963 affected the progress and development of the CAP plan. President Kennedy's death had many ramifications, including that of putting considerable pressure on the new President to produce a legislative record of his own on which to campaign in the 1964 election. Johnson decided that such a package, aimed at the problem of poverty, offered the best potential in terms of short-term gains.

President Johnson had less than a year in which to make an impact, and so quick, high-profile returns were emphasized in the legislation he proposed, including provisions in the Economic Opportunity Act (passed on August 20, 1964) for work-training and work-study programmes, a Jobs Corps, and small business incentives. Johnson recalled the frantic pace of those early months in office in his memoirs. '[Sargent] Shriver took over directorship of the poverty program on 1 February 1964. I told him he would have to work fast. Not only did I want to propel a program through the Congress immediately but I wanted to produce visible results ... Only six weeks after the task force had first assembled, the program was ready to go. On 16 March I approved it and sent it to Congress.'[20]

Many of the proposals, which became known as the War on Poverty, were produced in a hurry. Much of the programme was rushed and poorly researched. The CAP idea, although still popular with the Council of Economic Advisers (CEA), lost some of its attraction when the new administration realized that it was a medium-term project, taking several years to show benefits.[21] Moreover, it was regarded by many as a Kennedy idea, championed by the late President's HEW committee.

According to Moynihan, when Johnson heard that the CAP would not start to work before the 1964 election, as under Shriver's proposal each project would be given twelve months to make a formal application for funds, the President lost interest in the plans. Instead, provisions which promised quicker results were concentrated on by the White House, including employment programmes for the elderly, loans for college students and lighting provisions for schools.

Although there is no reason to believe that Johnson was against the idea in principle, the CAP plan clearly did not serve his immediate purposes, and had Robert Kennedy not lobbied for it so vigorously it might not have been included in the Economic Opportunity Act of 1964 at all. In the Congressional hearings on the legislative package, Robert Kennedy was the only administration official to refer to the HEW committee/ Ford Foundation idea of 'maximum feasible participation' by the poor.[22] The rest of the debate on Johnson's Economic Opportunity Act centred on funding for parochial schools and whether the measures would be seen to be working by the November election. Years later, when much of the programme was regarded as failure, Moynihan wrote: 'Congress ... wanted action without too much forethought, preparation, planning, negotiating, agreeing, staging. That is what it got.'[23]

The War on Poverty dominated the political agenda until it was over-taken by Vietnam. Many blamed the war for its downfall, claiming that the funds for domestic legislation went to pay for weapons in Asia, and believed that without the foreign war more resources would have been available for America's cities. It did have its successes, however, and some poor people undoubtedly benefited from its programmes, but as the decade wore on it became clear that the CAP idea, although theoretically a good one, was not working. In 1965, for example, there were 16 million households with income below the poverty line. Over two-thirds received some assistance from government programmes, lifting 4.7 million above the poverty line, but a hard-core underclass remained untouched.[24]

By 1965 Robert Kennedy's immediate concerns had shifted from those of federal law enforcement to provisions for his New York constituents, and to the development of a national following which might offer him the chance to return to the White House as President. Already associated with the idea of 'maximum feasible participation' by the poor, Kennedy never fully abandoned it. Later in his Senate career he refined it, advocating a much greater role for private enterprise. By the time of Kennedy's death, 'Community action was an idea that came more and more to be associated with Robert Kennedy, even as he grew further from the centers of power in Washington where ... its official fate was determined', wrote Moynihan in 1969.[25]

Apart from Vietnam, Kennedy's major differences with the centres of power in Washington during the period from 1964 to 1968 focused on the urban crisis and the best ways to move forward in fighting poverty. The CAP, like Robert Kennedy, soon spun out of White House control and in time both became symbolic of how out of touch the adminis-tration was with the problem of poverty.

Those on the HEW committee who had conceived of 'maximum feasible participation' were probably as surprised as everybody else at what they had created. In fact, had Kennedy been told in 1964 how radical some of the projects would become, he might not have endorsed them, but as his political development progressed in the Senate he called for their extension and personally helped develop a CAP in New York City (see below).

Problems with community action were largely rooted in gaps in perception between poor communities and Washington. Both wanted the alleviation of poverty, but neither knew how best to bring it about. Moynihan, an early critic of the plans, recalled: 'At that time [1964] I began to feel that official Washington had an entirely different, almost antithetical, view of the style and function of "community action" from that of its proponents in the field, and that the intermediaries who had transmitted the idea were either unaware of this discrepancy, or if not aware not perhaps entirely candid about it.'[26]

Those in Washington who had first proposed the idea of the CAP (including Kennedy) had intended that it should be a tool of integration. However, peaceful integration was often the last thing wanted by some of those Washington ended up funding. For instance, Bobby Seale, later to become a Black Panther official, was on the CAP payroll in Oakland in 1966. He remembered, in an essay called *Using the Poverty Program*, how he used the money to raise black consciousness.[27]

'One of the things that hurt the poverty program was that they were always trying to do things by pulling that authoritarian stuff. They were citing the Marquis of Queensberry's rules and stuff like that ... Most of the brothers were from the streets. They wanted to be slick, they wanted to be pimps', said Seale.[28]

Instead of increasing respect for the government, the War on Poverty was often regarded as tokenism by many in the inner cities. 'We don't want a war on poverty,' said Black Panther Eldridge Cleaver. 'What we want is a war on the rich.'[29] Funding for local groups also coincided with the rise of black separatism in many urban centres, which attacked conventional ideas of integration and so worked against the original aims of the HEW committee and the Economic Opportunity Act. Some officials in Washington must have thought they had created a monster.

When the CAP plan was up and running in August 1965, Jack Conway became chairman. A radical union leader who had been working at the AFL-CIO headquarters in Washington, he expanded the idea of 'maximum feasible participation' to its maximum feasible limits. He advocated grass-roots action, newsletters, local political leaders, the poor 'forming their own institutions'.[30] Adam Yarmolinsky, Shriver's former deputy at the Office of Economic Opportunity, which was to supervise CAP projects, recounted how those who had devised the plan of local input had 'no intention of getting the poor to think of themselves as a political force. It did not occur to us, and it did not occur to any of the highly professional politicians we consulted.'[31]

'The government simply didn't know what it was doing,' confessed Moynihan.[32] Previous generations of ethnic groups had managed to use the local political system to their advantage, and many cities had been divided up and run according to local ethnic representation. The Irish and Italians had carved up much of New York, for example, and had run the city's politics for generations. Urban blacks in the 1960s had no such strong tradition to draw on, however, and had never controlled cities the way other ethnic groups had in the past.

The Kerner Commission, set up by the President in the wake of the 1967 riots to investigate the urban problem, found that every riot studied started with a grievance against the local City Hall, from which the local black community felt alienated. 'It is plain that the negro ghetto resident feels deeply that he is not represented fairly and adequately under the arrangements which prevail in many cities,' noted the Commission.[33]

However, by the mid-1960s, it was rather late to turn back the clock on the New Deal, or even on the CAP idea, which despite advocating community participation envisaged it on a federal to street level, which often bypassed the local political machinery. Moreover, the question of jobs had not been adequately considered. Little planning seems to have gone into how employment programmes should be set up, what sort of jobs were appropriate, and who should pay for them. A company set up in the Watts district of Los Angeles with federal help in 1966, clearly prompted by riots in the city a year before, 'was formed in such a hurry that it incorporated and hired a black president and general manager before anyone decided what it would produce'.[34] Eventually the company was awarded a contract from the Defense Department to make military tents, and was saved by the expansion of the war in Vietnam and a greater demand for tents.

Kennedy's main criticism of the War on Poverty focused on the dependence on contracts financed by federal money to create employment in the ghetto, and he proposed a greater involvement of the private sector in job-creation schemes. According to War on Poverty historian John C. Donovan, Kennedy 'was perhaps the most outspoken of all Senate liberals in his criticisms of the administration's budgetary policy.'[35] A journalist covering the Senate committee on poverty reported that Kennedy opened one session 'denouncing our whole system of relief as an assault on human dignity'.[36]

Kennedy's plans represented a significant break with the Johnson administration and proved sufficiently different from traditional methods of fighting poverty for him to convince many voters in the 1968 presidential primaries (not least blacks) that he was offering something genuinely new in dealing with urban unrest. This departure was based mostly on his Urban Employment and Urban Housing & Development Bills of 1967 which sought to finance metropolitan area planning and provide land-development mortgage insurance to rehabilitate ghettos with use of local labour, and on his record in helping to rejuvenate the Bedford Stuyvesant ghetto with funds from the private sector.

'No welfare system can take the place of a serious programme of employment and economic development in the ghetto', he declared.[37] Under Kennedy's proposals the economic encouragement to private investors would take the shape of lucrative tax breaks and was intended to involve the local municipality. Under the legislation for employment, for example, he suggested that a business wishing to locate in a low-income area would have to gain approval from the municipality and from the residents of the area itself. It would be required to hire a minimum of twenty people, two-thirds of whom would be either poverty-area residents or low-income individuals. In return for participating, a business would be offered a 10% credit on machinery and equipment (an increase of 3% of what was permitted at the time), a 7% credit on costs of constructing a facility of leasing space (none was offered at the time) and a 25% subsidy towards salaries paid to workers hired to meet the requirements of the bill (no help was given at the time). Other methods had been tried in an attempt to attract industry to the ghetto, and Kennedy warned big business that, if conditions in the inner cities did not improve, the long-term risks to capitalism were substantial.[38]

However, this approach appeared to have little impact on those executives who were more interested in short-term economic gains than the larger threat to the fabric of society which might destroy their company in a generation or two. The tax-break scheme designed to encourage business into the ghetto was an important ideological departure from previous proposals, including some Kennedy had sponsored.

In his first year as Senator, he had joined with other orthodox liberals such as Walter Mondale, Eugene McCarthy and George McGovern in sponsoring a bill 'to provide grants for public works ... to alleviate conditions of substantial and persistent unemployment' and he co-sponsored a bill to set up a Department of Housing and Urban Development.[39] In January 1966 he supported a proposal in the Senate that a series of 'new towns' be established outside the most deprived cities, where the residents – at least 15% of whom would be black – could afford to pay for their accommodation through a series of federal subsidies disbursed by the new government department.[40] The proposal also sought to provide money to bus inner-city blacks to schools in these new towns and so force the pace of integration.

His 1967 ideas on attracting business money were a good deal more imaginative than his previous efforts, and he also began to appreciate what local participation might entail. 'Community action is going to be directed against the establishment. That means it is going to be directed against us,' he noted.[41] His shift in emphasis on funding proved even more significant. 'The lack of private enterprise participation is the principal cause of our failure to solve the problem of employment in urban poverty areas,' he declared in 1967.[42]

The federal single-weapon approach had not been successful in tackling the problem of providing suitable housing, Kennedy suggested. Of federal efforts at improving the situation he said: 'In its 30 years of operation, the public housing program has completed only 639,000 units ... [and while] the building of luxury housing in the city has been assisted by favorable treatment in the Internal Revenue Code ... similar assistance has not been available for low-cost housing in the slums.'[43]

Through a series of tax incentives to businesses, including home building loans set at 2%, Kennedy wanted to 'produce two- and three-bedroom units that will rent for under $100 a month'.[44] To involve the private sector was not Kennedy's idea, and not a particularly new one. The private sector had played a major part in the development of America, as Kennedy himself was not slow to point out: 'Throughout the Nineteenth Century, the government induced the building of railroads, including the great transcontinental railroads, by offering liberal grants of land on either side of the right-of-way; the railroads sold this land to help repay their investment.'[45]

Kennedy's proposals of 1967, which drew on traditional Republican principles of private funding, together with his experience on the HEW committee and his representation of New York in the Senate, were taken up by others, including the Kerner Commission and, to some extent, the Johnson administration. In his State of the Union address to Congress in January 1967 the President called for 'a new partnership between government and private industry to train and to hire the hard-core unemployed persons'.[46]

Nevertheless, what the President had in mind was markedly different from the Kennedy proposals, which regarded private business involvement as a long-term prospect, with the major corporations of America investing generations of resources into the cities. By 1968 sociologist Kenneth B. Clark agreed that 'business and industry are our last hope'.[47]

In a curious change of direction for radical liberals at the time, it was those on the left of some progressive movements who were championing free enterprise, while the moderates often stuck by the old approach.

The discussion was not a new one, and the federal/local dichotomy had shaped the American Constitution, its party system and its Civil War. However, for the first time in several generations, it surfaced on the left of the Democratic Party, which hitherto had been bound by a consensus on federal intervention, as realized in the shape of the New Deal.

By the mid-1960s, as the New Deal electoral coalition began to disintegrate completely, so too did its philosophy of central government funding. Kennedy, despite his ties to the old school, was among the first on the left to call for its replacement. The debate was also being aired in fora other than the Democratic Party. Martin Luther King aide Andrew Young recalls how King was 'quite rough on Jesse [Jackson]' for putting too much emphasis on the private sector in improving conditions in ghettos.[48]

King, according to Young, insisted that 'jobs would finally have to be provided by the public sector rather than the private sector, and that [Operation Breadbasket] was essentially a private sector program'.[49] Operation Breadbasket was a food relief programme for low-income urban areas. After King's death, when Jackson encountered less resistance to his private enterprise proposals, the thrust of Breadbasket shifted from employment to black capitalism. 'Jackson sought to induce the mighty corporations to buy from, bank with, and invest in black-owned businesses. Blacks should develop their own "private economy" he insisted; they needed a "capital base in the black community."'[50] Apart from the ideological attraction to Kennedy in pioneering a new, radical thrust in urban policy, there was also the question of cost.

With the Vietnam War threatening to go on indefinitely, the federal government was not capable of keeping the promises of the earlier years, when money had apparently been no object in the relief of poverty. *Stone's Weekly* noted in April 1966 that 'although 650 CAPs are now in operation, barely 10% of the nation's poor have been reached. In spite of this, the OEO [Office of Economic Opportunity] has recommended that program development funds ... be cut from $18m. to $6m.'[51]

Civil rights leaders, including Walter Fauntroy and Andrew Young, met Kennedy that year and proposed a domestic Marshall Plan to 'solve poverty', which would cost $100 billion. He told them that with the war in Vietnam costing $2 billion a month no such figure was likely to be appropriated in the near future. 'If the Vietnam war ends, maybe in five years we can think in those terms,' he said.[52]

Part of the credibility of Kennedy's private enterprise proposals was staked on the success of his experiment at Bedford Stuyvesant, an especially poor ghetto in New York. The project was considered by Kennedy to be a prototype for community rehabilitation, and thanks largely to his personal involvement and contacts it flourished in its first years.

By 1968 a community hall was being successfully rebuilt, over 300 homes had been renovated, IBM was planning to create 300 jobs in the area and several local businesses were expanding. Eighty banks and insurance companies agreed to offer conventional-rate mortgages guaranteed by the Federal Housing Administration. *Newsweek* described the project as 'the most sweeping and comprehensive rehabilitation effort ever brought to bear on a single American community'.[53]

The project succeeded where others failed partly because it had been properly worked out in advance: partly because it was paid for with injections of cash from Kennedy's contacts in the private sector, including money from the Ford Foundation, the Taconic Foundation and the Astor Foundation, which gave the project a certain dynamism that earlier government initiatives had lacked, and partly because Kennedy's personal involvement ensured it enjoyed a status which was missing from lesser-known projects.[54] Compared with other schemes of its kind, for example one set up in the Roxbury area of Boston, the Bedford Stuyvesant project was well thought out and properly planned.

In March 1968 EG&G, a major nuclear research corporation, opened a metal fabricating plant in Roxbury, and a *Newsweek* study of business in the ghetto compared its success with that of Kennedy's New York scheme.[55] Not only was EG&G inexperienced in light metal fabrication, but it proceeded to hire a group of disadvantaged workers and four black managers, all of whom were totally unfamiliar with such operations. EG&G had little internal demand for such metal products, and so outside markets had to be cultivated, which the company found almost impossible to find. The inexperience of the workers and managers meant that overheads ran at about three times wages – whereas under normal conditions they would be only about twice as much. Despite a $575,000 training grant from the Labor Department, the plant lost $75,000 in 1968 and was forced to make two of its four black managers redundant.[56]

The Watts-based company mentioned earlier, which was saved only by Defense Department contracts, had encountered similar problems, as it found its training costs to be nearer $5,000 per worker than the $1,300 provided by the Labor Department. Two years after its inception, one of its executives reported: 'There was a lot of flag waving in the beginning, but when the hurrahs died down, we were caught in the middle of it.'[57]

IBM's involvement in Bedford Stuyvesant, on the other hand, is still prospering today. Beginning operations in July 1968, the plant originally produced computer cables for IBM, but this proved unprofitable. It gradually shifted to producing power supplies, which it was able to do at less than outside vendor costs (though still more expensively than at other IBM plants).

IBM succeeded where others failed because at the outset it consciously underplayed its goals to the public and did not go in for the fanfare which heralded other business entries into ghettos. It also produced for an internal and guaranteed market: the demand was known and only the question of supply remained to be worked out. The project depended on more than just IBM, of course, and two organizations were set up to monitor the rebuilding of the ghetto.

The Restoration Corporation represented the residents of the local community and was responsible for the development and implementation of programmes, whereas the Bedford Stuyvesant Development and Services Corporation was established to represent the business community. In 1973 the two organizations merged to create the single corporation which now runs the project. In its first fifteen years of operation the project in the ghetto received 25% of its funding directly from government, 15% from business subsidiary income, 20% from mortgage and loan financing, 18% from rent, 11% from special contributions and grants, with the rest generated from other projects.[58]

If there had not been so much pressure on the community action programmes to work so quickly, and had they been given sufficient time to be properly researched and developed, more projects might have enjoyed the benefits which were afforded to Bedford Stuyvesant. Moreover, if the large corporations could have been attracted into the ghettos through a series of economic incentives, parent companies might have taken over from the government in providing many necessary services.

These might not necessarily have been any more efficient in providing long-term job prospects, but in some ways they were more stable than government agencies, whose funding could appear and disappear as regularly as there were elections. Kennedy's plans for the ghetto were not revolutionary, but he did help to pioneer ideas which were not realized until some years after his death. Through Moynihan's influence in the Nixon White House, for example, when business was encouraged to play a greater role and where more planning was required before a community was awarded government money. In fact much of Kennedy's community bias was echoed in Nixon's urban policy, which discouraged the federal government's participation in renewal programmes. Kennedy may not have been ready to go as far as Nixon, who preferred awarding block grants to local mayors to allocate money to specific projects in their cities, but it would not be stretching the parallel too far to submit that Nixon's policy bore hallmarks of Kennedy's legacy.

These principles of private funding and local control have grown in strength since they were proposed by Kennedy and have often been cited by politicians on the right as sensible approaches to the alleviation of poverty. In the early 1980s they were commended by Peter Walker, then a British cabinet minister in the Conservative government and later head of the country's Urban Regeneration Agency. He suggested that Kennedy was acting in the tradition of former British Prime Minister Harold Macmillan in advocating 'The Middle Way'. 'Bobby Kennedy ... drew attention to the powerful role that free enterprise needs to play in tackling the urban problem. He wanted private enterprise to have the ingenuity to provide decent housing ... He recognized that welfare wrongly applied would destroy self-respect and encourage family disintegration.'[59]

In the early 1990s the Bush administration also appeared to be reverting to Kennedy's ideas of the mid-1960s to fight American poverty. Secretary of Housing and Urban Development Jack Kemp suggested a cut in capital gains tax for those investing in the inner cities and an expansion in inner-city home ownership – both plans pioneered by Kennedy during his Senate career.[60] In recent years these tax incentives for inner cities have become known as 'enterprise zone' schemes.

Whether the enterprise zone idea proves ultimately successful remains to be seen. So far these ideas have failed to stem the drug trade or the increase in violent crime. That Robert Kennedy's ideas have not achieved total victory in the war against poverty does not mean they have not made a significant contribution. They were new approaches to historic problems, and Kennedy should at least be credited with being far ahead of his colleagues in his proposals for inner-city renewal.

After the 1992 Los Angeles riots, the two largest gangs in the city drew up a truce and an economic plan for the future of their community. It demanded that private companies be forced to invest in the area. IBM, for instance, was asked to provide ten computers and three staff members. In return 30 gang members would be trained as computer operators and repairmen. Computer manufacturers Apple and Micro were asked to train young blacks as software writers. 'We demand that welfare be completely removed from our community,' declared the gangs, 'and these welfare programmes be replaced by state work and product manufacturing plants that provide the city with certain supplies. State money shall only be provided for invalids and the elderly.'[61] The demands echo Kennedy's ideas for Bedford Stuyvesant, which appear to have been two decades ahead of their time.

There is no denying that Kennedy was particularly sensitive to black aspirations, and his popularity among black voters was remarkable. His support from their leaders was often less enthusiastic, as they were worried by his previous involvement with FBI surveillance of Martin Luther King and his initially lukewarm response to civil-rights activists in the early 1960s.[62] Nevertheless, his popularity with the majority of blacks was undoubted. How much of this support came from his legislative proposals, and how much from his past relationship with President Kennedy is impossible to quantify.

Kennedy had been exposed to the idea of black consciousness as early as 1963, when he met novelist James Baldwin and other prominent blacks shortly before the March on Washington in August of that year. Kennedy felt he had no reason to be ashamed of what his brother's administration had done for civil rights, but this record carried little weight in his New York meeting. He was met with a barrage of criticism from those like playwright Lorraine Hansberry, psychology professor Kenneth Clark and Baldwin who thought the President had not done enough to recognize the difficulties being experienced by urban blacks at the time.

It was, by several accounts, the first direct encounter that Kennedy had ever had with the idea of black consciousness.[63] Hansberry launched a virulent attack on the administration, warned of gun battles in the streets, and introduced notions such as black separatism to the Attorney General. Kennedy was shocked by the verbal assaults and largely ignorant of the blacks' motives in criticizing him. In an oral history programme recorded in 1964, he told the interviewer that 'A number of them ... have complexes about the fact that they've been successful. I mean, that they've done so well ... so the way to show that they hadn't forgotten where they came from was to berate me and berate the United States government.'[64]

He also questioned the credentials of the blacks he met to speak on behalf of others. 'They didn't really know, with a few exceptions, any of the facts. James Baldwin couldn't discuss any legislation, for instance, on housing or any of these matters. He didn't know anything about them. Harry Belafonte said afterwards – and he was right – that it was a mistake having them there because they didn't know anything.'[65]

Kennedy's position as Senator for New York, which had one of the most militantly black separatist traditions in the country, also exposed him to some of the most radical blacks of the time. (According to Tom Hayden, 'Kennedy met with [militant Committee on Racial Equality (CORE) leader] Floyd McKissick and continually gave him money.'[66]) Assigned to the Committee on Labor and Public Welfare, and to the Committee on Washington, DC, he was as familiar with the problems faced by the urban poor as was any other national legislator.

Kennedy was also an assiduous constituency Senator. Having won a Senate campaign during which he had been attacked for being an outsider from Massachusetts, he immediately expanded his Senate staff so that it soon became the largest in Congress. His staff included Earl Graves, the only black aide on any Senate staff at the time.[67]

On entering the Senate in January 1965, he is recorded as having twenty administrative staff on the payroll. Within six months 36 more had joined, making a total of 56 – appreciably larger than the staffs of either his brother (who had 23), other Senate newcomers such as Walter Mondale (who had 26) or even New York's senior Senator, Jacob Javits, who had 38 staff members. By 1968 Kennedy's Senate staff of 70 was by far the largest in Congress.[68]

With such resources (a Senator was given a certain allowance by the government, which he could augment from his own pocket), Kennedy proved a competent, if unprolific, legislator and earned a reputation for keeping in close touch with his constituents. He was the first Senator from New York to run an upstate office, and the 'carpetbagger' charges were soon dropped (in fact Kennedy had been born in New York, although he had left it as a child). Although he never favoured the approach of separatists such as Malcolm X over the integrationist views of, for instance, Martin Luther King, Kennedy was aware that lifting the legal obstacles to equal opportunity and voting rights was not enough. 'You may remember that when the Civil Rights Act went into effect, Mississippi civil rights workers had to go to great lengths to ensure that all negroes who tested the law had enough money to pay for a single cup of coffee,' he told the Senate in a remark which challenged the liberal consensus based on Myrdal's analysis that the issue was primarily a moral one.[69]

Once Kennedy had accepted that substantial economic independence was a prerequisite for real black emancipation, it was a short step for him to concede that other disadvantages experienced by the black community might also have to be dealt with before real integration could begin. There was nothing new in this, of course. Malcolm X had been saying it for years before, and Frantz Fanon had been saying it years before him.[70] Nevertheless, Kennedy spotted the political potential of Black Power before any other major white politician (and a whole decade before the rise of Steve Biko and black consciousness in South Africa). 'Blackness,' he said, 'must be made a badge of pride and honor'.[71]

Probably only Edward Brooke, the black liberal Republican Senator from Massachusetts, rivalled Kennedy in Congress for his appreciation of the phenomenon of black power, and his major statement on the issue did not appear until July 1967. Brooke suggested that 'Black Power is, more than a slogan, an idea with very many promising uses for negroes and for the country generally ... If the idea of Black Power assists the internal organization of political strength in the negro slums, then it will have served a very useful national purpose indeed.'[72]

Black Power, coined in October 1966 as a political slogan by Stokely Carmichael, was an effectively vague phrase which was used to suggest varying degrees of self-determination, from revolution to cultural pride. (Floyd McKissick claimed to have used it before Carmichael.) Kennedy's idea to develop Bedford Stuyvesant was one manifestation of Black Power, as local blacks were to be awarded an unprecedented measure of self-determination. But it was not without its paradoxes. The power could not be said to have been genuinely black if it had been granted (and could be withheld) by white money and white enthusiasm.

Moreover, Kennedy's project was viable only with a certain kind of pliable local leadership. According to former Kennedy staffers, Bedford Stuyvesant was chosen over Harlem because the local black leadership in the latter district was too close-knit to allow for such outside initiatives.[73] Harlem was declared unsuitable because of its 'highly structured political leadership, the strong influence of the militant anti-white groups which would create barriers, as would his own arm's length relationship with Adam Clayton Powell, who was at the time chairman of the House Education and Labor Committee,' conceded members of Kennedy's Senate staff.[74]

Bedford Stuyvesant, on the other hand, was eminently appropriate partly because 'it had no congressman of its own, its borders having been cut up and distributed between three congressional districts, [and] ... no dominant negro leaders'.[75] When some locals did object to Kennedy's plans for the ghetto, they were co-opted into the scheme, just as radical blacks had been co-opted into the March on Washington. (Kennedy later recalled how the administration was concerned about Communist infiltration in the march and stopped an official from the Committee on Racial Equality from delivering an 'inflammatory speech' because it was 'an attack on the country. It attacked the President.'[76]) 'At one point, some of the neighborhood groups threatened to discredit the project, but Kennedy ... turned them back by broadening the membership of the community corporations to include younger and more militant elements,' recalled the Senate aides.[77]

However, the Bedford Stuyvesant project did complement the notion of black assertiveness. 'In the long run, it is only by a rebuilding process of which physical reconstruction is part, that we can achieve the comparability of housing which is an independent requirement of full integration,' Kennedy declared to Congress.[78] The ultimate aim was still one of integration but from a position of black strength, although this point proved too sophisticated for some of his most liberal colleagues in the Senate.

Eugene McCarthy, Democratic Senator for Minnesota and later Kennedy's rival for the 1968 presidential nomination, was against the idea and suggested that 'He [Kennedy] was really for apartheid; "keep 'em in lots" was in effect what he was saying. I was saying that you had to have physical integration ... He was big on Bedford Stuyvesant, which was segregated residential apartheid. There was even talk of putting industry in Watts – some[one] proposed to build a factory making baseball bats. Baseball bats! – the last thing you'd need in Watts. Perhaps pillows ...'[79]

McCarthy was not the only one who was confused about the project's philosophy. John Bartlow Martin was an important figure in the Kennedy circle, who had known Robert Kennedy since the 1950s, when he covered the union hearings as a journalist. After campaigning for JFK in 1960, he was rewarded with an ambassadorship to the Dominican Republic. In 1968 Robert Kennedy asked him to organize his presidential campaign in Martin's native Indiana. Charged with the responsibility of encouraging black support in places such as Indianapolis, Martin relied primarily on Kennedy's record as Attorney General rather than his new enthusiasm for black consciousness. 'He talked about that [Bedford Stuyvesant] endlessly,' recalled Martin in 1985. 'I couldn't make head or tail of it. I didn't understand it. I remember talking to him early on in the campaign. He went on about Bedford Stuyvesant and I was bored ... I didn't listen to that. I just literally didn't understand it.'[80]

It is difficult to judge if Kennedy himself really understood the limitations of his position as a white liberal in such a project. 'If I could do what I really wanted to do, I would resign from the Senate and run Bedford Stuyvesant,' he said in 1967, apparently missing the essential point that part of the project's *raison d'être* was that it would not be run by outsiders, especially white ones.[81]

Whatever his understanding of the principles involved, there is no doubting Kennedy's genuine popularity in the ghettos. In an immediate reaction to the death of President Kennedy, Islamic leader Elijah Mohammed forbade public discussion of the assassination in case it offended blacks who idolized JFK. Within a week of the killing, however, Malcolm X addressed a black Islamic service at Temple Seven in New York and referred to President Kennedy as a segregationist and to the Kennedys (John, Robert and Edward) as the KKK. The congregation, according to reports, left disappointed, unenthusiastic about Malcolm X's attack on the Kennedys.[82]

It has been suggested that some of Robert Kennedy's popularity with blacks relied on his anti-war position, as money spent on the war effort in Vietnam could otherwise be used to improve inner-city areas. Although the war hit ghetto communities severely, and Martin Luther King took up strong anti-war positions before his death in April 1968, it does not appear that by the time of Kennedy's death the war was a major concern of black voters. Martin and McCarthy saw the issues as distinctly separate, and suggested that dovish candidates did not especially emphasise their dovish war voting records in black areas.[83]

In 1966 Kennedy made a much-publicized trip to South Africa, where he spoke out against racial injustice and met banned Nobel Peace Prize winner Albert Luthuli. There is little evidence that American blacks were especially drawn to him because of this sort of stand. Nevertheless, just as his brother's speech in 1957 calling for Algerian independence was probably not significant in attracting black support in 1960, it may have had a slight electoral impact.

According to McCarthy, 'blacks didn't know what [Kennedy] was saying and they didn't care anyway'.[84] Kennedy's phenomenal popularity in black areas did not necessarily reflect his views on the war, or even his sensitivity to the emergence of Black Power. It could simply have been glamour or charisma. According to classic studies of charisma, charismatic leaders (i.e. those who are perceived to have extraordinary abilities or supernatural talents) emerge at times of great change or confusion.[85]

By the mid-1960s in America there is little doubt that many perceived the social situation to be critical, and a crop of charismatic leaders surfaced. John Lindsay, Ronald Reagan, George Wallace, Martin Luther

King and Barry Goldwater all emerged at this time offering strong and attractive leadership, while the fringes produced Bobby Seale, Malcolm X and Tom Hayden. How the Robert Kennedy of the early 1960s became the most worshipped of these figures (even to the point of messianic reverence) is still unclear, although, according to Max Weber's classic study of the phenomenon, charisma can be 'transferred' from one charismatic leader to a nominated successor, often 'to the kinsmen of its bearer ... this is the case of hereditary charisma'.[86] Assuming that some of Robert Kennedy's appeal came from his relationship to John Kennedy, it is conceivable that his charisma was 'inherited' in this way.

In a more recent study of the charismatic appeal of Jesse Jackson, Ernest House contends that 'it is critical for charismatic figures to become attached to the primary myths of the culture ... Thus John F. Kennedy, a glamorous but hardly charismatic figure for most Americans, became a charismatic figure after his assassination by being assimilated to the Lincoln myth.'[87] (The author describes how Jesse Jackson tried to align himself to the myth of Martin Luther King immediately after he was assassinated by wearing a shirt on television which had apparently been stained with King's blood.)

A lieutenant of Martin Luther King during the 1960s and later Washington DC's Representative in Congress, Walter Fauntroy, suggests that Kennedy's popularity among blacks was partly rooted in 'the feeling that his brother was assassinated for the forthright stand he was moved to take in 1963 around the Birmingham movement ... and at a subliminal level, blacks felt that for whatever reasons he was killed, among them was his forthrightness on the question of civil rights ... There was a desire to reward [Robert Kennedy] with what the people would've rewarded his brother had he lived.'[88] Certainly Kennedy's presidential campaign team of 1968 felt confident enough to leave out a great deal of political substance during his appearances in ghettos, preferring to rely more on the simple pull of his presence. His campaign manager, Fred Dutton, believed that 'blacks need a high-intensity, high-visibility style of campaigning (so do blue-collar whites, but not as much). We made an intentional pitch to the blacks and made the most out of dramatic situations.'[89]

A rough 'line of descent' appeared to emerge in popular culture in the months after Robert Kennedy's assassination, as a Motown song, *Abraham, Martin and John* – which reached number four in the US charts of November 1968 – grouped Robert Kennedy with fallen heroes Presidents Lincoln and Kennedy and Martin Luther King. Kennedy's links with popular black culture did not end there. Musician James Brown 'had just about decided to endorse Senator Robert Kennedy' when he was assassinated, and Diana Ross and the Supremes played a $1,000-a-plate fundraiser concert in April 1969, the proceeds of which went towards paying off Kennedy's campaign debts. In June 1971 Motown subsidiary Mowest released *What The World Needs Now Is Love* where the lyrics were interspersed with extracts of speeches from King and John and Robert Kennedy.[90]

The line of descent appears to have been extended, but Robert Kennedy is still part of it. Addressing the 1984 Democratic Convention in San Francisco, Jesse Jackson referred to the achievements of the civil rights movement in the 1960s: 'We lost Malcolm, Martin, Medgar, Bobby and John and Viola. The team that got us here must be expanded, not abandoned.'[91] Whatever Kennedy's real place in black culture, he appears to have joined the pantheon of black heroes and heroines credited with fostering black progress.

Kennedy was primarily concerned, of course, with how far this affection translated into electoral support. He swept ghetto areas in the presidential primaries with overwhelming majorities (and lost only in Oregon, which was virtually ghetto-free). In fact Kennedy's popularity in the ghettos threatened to damage his image with suspicious white voters. The urban response to Kennedy was often overwhelming. While McCarthy stayed away from ghettos because he 'didn't want to stir them up',[92] George McGovern recalls how he 'would watch the nightly news and you'd see these largely youthful, black, poor crowds crushing around [Kennedy] and it frightened a lot of people. The majority may not have been quite ready for Robert Kennedy in 1968.'[93]

John Bartlow Martin had similar memories of organizing Kennedy's primary campaign in Indiana. 'I remember he was at Monument Circle in Indianapolis and he got a crowd there such as I've never seen. I've seen Eisenhower's crowds there and Stevenson's and I've never seen anything like this ... I was scared physically. I fell and broke a tooth and it was just a mess.'[94]

The pop-star image of Kennedy in his latter days as a Senator proved effective in primary campaigning, especially in low-income areas. Stokely Carmichael had complained to a Kennedy aide about the candidate's popularity: 'I would not want to see your man run for president because he can get the votes of my people without coming to me. With the other candidates, I'll have bargaining power.'[95] Even Eldridge Cleaver, one of the most militant black leaders and a Black

Panther official, described Kennedy's performance at a Senate hearing in 1967 with reticent respect, before dismissing him as 'too white to be all right'. 'He wore the aura of an idol-smasher. He was the bad boy on the committee, the only one who contained the potential in his image to ask the scandalous questions … The other two members of the committee … bore no promise,' wrote Cleaver.[96]

Moderate black leaders also respected Kennedy much more in these years. In the summer of 1967 King suggested that Kennedy would 'make a great President', although he said he did not believe Kennedy could win the nomination from Johnson.[97] National Association for the Advancement of Colored People (NAACP) leader Roy Wilkins also conceded that 'When Sirhan Sirhan shot Bobby Kennedy in Los Angeles, I came as close as I ever have come to losing faith in the workings of democracy. I had always felt a degree of distance from Bobby Kennedy, partly because he had become Senator in New York by defeating Kenneth Keating, a Republican who had always been a very good friend of the NAACP. But the older Bobby grew, the more clear matters of race relations became to him. By 1968 he obviously felt the problem deeply, and he was poised to offer considerable help.'[98]

On the night of King's assassination in April 1968 John Bartlow Martin had arranged to meet Kennedy at Indianapolis airport. Kennedy was due to open his primary campaign headquarters in the city and attend a rally in the ghetto. While waiting for Kennedy's plane to land, Martin asked a police inspector if the candidate should still attend the rally in the light of King's death. The police inspector, according to Martin, replied: 'If he doesn't, they'll tear this town apart tonight. He's the only one that can do it.' Martin remembered: 'The negroes did burn the cities that night, except Indianapolis … Bobby did exactly what the policeman wanted him to do without knowing the policeman wanted it …'[99] This notion of understanding blacks was certainly one of Kennedy's main attractions among whites, who often believed he could keep blacks under control.

According to Walter Fauntroy, when Kennedy was assassinated, the police authorities in Washington, DC, deployed extra troops in the areas which had rioted after King's death, believing that blacks in the city might become violent on hearing of another of their leaders murdered. On the outskirts of the city 10,000 soldiers were placed on alert in case Kennedy's death triggered rioting.[100]

One of the areas which the police believed offered potential for violence was around the Lincoln Memorial, which had become home to those who had arrived in Washington at the end of the Poor People's March. The march was designed to embarrass the government into doing something for the poor of the country, and poor people from all over the nation converged on Washington in 1968 and set up camp near the memorial. According to NAACP lawyer Marion Wright, the march was Kennedy's idea. 'I had told him [in August 1967] that I was going to stop back in Atlanta and see Dr King – he said "Tell him to bring the poor people to Washington." And as simply as Bobby Kennedy had said it, King instinctively felt that that was right ... Out of that, the Poor People's Campaign was born.'[101] The suggestion was typical. By encouraging thousands of poor people to Washington, Kennedy could ensure that the President was embarrassed on the issue of poverty and could claim extra credibility for himself with radical leaders by adopting the mantle of direct (if non-violent) confrontation.

For cynics, Kennedy's position at the cutting edge of civil rights may have been nothing more than part of a master-plan to capture the presidency. But there is no doubt that his position on civil rights had evolved remarkably between his time as Attorney General and his death. Anyway, his motivation in embracing some of the most radical ideas of black self-determination is not as important as the fact that he was successful at it. This radical appeal to blacks' self-sufficiency proved a formidable vote-winner and has not been emulated by a white candidate since.

Chapter Two

Kennedy and Industry

'The South regards the Senator as only slightly less dangerous than Mao Tse-tung' – *Wall Street Journal*, April 1968

According to an FBI report, Southern Californian ranchers paid towards a $500,000 contract to kill Robert Kennedy in June 1968.[1] He had, it is fair to say, never been recognized as a friend of big business, and some of the larger ranchers in California were angry at Kennedy's support for Cesar Chavez, who was trying to unionize their employees.[2] It would also be fair to say, however, that Kennedy had never been recognized as a friend of big unions either. In February 1963 President Kennedy told *Newsweek* journalist Benjamin Bradlee that Jimmy Hoffa of the Teamsters Union had sent an assassin to Washington to kill Robert Kennedy.[3]

Kennedy's problems with organized labour went back to the late 1950s when he was part of a Senate investigation which exposed corruption in several large unions, including Hoffa's International Brotherhood of Teamsters (IBT). The investigation was where Kennedy's 'ruthless' image first emerged, as he hounded several union officials to breaking-point in the Senate caucus room where, a decade later, he would announce his presidential candidacy. The hearings of the Senate Select Committee on Improper Activities in the Labor or Management Field began in January 1957, chaired by Senator John McClellan of Arkansas. In its three years, the 'McClellan Committee' held over 500 public hearings and heard more than 1500 witnesses as it probed corruption in union managment.[4] One Teamsters official, John O'Rourke, was badgered so fiercely by Kennedy during the hearings in 1957 that he broke down and cried.[5]

The Teamsters had begun at the turn of the century to represent city delivery crafts – drivers of coal, milk and bread trucks. They grew steadily but slowly until the 1930s, when younger leaders organized the union more vigorously, realizing that the Teamsters could exert national political influence.[6] With the proliferation of motor transport, the Teamsters were in a powerful position to demand substantial improvements in pay and conditions, as they controlled much of the country's commodity transportation network.

One of the young organizers was Jimmy Hoffa. He had started as a junior official with the Teamsters in Detroit, and had helped organize its first city-wide strike in 1937. The strike was violent, and Hoffa later claimed he had been beaten up 'at least two dozen times' that year.[7] To help his members in their struggle, the young Hoffa had used contacts in organized crime to fight off the bosses' thugs, and when relations between the Teamsters and the governing union body, the Congress of Industrial Organizations (CIO), soured in 1941, Hoffa brought in his mobster friends to help sort things out. Within a month CIO control of Detroit was over, and Hoffa's IBT was in control. The war years saw Hoffa standing trial for racketeering in 1941 and 1942. (He had persuaded local Teamster official R. J. Bennett to write to the draft board claiming Hoffa's union work was crucial to the nation's transport industry, and therefore war effort. He was exempted from military service.) Although Hoffa was acquitted, a 1953 Congressional investigation into corruption found evidence of racketeering in the IBT, with union officials being accused of taking members' money (one car-washer told the investigation that his weekly earnings had dropped from $30 to $18 after he had joined the union).[8]

Nevertheless the Congressional hearings were abruptly ended in 1953, and Hoffa was temporarily spared further investigation. In 1955 he moved the IBT headquarters from Detroit to Washington, DC, and managed to gain an innovative benefit for his members whereby employers agreed to pay $2 a week per employee into a pension fund. This provided Hoffa with considerable support from his members and a huge war chest which he could use to extend his influence. Within a year he had taken control of most of the eastern states' Teamsters operations by winning dubious elections with the support of 'paper' locals (i.e. local branches which existed only on paper) and became the second in the union hierarchy to Teamsters President Dave Beck.[9]

One of the first McClellan Committee targets, Dave Beck was found to have siphoned off $320,000 in union funds to build a private home. Beck was ruined within the first month of the hearings, being forced to take the Fifth Amendment (a safeguard against self-incrimination) 140 times in one session.[10]

Hoffa proved a wilier adversary. A series of appearances before the committee during 1957 left his public reputation in tatters, but the union boss's skirmishes with Kennedy seemed only to enhance his popularity with his members.

With Beck about to go to prison at the end of 1957, Hoffa won the Teamsters' presidency by a majority of three to one, although he was barred from taking up the position by a legal ruling which found some of the delegates voting for him at the IBT convention to have been improperly selected. Moreover, the wider labour movement was embarrassed by Hoffa, and the governing AFL-CIO (the CIO having merged with the American Federation of Labor in 1955) expelled the IBT from its organization in 1958. Hoffa dismissed the expulsion as 'back-alley politics by the Kennedys'.[11]

Nevertheless, Kennedy earned a reputation at this time as a prosecutor given to excess in investigating unions, an image which his father thought might damage John Kennedy's chances for the presidency in 1960. To emphasize his interest in union reform, rather than his interest in persecuting union officials, John Kennedy introduced a bill in 1957 which required union officials to guarantee regular elections with secret ballots, to file financial reports with the Labor Department and to disclose financial deals which might involve conflicts of interests. The Kennedy-Ives Bill had the support of the AFL-CIO and passed the Senate 88–1 in June 1958, but after intense Teamster lobbying in the House of Representatives, it was defeated.[12]

The AFL-CIO, aware that the hearings had damaged the image of organized labour across the country, endorsed the bill and took every opportunity to distance itself from the corrupt exploits of the Teamsters. (It had also forbidden its representatives to cite the Fifth Amendment before the Senate committee and had thrown out the East Coast Longshoremen from its movement for thuggishness.)[13]

The Kennedy-Ives Bill, reintroduced in 1959, was passed after complicated negotiations and provided John Kennedy with a significant piece of legislation to his credit for the 1960 election campaign.

Robert Kennedy's time as prosecutor had helped to create a climate for union reform, enabling his brother to take advantage and pass a popular bill. Throughout his Senate career, however, the 'ruthless' tag would remain, and many in the labour movement never trusted him for damaging its reputation during the late 1950s. Among those criticized as a result of Kennedy's investigations were unions of bakers, operating engineers, textile workers, meat-cutters, carpenters, hotel and restaurant workers, and sheet-metal workers.[14] Of course Kennedy's prime concern at this stage of his political career was not electoral success for himself, and if making such powerful enemies did not interfere with his brother's chances of the presidency, he had no compunction in upsetting union chiefs. Moreover, the labour movement was not a monolithic bloc, and there were significant pockets of influence which remained loyal to Kennedy throughout his Senate years. Apart from the various disaffected local Teamsters, who had fallen on the wrong side of Jimmy Hoffa at one time or another, powerful figures such as Walter Reuther, president of the influential United Auto Workers (UAW), remained close to Kennedy, and any new coalition would have to include other similarly progressive labour leaders.

Reuther, like Hoffa, had come up through union ranks the hard way. For years he was suspected as a secret Communist by many on the right because of the trip he made to the Soviet Union with his brother Victor during the 1930s, but Reuther shared Kennedy's capacity to learn politically. In December 1947 he helped found an anti-communist organisation, Americans for Democratic Action (ADA), with fellow liberals Reinhold Neibuhr and Arthur Schlesinger, and the following year was shot in an assassination attempt.

Reuther too first met Kennedy during the racketeering hearings, when the latter went to Wisconsin to investigate a strike backed by the UAW and ended up supporting the strikers' demands for longer lunch-breaks. John Kennedy remembered how his brother at this time 'might have been intolerant of liberals as such because his early experience was with that high-minded, high-speaking kind who never got anything done. That all changed the moment he met Walter Reuther.'[15] During the investigation into the Wisconsin strike, John Kennedy told the labour leader that 'you fellows are educating Bobby' and throughout the next decade Robert Kennedy would look to Reuther as his most important political ally in the union hierarchy.[16]

Although powerful in his own union, Reuther's increasing radicalism in the 1960s meant he was losing influence with the wider movement. While the AFL-CIO did not support the March on Washington in August 1963, for instance, Reuther was there, persuading SNCC leader John Lewis to tone down his attacks on the Kennedy administration.[17] Later he supplied Tom Hayden's Students for a Democratic Society with funds for a revolutionary ghetto rehabilitation project.[18]

Reuther was politically light years ahead of his AFL-CIO colleagues (and the UAW would later officially split from the organization). Virulently anti-Communist, the AFL-CIO was never part of the international left and remained a strident supporter of American involvement in Vietnam throughout the 1960s. AFL-CIO leader George Meany disliked the more progressive Reuther and took it as a personal insult when Kennedy praised Reuther at a speech in Detroit in 1964 for all he had done for John Kennedy.[19] Meany had thought himself a greater ally of the late President and was outraged. It was the beginning of Kennedy's difficulties with the AFL-CIO.

However, it was leaders like Reuther to whom Kennedy looked in forging a new electoral coalition of workers. In 1966 he went to support the striking grape-pickers in California because Reuther asked him to.[20] The grape growers in California were an extremely powerful lobby, and Kennedy was the first politician to visit the strikers in Delano in 1966. 'Politically speaking, in California at that time, it was probably a stupid thing to do', said Michael Harrington.[21]

The Senate Migratory Labor Subcommittee was due to hold hearings on the issue in Delano, and Kennedy agreed to attend. He became a hero among the grape-pickers almost immediately for his aggressive prosecution of the local law-enforcers for their treatment of the pickers, in one memorable incident suggesting that the local sheriff use his lunch-break to read the Constitution of the United States.[22]

It may have been stupid politics, as Harrington suggested, but Kennedy needed the support of those electoral blocs like the migrant workers who were not already organized and controlled by traditional union leaders. The emerging workers' organizations, like the National Farmers Association led by Cesar Chavez, were not directed by AFL-CIO powerbrokers, and so Kennedy could go straight to them without having to barter with the (often antagonistic) old guard. This principle – which also extended to the other pools of unorganized poor such as Indians and some blacks – could be stretched only so far. It was not as if there were enough people outside the old-style voting blocs to elect him, and he would have to barter with the traditional bosses in the traditional way during the presidential election.

Unfortunately for Kennedy, his main rival in the primaries turned out to be Vice-President Hubert Humphrey, who was hugely popular with the AFL-CIO leadership. Even Reuther could not go against Humphrey and declare himself for Kennedy, which left Kennedy with only a handful of endorsements from local union leaders during the 1968 election. In the Indiana primary, the only union support which declared for Kennedy were the local UAW branches in Indianapolis and Kokomo. The rest went to local Governor Roger Branigan, widely recognized as a stand-in for Humphrey. The President of the Labor Council in

Indianapolis, Max E. Brydenthal, stated that 60% of union members who were Democrats favoured Branigan.

Given the indifference, and sometimes hostility, that Kennedy faced in securing the support of union bosses, he aimed his pitch straight at the members. Union members could, of course, be approached at levels other than that of employment: they may have fallen into other sociological categories where Kennedy was stronger. For example, many union members were young, some black, some Catholic, and Kennedy could garner a significant number of union votes by appealing to voters on those levels.

In 1967, for example, 25% of union members were under 30, and 50% under 40, a whole generation younger than most union officials. At the AFL-CIO convention in Miami on 12 December that year, Kennedy shrewdly sent a young emissary who identified with the membership more than the leadership. The *Wall Street Journal* noted how 'the Senator's Labor Aide, Carter Burden, Harvard '63, stands out in the informal convention setting with his long hair and British-style suits'.[23] In a bid to counter the influence of national union leaders on their members, Kennedy's strategy in the primaries was aimed at leaders of local unions and the younger staff members of the large international unions, but official support either remained neutral (like Reuther) or went to Humphrey.[24]

There is little doubt that there was still enough of the old politician in Kennedy to have gained AFL-CIO backing had he won the nomination in 1968, despite his opposition to the war (although such support was withheld from Democratic nominee George McGovern four years later). Nevertheless, traditional union support would have swung heavily behind Humphrey at the Chicago Convention and would have been a major obstacle to Kennedy's securing the nomination. According to the estimates of Kennedy aides in 1968, about 300 delegates to the Democratic Convention were union members, but 'between 500 and 600 others [of a total number of 2,622] were men whose votes could be influenced by the recommendations of the powerful unions in their area'.[25]

While Kennedy could probably have counted on the support of organized labour after he had won the nomination, backing from the country's business community would have proved far more elusive. Anyway, business endorsements were not crucial in deciding the outcome of the Democratic primaries, and were mainly useful to the candidates for fund-raising purposes. Moreover, Kennedy's personal wealth, and his willingness to spend it on campaigning, meant he did not have to bargain with the usual series of business interests which clustered around other candidates. Kennedy's wealth had come from his father's legendary stock-broking deals in the 1920s and 1930s, and, although Joseph Kennedy Sr. enjoyed some influential business contacts, he had always been far from the inner circle on Wall Street and was regarded by many in the business community as a conniving cheat, amassing wealth for political ambition. He had regarded them with similar affection, and in a famous remark described all businessmen as 'sons of bitches'.[26] Asked in December 1964 about his father's remark, Kennedy said that businessmen were like liberals: 'The people who are selfish are interested in their own singular course of action and do not take into consideration the needs or require-ments of others or what ultimately can be accomplished.'[27]

Kennedy's opinion of businessmen remained much the same in the coming years, that they were essentially selfish people uninterested in working for the common good. However, although relatively unim-portant in the primary tussles, the business community would be a significant national constituency when it came to the November elec-tion, able to apply powerful lobbying forces on candidates throughout the country, candidates whose support Kennedy would need in order to win the presidency.

Consequently he made sporadic efforts to improve his poor image with big business.[28] Memories of the steel crisis in 1962 did not help. Nor did his association with Cesar Chavez and the migrant workers, and nor did his constant harassment of the cigarette industry, which could also have been called 'stupid politics'. The tobacco lobby was much stronger at this time than the anti-smoking lobby in terms of money and political clout, and in attacking the industry Kennedy was making powerful enemies over an issue where, in strictly electoral terms, he did not have to risk political capital. Nevertheless Kennedy was a vigorous opponent of cigarette advertising in his Senate years, introducing bills to curb tobacco advertising on television and proposing that stronger brands of cigarettes be taxed more heavily.

The tobacco industry was, to be fair, mostly concentrated in the South, whose business class would have been hostile to Kennedy anyway. However, his badgering of tobacco interests and his readiness to call for federal regulation to control them must have worried business magnates in other industries.

In June 1965 Kennedy opposed a bill calling for health warnings on cigarette packets because it was too weak, and he continued to push for stronger legislation. He told the Senate that while 'the cigarette lobby spends more than $300m a year on advertising ... 300,000 people each year die from diseases associated with smoking'.[29] In April 1966 he suggested that the warning on packets be extended to all kinds of cigarette advertising and threatened the tobacco industry that if it did not regulate itself 'within the next few months ... the administration should act'.[30] He criticized the industry (as he had the previous year, in exactly the same phrase) for 'portraying smoking as the smart, sophisticated thing to do' and said that federal controls on cigarettes would be as sensible as those banning dangerous cars.[31]

Kennedy attacked the equally powerful broadcasting industry for conspiring with the cigarette manufacturers to sell death. 'As to young people, the advertising is a weapon to lure them to their ultimate destruction, a tool to lead them to snuff out their own lives at an early day. Both industries, therefore, must come up with realistic programs to police themselves.'[32] If they did not, he warned, the government would do it for them.

Of course they did not, and the following year Kennedy sponsored five different bills to limit the sale and advertising of cigarettes, including one to forbid the broadcast of such advertising after 9 p.m. and during sports coverage.[33] The day before he introduced this proposal to the Senate on 12 September, 1967, he addressed the World Conference on Smoking and Health. He proposed that anti-smoking commercials be broadcast on television. 'One suggestion that I thought appropriate,' he said in a jibe at the famous Marlboro ad, 'would place the tough, rangy man with the tattoo on his hand in front of a hospital ward and have him say: "This is Emphysema country."'[34]

Kennedy regarded the rest of the business community with hardly more respect than he gave the tobacco barons, and the feeling was mutual. There were exceptions, of course, and IBM, for instance, was helpful in supporting the Bedford Stuyvesant project, but businessmen generally distrusted Kennedy, and he distrusted them. '[President Kennedy] never liked them', Robert Kennedy said in 1964. 'He always just felt that you couldn't do anything with them; there's no way to influence them. We were brought up thinking they were ... My father thought businessmen didn't have any public responsibility. And we just found that they were antagonistic and you couldn't do anything with them.'[35]

The Kennedy administration's relations with big business had soured badly over the steel incident, although local businessmen were used as a powerful lobbying group by the Kennedys during the integration of the University of Alabama. 'We wrote down in a book the name of every company with more than 100 employees – I think – in the whole state of Alabama. All those names were distributed at a Cabinet meeting ... A Cabinet member or somebody called, I guess, every one of them ... We built up a reaction to what Wallace was doing', Kennedy recalled in 1964.[36]

Such co-operation with business interests was rare, however, and in an October 1966 feature on Kennedy the *Wall Street Journal* noted that, although he proved a popular campaigner in the mid-term elections, 'the South and business community remain areas of substantial resistance'.[37]

Kennedy's entry into the presidential campaign seriously worried many business leaders, and the *Wall Street Journal* wasted no time in outlining the reasons why a Kennedy candidacy was a bad idea:

> The South regards the Senator as only slightly less dangerous than Mao Tse-tung. AFL-CIO president George Meany and other key labor barons have disliked and distrusted him since his days on the staff of the Senate's Labor Racketeering Investigation Committee. Businessmen in both parties have feared him ever since he was his brother's tough lieutenant in the fight against Big Steel.[38]

The business magazine *Fortune* was no more encouraging:

> During recent weeks, *Fortune* has surveyed the political views of business leaders in cities scattered across the nation. At each meeting with the businessmen, mention of the name Bobby Kennedy produced an almost unanimous chorus of condemnation ... Although the traditional alignment of business with the Republicans has weakened, there is agreement that Kennedy is the one public figure who could produce an almost united front of business opposition ... If Kennedy should become the Democratic candidate, this hostility would stuff the Republican coffers, and if he were elected it might seriously impair his ability to govern.[39]

Hubert Humphrey noted that during the early stages of the 1968 presidential campaign 'a large share of the money pledged to me came from New York business leaders who feared and distrusted Bob. With his death, their interest in me waned.'[40]

In an effort to counteract the hostility, Kennedy met with a few business leaders sympathetic to his candidacy, and they agreed that he should make a major address to a business audience and have *Fortune* or the *Wall Street Journal* conduct an independent investigation into what had happened during the steel crisis. Kennedy's version of events was that, although he had ordered the questioning of steel executives, it was the FBI, perhaps being deliberately heavy-handed to discredit him, who burst into the bosses' homes in the early hours of the morning in Gestapo-like raids.

The business address was scheduled for 5 April to the City Club of Cleveland. It was the only appointment Kennedy kept that day, the rest of his schedule having been cancelled owing to the assassination of Martin Luther King the day before. At it, however, he dispensed with his prepared speech on the economy and spoke instead about violence.

Had he delivered his address on the economy, many of the businessmen might have been surprised at his ideas for urban renewal. His proposals for ghetto redevelopment were, of course, heavily dependent on private investment and tax breaks for businesses willing to help fight social problems. The war, too, was not overwhelmingly popular with the whole business community – it increased the tax burden significantly. However, most liberal businessmen at this time favoured the Republican Nelson Rockefeller, and Kennedy was unlikely to win many supporters from this group.

He did not have a strong grasp of macroeconomics, but then neither had President Kennedy (who had once reportedly remarked that asking Kennedys about economics was like asking nuns about sex).[41] In fact, the Kennedys' only real political disagreement with each other during John Kennedy's administration (besides a minor skirmish over the building of a dam in Ghana) was over a cut in the rate of income tax.

At the start of the administration, the Attorney General was in favour of increasing income tax to 'bring home to the American people ... the fact that everybody was making a sacrifice'.[42] The President opposed the idea, as did most financial experts, and the disagreement nurtured the idea that Robert Kennedy was a lightweight economist, prepared to mess with the economy for political points. (Speaking about this with Kennedy in 1964, John Bartlow Martin suggested: 'I think at the time the general impression was that you were alone in this position.'[43])

The image was hard to shake off in business circles, and the Bedford Stuyvesant project was regarded by some businessmen as little more than gimmickry. The *Wall Street Journal* made it difficult for its readers to take the Kennedy candidacy seriously. 'He must push the jet setters further into the background of his entourage. Many campaign aides are breathless young dilettantes with names like Pebble and Muffie, who create the impression that the Kennedy headquarters has replaced Acapulco as the place to be this year,' it noted a month before Kennedy's first primary.[44]

For all his efforts in attracting top industrialists to his campaign, by the end of May 1968 a national Citizens for Kennedy advertisement included only two significant business names: Jerold Hoffberger of the National Brewing Company, an old friend of Joseph Kennedy Sr., and Harold Williams, President of Hunt Foods and Industries.

The business community was a low electoral priority for Kennedy during the primaries, however, and was unlikely ever to form part of any radical alternative coalition. No doubt many of its members would have been distraught at the prospect of a Robert Kennedy presidency, but despite apocalyptic warnings, they would not have sabotaged the economy just to make life difficult for him. Business had, after all, put up with John Kennedy and (unless certain assassination conspiracy theories are to be believed) had not prevented him from governing the country.

Traditional labour organizations probably had more to fear from a Robert Kennedy presidency. In dismantling the old New Deal structure to build an alternative Democratic one, union bosses – along with some southern politicians – may have found themselves early casualties of Kennedy's new power base. Little love would have been lost on either side.

Chapter Three

Kennedy and the New Left

'George Wallace is Robert Kennedy in drag ...' – Jerry Rubin

When Allen Ginsberg visited Robert Kennedy's office and was quizzed about his political links with the Black Power movement, the conversation lurched from LSD to religion to reconstructing the human universe and finished with Ginsberg chanting the Hare Krishna mantra for the Senator.[1]

Kennedy, not much the wiser about youth politics, made his excuses and left, still wondering if a coalition of youth groups could be put together and, if so, how strong it would be. During the mid-1960s the demographic changes in America meant that there were more people aged under 35 than at any time in the nation's history.[2]

Children born after the Second World War also enjoyed an unsurpassed material security which allowed them to indulge in self-conscious social and political behaviour. Whatever the reasons for the tumultuous changes in youth culture, there was no denying its existence or the possible impact it could have on the political agenda as the universities in particular became increasingly politicized.

Kennedy's interest in this new generation was primarily political, and as the new leader of the radical left in his party he would have to establish links with the larger youth organizations who were at the forefront of dissent. The new radicals were remarkably different from those on the old left who had emerged in the 1930s and became either New Dealers or Communist sympathizers. The New Left was broadly anti-Communist (although this distinction was difficult for many in the US government to understand), anti-authoritarian, libertarian and often unfocused in its political objectives. Thus Kennedy could identify more easily with the New Left, with its evolving and uncertain policy direction, than with the old-style left, many of whom distrusted him anyway for his part in the labour racketeering hearings of the 1950s.

In June 1964 the Socialist Youth Conference (made up broadly of university students, but decidedly old left in its traditions) voted on a resolution chastising Kennedy for his record as Attorney General. The motion failed (229 to 202) but is revealing if compared with his relations with New Left groups at this time.[3]

These, of course, were early days in terms of Kennedy's links with the new radicals, but as Attorney General he had already had significant dealings with one of the two most important New Left organizations to emerge in the following years – the Student Non-violent Co-ordinating Committee (SNCC). Born in 1960, SNCC had resisted being co-opted by any of the adult organizations such as the National Association for the Advancement of Colored People (NAACP) or the Committee for Racial Equality (CORE) which offered it financial support but were often perturbed by its controversial tactics.[4]

SNCC had been involved in the sit-ins to highlight segregation in southern states and later had injected impetus into the Freedom Ride movement at a time when it appeared the Freedom Riders would have to call off their attempt to integrate interstate bus terminals. Robert Kennedy, in fact, had tried to get the Freedom Riders to call off their trip after they had been surrounded in the First Avenue Baptist Church in Montgomery, but SNCC Freedom Riders urged that they push on to Jackson, Mississippi, which they did.[5] As Attorney General, an exasperated Kennedy had been asked to ensure the safety of those involved in the Freedom Rides and he had taken some steps to make sure that the buses progressed (including a famous call to 'Mr Greyhound' to get a driver for one group of riders threatened with violence).[6]

Nevertheless, Kennedy had regarded the Freedom Rides (with some justification) as publicity stunts designed to cause his brother's administration international embarrassment.[7] Kennedy had urged SNCC to concentrate on voter registration for blacks in the southern states instead of sensational media events. As Attorney General, he argued, he could afford them more vigorous backing if they concentrated on registration, as the federal role in such matters was much clearer, and hence more easily enforceable, than in the desegregation of public facilities. Voter registration drives also provided more positive photo opportunities than, for instance, mobs stoning a bus. SNCC did do a lot of voter registration work at this time and were given significant backing by the Kennedy administration, which was sometimes identified in the south with the SNCC radicals urging blacks to register. The deputy sheriff in Dawson, Georgia, interrogated SNCC activist Ralph Allen in 1963 and demanded: 'Did Bobby Kennedy send you?' 'Indirectly,' replied Allen.[8]

The SNCC's relationship with the Kennedy administration was far from one of mutual admiration, however, and during the March on Washington SNCC leader John Lewis was persuaded at the last minute to refrain from publicly criticizing the administration's record on civil rights.[9] Lewis represented the moderate wing of SNCC, however, and in May 1966 he lost the chairmanship of the organization to the far more radical Stokely Carmichael. Carmichael was too extreme for Kennedy to deal with directly, but Kennedy appealed to much of Carmichael's political base, a fact Carmichael acknowledged.[10] However, SNCC joined Kennedy in backing the grape-pickers at Delano, and (Carmichael apart) SNCC supporters would be an important part of any youth coalition sought by Kennedy.

Another block in any new political framework would be the Students for a Democratic Society (SDS). Described by Carl Oglesby, its president in 1965, as 'the SNCC of the north', the SDS was to prove the most influential youth group during the latter half of the decade and is credited with organizing huge anti-Vietnam War demonstrations.[11] However, the SDS was more than a single-issue movement. In its earlier years of 1963 and 1964, the emphasis was on ghetto renewal and community action politics. Founded in Michigan in 1962, the SDS was based on the famous 'Port Huron Statement', which eschewed the old materialist values of American capitalism and declared 'that work should involve incentives worthier than survival' and be creative and educative.[12] Student radicals, invited by SDS President Tom Hayden, met to draw up a blueprint for their activism:

> SNCC could not go on alone. There was an entire generation to arouse, primarily about civil rights but also about the larger issues that SNCC itself had begun to raise … the time was ripe, vibrating with potential. Students like ourselves were struggling for something more than a twenty-five cent hamburger in the South. We needed to put our goals into words. Many of us were student leaders who were conditioned to believe that if you spoke out, you would get a hearing from the Kennedy administration.[13]

Sixty people turned up to Hayden's invitation, and considered a 75-page document he had drafted on how students could best influence national politics. The eventual Statement, based on Hayden's draft, attacked the alienation of the American workforce and drew on the writings of C. Wright Mills to insist that 'a new left must transform modern complexity into issues that can be understood and felt close-up by every human being ... In a time of supposed prosperity, moral complacency and political manipulation, a new left cannot rely on only aching stomachs to be the engine for social reform.'[14]

Hayden persuaded Walter Reuther, the leader of the Union of Auto Workers, to donate $5,000 to the SDS ghetto projects. Reuther, as stated in the previous chapter, was also the sort of union leader Kennedy regarded as important to an alternative Democratic coalition, representing as he did links to the new and old left. Despite his associations with the old socialist factions, Reuther had maintained credibility with the emerging New Left, who regarded him as a different breed from the more traditional union bosses.

The programmes Reuther's money funded for the SDS were not unlike those advocated by Kennedy in his urban renewal proposals. The money went to the Economic and Research Action Project (ERAP) in Newark, which Hayden described as 'like a SNCC programme' and which encouraged participatory democracy and community action.[15] Kennedy was one of the few national politicians who enjoyed significant credibility in SDS circles, and at least one ERAP activist worked for Kennedy's 1964 Senate campaign. Hayden notes that by 1967 'the only politician who expressed an interest in what I was doing was Robert Kennedy', although Kennedy's interest in Hayden often centred on what sort of political links he could offer to other organizations.[16]

The SDS saw itself as very different from the old leftist student organizations, and it deliberately moved its headquarters away from the tribal feuds of the old left in New York and set up in Chicago. By 1965 the Vietnam War began to dominate the SDS agenda and national politics and a march organized by the group in April 1965 attracted 60,000 demonstrators to Washington. (Two months later, SNCC activist Julian Bond was elected to the Georgia state legislature on an anti-war platform. Bond was refused permission to take up his seat because of his stance on the war, fought the case up to the Supreme Court and ultimately gained his seat.[17])

In November another SDS anti-war rally attracted tens of thousands to Washington, and in the following February Kennedy broke with the White House in calling for a coalition government in South Vietnam. However, the anti-Vietnam War movement was certainly not a majority at this time (or at any time before Kennedy's death), and Kennedy had to ensure that he was not too closely identified with the anti-war demonstrators. Once he had made his break with the Johnson administration, and claimed some of the radical ground to the left of the party, he fell into a long silence about the issue and did not speak out again as forcefully for another year.

Elsewhere in the country, meanwhile, the SDS and other New Left organizations were trying to mobilize opposition to the war on a variety of fronts. Demonstrations were fine for politicizing the public but did not appear to be changing policy. During the summer of 1966 Bob Scheer, editor of *Ramparts*, organized an electoral campaign for the Democratic Party nomination to Congress in the San Francisco Bay area. He won 45% of votes on a radical platform firmly opposing the war.

However, the anti-war policy, though potentially powerful, was not strong enough for Kennedy to base his national constituency upon it. The issue, and with it his political base, could disappear within a week, and he was careful not to ally himself solely with those New Leftists opposing the war.

The poverty, or black, issue, provided some scope for relations with the new activists, and in ideological terms they were more receptive to Kennedy's ideas for private capital helping to renew urban centres than the old-style socialist left would have been. Of course, not all Americans under 30, or even the majority of students, were New Leftists. However, it was New Left philosophy which was becoming increasingly influential on campuses throughout the mid-1960s. For example, the relatively conservative National Student Association (NSA), which represented the respectable face of student politics, passed resolutions at its 1965 convention for a halt to offensive action in Vietnam, the admission of China to the UN and the establishment of a national police force to protect civil rights.

While NSA students were eventually drawn to the Eugene McCarthy presidential campaign in 1968, Kennedy's appeal appears to have skipped over much of this moderate faction, and he was to find a surprising amount of support in the more radical youth elements. However, one radical New Leftist who was not impressed by Kennedy's image of developing radicalism was Bob Scheer. 'He's been raised in a traditional, political bag, and he was fundamentally a hack,' he noted, but he conceded that Kennedy 'could be awed by radicals'.[18]

Scheer wrote a lengthy and critical profile of Kennedy for *Ramparts* in February 1967, which warned New Leftists not to trust the Senator. 'What Bobby learned during the course of the [1964] campaign was that it was possible to gain liberal support without losing the other; for while "bosses" care about the substance of power, liberals remain suckers for mere rhetoric.'[19] Scheer was determined not to believe the hype: 'The Kennedy people have raised co-option to an art form. At hearings of his subcommittee, his tours through New York's ghettos, and during speeches before dozens of college audiences, they have hooked on to the mood of crisis and, as with everything else, have come to use it.'[20]

However, while Scheer accused Kennedy of relying on 'standard Cold War mythology' in foreign affairs, Scheer himself was guilty of standard class-war mythology in criticizing the plans for fighting poverty. 'On relying on private investment as a panacea for Latin American problems, he is clearly to the right of the New Deal,' he declared, not grasping that Kennedy's 'hack' background enabled him to break out of the old right v. left equation.[21]

Andrew Kopkind, writing for *Ramparts* during the 1968 primaries, made the same mistake of viewing Kennedy through a lens of old ideology, but this time came down admiringly on the Senator's side: 'The Kennedy men have been interested in reorganizing Democratic politics ... but they put little stock in the peace movement as their agent. Rather, they favour the "urban" route; the angry and oppressed masses in the cities are a tougher force than the suburban [anti-war] SANE-niks. The Kennedys don't forget their Marxism.'[22]

Both Scheer and Kopkind got near to the point but missed it. Kennedy's overriding motivation was neither Marxism nor to the right of the New Deal. He was trying to put together a vaguely liberal (and the vaguer the better, as it would exclude fewer participants) coalition to form a national constituency. He had severe image problems with some of the older leftists (I. F. Stone and James Baldwin both backed Keating in the Senate race), but the New Left liberalism offered him the chance to develop a new base without relying on the old unions and former New York socialists. It was the very lack of ideology in the New Left which attracted him to them, and them to him. New Left leader Abbie Hoffman, for instance, acknowledged Kennedy's attraction for many radicals. In December 1967 Hoffman founded the Youth International Party (Yippie!), designed to obstruct the Democratic Convention in Chicago during the following summer. Hayden regarded Yippie! as a politicising force on youth culture. 'Instead of a weighty manifesto like the Port Huron Statement, a radical message was communicated by appearance, not by new ideas but by a seemingly new species, the "freak," who would first alienate, then challenge, and ultimately dispel the repressive attitudes of the majority culture.'[23] The Yippie! Party was part of a wider New Left movement, which included organizations such as the National Mobilization Committee to End the War in Vietnam, formed to protest at the forthcoming convention.

The New Left rallying cry from the end of 1967 was 'On to Chicago!', and various schemes (including the 'nomination' of a pig) were planned to create disturbances in the city. Hoffman explained how Yippie! drew support from many of those supporting Kennedy's presidential campaign. 'Bobby, there was the real threat. A direct challenge to the theatre-in-the-streets, a challenge to the charisma of Yippie!' When Kennedy announced his candidacy in March, 'it was no contest,' says Hoffman. 'When young longhairs told you they'd heard that Bobby turned on, you knew Yippie! was really in trouble.'[24] By the end of May, Hoffman's constituency had been so severely eroded by the Kennedy campaign that it was disbanded. After Kennedy's death it was resurrected and duly caused chaos in Chicago.

As with his campaigns in black areas, Kennedy appears to have relied heavily on style, leading Scheer to warn in *Ramparts* that Kennedy 'could easily co-opt the prevailing dissent without delivering to it ... providing the illusion of dissent without its substance'.[25] Yippie! co-founder Jerry Rubin was similarly unimpressed with Kennedy's reliance on glamour: 'The right-wing menace exists but it's not George Wallace. It's the Kennedy liberals ... George Wallace is Robert Kennedy in drag.'[26]

In his 1967 book *To Seek a Newer World*, which was to become his presidential campaign manifesto, Kennedy's opening chapter was on youth, and, in an emotional attempt to claim his brother's charisma by aligning himself with the martyred image of the dead President, Kennedy referred to 'the story of Moses, who brought his people within sight of the promised land and then died, leaving to Joshua the leadership in achieving goals that both completely shared'.[27]

Similarly direct appeals were made to youthful audiences throughout the presidential campaign, with a student audience in Kansas being told that they were 'the most important generation in history'. Nevertheless, the chapter on youth in Kennedy's manifesto was primarily concerned with outlining the part young people could play in a new coalition. He cited the example of the radical Provos in Amsterdam who stood for municipal elections with some success and whose ideas were incorporated into mainstream politics. Kennedy pointed out that the old left had little to offer the new generation and that liberals should be prepared to adapt to the New Left agenda. 'Nor, painful as it may be for liberals to acknowledge, are these young people enchanted with liberal institutions ... They think labour has grown sleek and bureaucratic with power ... occasionally even corrupt and exploitative, a force not for change, but for the status quo,' he explained.[28]

The tone of the chapter was one of Kennedy interpreting the younger generation's grievances for the adult world. In an passage which is peppered with quotations from Bob Dylan, John Lennon and the radical Free Speech Movement at Berkeley, Kennedy appeared to offer himself as a go-between between the young dissenters and the older voters, just as he often presented himself to white audiences as a person who understood black frustrations and could deal with them.

Traditional liberals were often particularly suspicious of the New Left. The radicals, after all, threatened liberal symbols such as the universities and attacked working-class heroes such as Mayor Richard Daley. The tension between the old and new liberals who supported Kennedy was evident during his Senate career and was exacerbated during his presidential campaign.[29] Traditional New Deal liberal Arthur Schlesinger remains bitter towards the New Left. 'If you look at the leaders of the New Left, where the hell are they?' he said in 1985. 'They're selling real estate or they're on Wall Street like Jerry Rubin, or they're in the State Assembly in California. I mean, these weren't highly principled figures. These were opportunistic figures ... none of them I know is a New Leftist today. I think it was an ephemeral movement ... [Adam] Walinsky [Kennedy Senate aide and speechwriter] was bitter on the left and now he's bitter on the right ...'[30]

Kennedy faced difficulties in trying to join the old and new leftists in any sort of coalition, let alone putting them together to work with more traditionally hostile elements such as blue-collar whites. Nevertheless he kept on searching out New Left ideas to incorporate into his new agenda and in February 1967 met with Tom Hayden and another New Leftist, Staughton Lynd, before delivering his major speech on Vietnam. At the end of the meeting Kennedy said he was going on to have dinner with two liberals from the old school, Schlesinger and John Kenneth Galbraith, and that Hayden and Lynd were welcome to carry on the discussion there. Both declined. 'I just had no desire to become part of that circle of intellectuals, because I didn't feel I belonged there,' remembered Lynd.[31]

As 1968 approached, however, Kennedy's links with the New Left became stronger, despite earlier resentment at his previous association with Republican Senator Joe McCarthy of Wisconsin, for whom he had waited for six months in 1952–53. He overcame revelations in early 1967 that as Attorney General he had approved CIA subsidies to the NSA and other 'moderate' student organizations designed to counter the activities of Communist and other radical student groups (which presumably included the SDS).[32] By the time of the election campaign many NSA members preferred Senator Eugene McCarthy, while the more radical student elements, such as those found in the SDS, supported Kennedy. The NSA membership, although broadly against the war, tended to be involved with local anti-Vietnam protests rather than national demonstrations.

McCarthy's much-vaunted appeal to disaffected youth was, according to one study of the New Hampshire primary, confined 'to quieter students, rather than radical demonstrators'.[33] Only a minority of McCarthy's student volunteers had taken part in any of the major anti-war marches, found Sidney Hymin in his study of *Youth in Politics*.[34] In fact, in a study of 800 McCarthy volunteers in the New Hampshire primary, it was established that the young were not represented any more than any other age-group, with as many volunteers aged between 50 and 55 as between 20 and 25.[35] The idea of a McCarthy children's crusade was rooted in media hype, and from the initial press reports to come out of New Hampshire one particular weekend in January, when students were heavily represented among the volunteers.[36]

Kennedy, on the other hand, had become increasingly associated with the more extreme elements among the New Left (or 'the beards' as he called them). In a confidential FBI memo dated 20 July, 1968, an unnamed agent reports 'that it was rumoured prior to the assassination of Robert F. Kennedy that substantial sums of "Kennedy money" were given to Tom Hayden and Renée Davis, both affiliated with the National Mobilization Committee to End the War in Vietnam, to create demonstrations at the National Democratic Convention, August 1968'.[37] The FBI report continues: 'These demonstrations, funded by "Kennedy money" were to be directed against President Lyndon B. Johnson, and for Senator Kennedy … a large meeting was called at an unknown lake outside Chicago, Illinois for the purpose of planning these demonstrations. Source related one [name deleted by the FBI] co-ordinated the invitations to this conference, and made free airline tickets available to various groups, through Hayden and Davis.'[38]

No doubt there were elements in the FBI willing to believe Kennedy was engaged in subversive operations, but there is no better example of how far he had come during his Senate years than the existence of this document: he was on the CIA's side in 1963 in countering the threat of groups such as the SDS, but five years later he was suspected of being in cahoots with their leaders to disrupt the Democratic Convention.

Although it would be an exaggeration to imply that Kennedy was very close to the SDS on many policy matters, he did respond to the sorts of concerns they expressed probably better than any other national politician (including McCarthy). He was not, however, in favour of a unilateral withdrawal from Vietnam and did not (overtly, at least) share the hippies' advocacy of free love and drugs, although New Left historian and Kennedy admirer Jack Newfield did point out in *The Nation* in November 1966 that during Senate hearings on drugs Kennedy 'was less tough on the pro-LSD witnesses than was his younger brother'.[39]

Newfield also declared that while Kennedy was 'not an advocate of reforming our repressive narcotics and abortion laws, he is not a headline-hunting crusader against the beards and beats'.[40] While Kennedy himself could not ever accurately be described as having been a New Leftist, his emerging liberalism incorporated much of the style and content of what the younger radicals were saying. In a standard campaign speech delivered dozens of times at stops in small towns during the 1968 presidential primaries, Kennedy told voters they would

> find neither national purpose nor personal satisfaction in a mere continuation of economic progress, in an endless amassing of worldly goods ... the gross national product includes air pollution and advertising for cigarettes, and ambulances to clear our highways of carnage ... it does not allow for the health of our families, the quality of their education or the joy of their play ...[41]

Hayden found the speech startling 'in its resemblance to Port Huron', and with several other leading figures on the New Left (including writer Pete Hamill) went to work for Kennedy in the California primary.[42]

Many planned to work for Kennedy in the New York primary, scheduled for 18 June, which of course he never entered. Kennedy's final speech on the night of his death ended with the New Left slogan 'On to Chicago!', the city where any chance of coalition between old and new liberals eventually died. If Kennedy had made it to Chicago, even without winning the nomination, the split might have been avoided, but as it was – with Democratic Mayor Daley ordering his police to attack the new radicals – the wound proved mortal.

Hayden and Hoffman were among eight New Leftists tried for inciting violence at the convention, in a trial that FBI Director J. Edgar

Hoover regarded as an opportunity 'to seriously disrupt and curtail the activities of the New Left'.[43] Humphrey proved an unattractive candidate to the New Left, and in 1972 George McGovern tried so hard to appeal to the new liberal vote that he could not carry the old labour left.

Kennedy, for all his misunderstanding of the hippie subculture, might have brought the New Left into mainstream liberalism as part of an electoral and governing coalition. No one else came close.

Chapter Four

Foreign Policy

Part I – The White House Experience

'The Americans ... had, on the whole, been open and candid with us, especially Robert Kennedy' – Premier Khrushchev, after the Cuban missile crisis

During the Senate vote on 21 January, 1961, to confirm Robert Kennedy as Attorney General, several senators expressed reservations about his lack of experience for the job. Although none actually voted against the appointment, a handful made long speeches pointing out that he had never practised as a lawyer. Senator Everett Dirksen of Illinois, the Republican leader on the Judiciary Committee, joined with several colleagues in recording that he had received a large amount of mail urging him to oppose the nomination, and also reminded the Senate that Robert Kennedy, if appointed, 'must advise the President not only on domestic problems, but on international problems as well'.[1]

In the following three years, Robert Kennedy would become involved in the execution of US foreign policy to an extraordinary degree. His influence on foreign policy increased throughout the Kennedy administration, and his role developed far beyond the constitutional boundaries of advising the President on foreign affairs to developing major initiatives on his own, and sometimes making key decisions on international affairs without the President's knowledge. By the time of his brother's assassination in 1963, Robert Kennedy was in effect deputy President in many areas of foreign policy, and on occasions when his brother was absent actually took presidential decisions on critical international events. His familiarity with world affairs on becoming Attorney General in 1961 was limited, although it was probably greater than his knowledge of many aspects of the law.

An early initiation into the world of foreign policy began at the age of thirteen, when in 1938 his father was appointed Ambassador to the

Court of St James. The appointment turned out to be a disastrous one for Joseph Kennedy's political career, as his reluctance to urge American entry into the Second World War branded him in some quarters an anti-Semitic appeaser.[2] Whether the streak of dissent on US foreign policy which Robert Kennedy was to reveal in his last years was rooted in his father's experience is difficult to assess, although as a Senator 30 years later Robert Kennedy would defend the rights of those opposed to US involvement in war.

With his father's policy discredited by the attack on Pearl Harbor and American entry into the war, Robert Kennedy's international education was halted, and his next venture abroad was a tourist trip to Latin America as a reward for his work in helping John Kennedy win a Congressional seat in 1946. The trip apparently made little impression on him politically, however, and it was only in 1948, when his father sent him on an educational mission to Europe and the Middle East that he first began to formulate his own serious ideas on international politics. Thanks to his father's contacts, Robert Kennedy left America armed with impressive letters of introduction from a number of influential figures, and an accreditation from the *Boston Post* to act as a foreign correspondent.

Kennedy (now 23) and college friend George Terrien found themselves in Israel when the British mandate ended. In Tel Aviv, Kennedy and Terrien 'went for a walk', according to Kennedy's notebook, 'but picked up by the police & as large crowd gathered were blindfolded & put in car ... taken to headquarters to be interrogated by Security Police. Advised to stay off streets unless with someone.'[3] In dispatches to his Boston readers he dutifully blamed the British for the mess in the Middle East, before travelling to Europe, where the threat of war over Berlin and Czechoslovakia appeared imminent.

Kennedy had by no means become an instant expert on international affairs during the trip, but he was no longer a novice, and another such fact-finding journey three years later in the company of his brother John and sister Pat proved significantly influential on his thinking in later years. The impressions he formed with John Kennedy in 1951 were to shape many of their attitudes to foreign policy matters when they took over the White House a decade later. His unfavourable opinion of Nehru, for example, was made during this trip and remained unchanged ten years later during the Kennedy administration. Speaking in 1967, he remembered how 'Nehru just talked to my sister Pat and directed everything to her. My brother always remembered that ... [JFK] really hated Nehru. Nehru was really rude to us when we went to India in 1951'.[4]

More significant, though, was the impression the brothers developed about struggles for national liberation. Robert Kennedy was shocked on his 1951 trip at how little American diplomatic staff knew about 'the people', and his own disdain for official diplomatic channels during his Senate years can be traced back to this experience.[5] The Kennedys' evaluation was largely based on their experience in Saigon, where Robert Kennedy noted that the French were 'greatly hated', and he blamed the Americans for not insisting 'on definite political reforms by the French towards the natives as prerequisites to any aid. As it stands now we are becoming more and more involved in the war to a point where we can't back out'.[6]

Although the assessment is not without irony when considered against the Kennedy administration's policy on Vietnam, this early judgement reveals much about John and Robert Kennedy's foreign policy principles. These ideas can be found in the Alliance for Progress and the various initiatives the administration undertook in Africa. This appreciation that it was in America's best interests to identify itself with those agitating for self-determination did not dawn on many other political figures until much later in the century, and not all have grasped it yet. However, this belief (though not always put into action) remained the most positive aspect of the Kennedys' foreign policy for the remainder of both their lives and made them heroes in a variety of unlikely places around the world.

The 1951 trip was set up (again with their father's help) to promote John Kennedy as a foreign policy expert and enhance his credentials for his Senate campaign the following year. Following his victory over Henry Cabot Lodge in 1952, John Kennedy's career in the Senate was generally marked by its moderation and blandness. The Senate for John (and Robert) was always going to be a platform from which to launch an assault on the presidency, and throughout his eight years John Kennedy was careful not to make enemies by championing controversial campaigns – except once.

JFK's only major break with mainstream political thinking in foreign affairs during his Congressional career was over national independence for Algeria. At a time when Washington was trying to maintain a discreet silence over the war against the French in Algeria, John Kennedy accused the Eisenhower administration of helping France continue a repressive colonial war and refusing to recognize legitimate Algerian claims for self-determination. In July 1957 he called on the United States to 'redouble its efforts to earn the respect and friendship of nationalist leaders'.[7] This belief, rooted less in ideological sympathy with the

Algerians than with basic common sense on what was best for US interests, surfaced in Robert Kennedy's decision several years later to receive Eduardo Mondlane in the Attorney General's office. Mondlane was head of Frelimo, the liberation movement in Mozambique which fought for independence from the Portuguese, and Kennedy's invitation was regarded by Secretary of State Dean Rusk as insulting to Portugal.[8]

It would not be fair to suggest that the Kennedys were secretly battling for the overthrow of colonial governments during their time in the White House. Nelson Mandela's arrest in 1962, it should be remembered, was reportedly the result of a CIA tip-off during the Kennedy administration.[9] Nevertheless John Kennedy's speech on Algeria was at least a recognition of the validity of one liberation struggle, and his time on the Subcommittee for African Affairs in the Senate presumably expanded his understanding of international politics during the 1950s.

Robert Kennedy, meanwhile, was not generally involved with international affairs in this period. During his brother's Senate career, Robert remained in government service, working for various Senate committees investigating the Teamsters' Union and organized crime. He had also spent the six months following John Kennedy's election to the Senate working for Senator Joe McCarthy as assistant counsel for the Permanent Subcommittee on Investigations, when he was given a foreign-related task: to research the trade carried on by the United States' allies with Communist China. Thus, by the time of his appointment as Attorney General, Kennedy's knowledge of international affairs was based on a spell as an ambassador's son, a short foray into the navy, his research for McCarthy on Chinese trade patterns, and a couple of trips around the world.

Despite these limitations, Kennedy had helped to engineer his brother's victory in an election which had been dominated by the Cold War and by which candidate was best able to deal with it. It was not crucial to global security in 1961 that the United States appoint an Attorney General who was an expert on international affairs, but, in his unique position as deputy President, Robert Kennedy's influence over world events was far greater than the framers of the US Constitution, or even Everett Dirksen, could have predicted. By the early 1960s the United States found itself taking over commitments for which it was ill prepared. Its decision to enter the Second World War had proved more far-reaching than had the decision to enter the First. At the end of the war, the United States found itself the outright winner – its country's infrastructure was intact, its enemies defeated, and much of the world looked to it for economic survival.

However, by taking up responsibilities which Britain and other colonial powers found they could no longer afford, the United States soon made itself significantly more unpopular in many countries around the world. It did not add to its popularity rating by backing oppressive regimes in Latin America, Africa and the Middle East to protect its economic interests. The bankrupt colonial powers were more than willing to cede their traditional spheres of influence to the new world superpower which, during the 1950s, appeared militarily and politically unassailable. However, centuries of diplomatic experience in dealing with the Third World could not be so easily transferred from the European powers to the United States, and American unfamiliarity with local concerns in Vietnam, Israel and dozens of other countries around the world was to prove disastrous. Dean Acheson observed that when British Prime Minister Clement Attlee refused to play any part in the partitioning of Palestine after the war, he 'deftly exchanged the United States for Britain as the most disliked power in the Middle East'.[10]

By the 1950s American foreign policy experts still lacked the intelligence-gathering agencies necessary to police the world, and the country's institutions were ravaged by a 'red scare', itself partly a result of failing to understand the motives of foreign governments. The United States made some staggering foreign policy assessments in this period. When Frank Bender, the CIA's chief expert on Latin American Communism met Fidel Castro in 1959 for a three-hour interview, he enthused: 'Castro is not only not a Communist; he is a strong anti-Communist fighter.'[11]

It was against this background that the Kennedys entered the White House. The American public, indirectly empowered to solve many of the problems of the rest of the world, had little understanding of international affairs. John Kennedy's Catholic religion had featured significantly in the 1960 primary campaign, primarily because of the electorate's xenophobia. It was not John Kennedy's belief in transubstantiation or the Immaculate Conception which bothered much of the public, but that he might somehow be open to manipulation by the Vatican. President Kennedy's inaugural address was a self-conscious acceptance of the United States' new role in the world. Inexperienced, like most of his fellow Americans, in international affairs, he promised too much and understood too little.

The President's new Attorney General, it should be added, understood even less, but was immediately involved in appointing representatives of the US government around the world. Although he had never negotiated with a foreign government, Robert Kennedy, now 36, spent his first days in cabinet advising his brother on major ambassadorial appointments.[12] In an oral history programme recorded the year before Robert Kennedy was killed, he was asked about various aspects of his involvement in foreign policy questions during the Kennedy administration. 'It is interesting to look back on all these things going on,' he said. 'I was involved in more things than I thought.'[13]

The extent of Robert Kennedy's influence on world events during those years is remarkable by any standards, especially in the light of his credentials. In the oral history he reveals that, before he was asked to become Attorney General, President Kennedy offered him the ambassadorship to Moscow. ('I didn't think it was a good idea,' he noted.[14]) Within days, however, he was being asked for his advice on who would be the best person to send to the Soviet Union in his place, and for suggestions to fill other ambassadorial vacancies. In 1967 he remembered those ambassadors who were appointed because they were colleagues of the President, and those who were appointed because they were colleagues of his own. 'Then a good number of them I knew. So, if there were a particular problem, I'd have correspondence with them, whether it's Jim Wine [then Ambassador to the Ivory Coast], or Bill Attwood [Ambassador to Guinea], or [William P.] Mahoney in Ghana, and some of the others ...'[15]

Within weeks of the Kennedy administration's entry into office, it was clear that Robert Kennedy was not bound by the constitutional limits on an Attorney General. He was the President's brother and so could apparently roam at will into other areas of responsibility and decision-making (although where he stood on the question of accountability if, for instance, a decision he made outside his remit turned out to be a mistake is not clear).

On occasions it appears as though Robert Kennedy actually thought of himself as an alternative President when his brother could not be reached. In May 1961 President Trujillo, the Dominican Republic's dictator, was assassinated, sparking off a major crisis in the region. President Kennedy was in Paris at the time, on his way to Vienna to meet Khrushchev, and so Robert Kennedy, in Washington, immediately assumed the mantle of the President. 'Nobody seemed to be doing anything,' he remembered in 1964. '... I guess I had the major responsibility of trying to work out some plans ... We moved the fleet in closer.'[16]

Robert Kennedy's memories of how the incident developed become even more revealing, as he practically claims to have been the President during the time when John Kennedy was in Europe. John Bartlow Martin,

interviewing Robert Kennedy in Virginia in April 1964, asked if the
Kennedy administration knew in advance of the Trujillo assassination.

Martin: 'I don't think they'd plan to assassinate a chief of state without telling the President.'

Kennedy: 'No. That's what I think. They wouldn't have done it without telling *me*' (my italics).[17]

However good the quality of advice Robert Kennedy gave to the
President, he was not empowered by the Constitution to think of himself
as President, and on another occasion – in dealing with Castro for the
return of prisoners captured during the Bay of Pigs – he was apparently
negotiating with the Cuban leader without John Kennedy's knowledge.
This is not meant to suggest, of course, that President Kennedy minded
in the least that his brother was willing to bear any burden in foreign
policy-making, but it does raise some worrying questions about accountability and the potential power of an unelected official in cabinet.

The Trujillo episode, where Robert Kennedy took charge in Washington, was presumably a strong reaction to what had happened the
previous month, when the Kennedy administration suffered its greatest
embarrassment at the Bay of Pigs. The Kennedys thought they had been
led into the disastrous invasion by experts who were badly informed,
and John Kennedy's instant reaction when news began to reach him that
the assault on Cuba had failed was to tell his assistant Kenneth
O'Donnell: 'I should have had Bobby in on this from the start.'[18] After
the Bay of Pigs debacle, Bobby was in on every major foreign policy
decision President Kennedy made. 'I then became involved on every
major and all the international questions', he recalled in 1964.[19]

Although inherited from the Eisenhower administration, the plan to
invade the Bay of Pigs proved typical of the Kennedys' thinking on how
best to cope with Communist revolutions. They had, after all, learned in
1951 that struggles for national liberation could be achieved by guerrillas operating out of small units in unconventional warfare. To combat
this, the Kennedys, and especially Robert, were drawn to the idea of
counter-insurgency techniques.[20] This fitted well with the athletic
but intellectual image of the administration. Robert Kennedy was
particularly associated with the elite counter-insurgents, the Green
Berets – top soldiers who would be able to compete with guerrillas on
their own terms and on their own terrain. The Kennedys encouraged
Third World military experts – even ambassadors – to read up on
local guerrilla techniques. John Kennedy urged his generals to read
Guevara and Mao.[21] The Green Berets were the American answer to

the Communist guerrillas and were regarded with a special awe in the administration. They were viewed, as David Halberstam notes, 'as brilliant, young, great physical specimens in their green berets, swinging through the trees, you know, arm in arm, and speaking six languages, including Chinese and Russian, and who had Ph.D.s in history and literature, and ate snake meat at night.'[22]

Robert Kennedy was much taken with the idea of the Green Berets, and even when their military effectiveness was largely discredited a few years later, and they had failed to make any significant headway in Vietnam, he still kept a green beret behind his chair in his Senate office. The idea that American soldiers, if they tried hard enough, could eventually become guerrillas, living off the land just as the enemy did, was a fatally flawed one. The Bay of Pigs proved that, no matter how well trained the troops, they could not function without local support.

The difference between guerrillas, who fight for a cause which they believe is long-term and political, and commandos, who are fighting for a medium-term military solution, or for money or prestige, is a fundamental one. The Kennedys, like many US military experts at the time, apparently believed that a commando could fight on equal terms with a revolutionary if he mastered the revolutionary's language and terrain. However, by failing to recognize the crucial difference in motivation between the Green Berets and, say, the Viet Cong, John and Robert Kennedy typified American inexperience in such matters. However, at least the Kennedys realized that a hearts-and-minds battle could be eventually decisive and made some attempt – through the Alliance for Progress – to counter the desire for Communist revolution in the first place.

At least in dealing with Latin America the Kennedys (and it would appear that on Latin American issues it was Robert as much as John who formulated official policy) could draw on a tradition of experience within the State Department. Unlike the rest of the world, Latin America was not uncharted territory for the new superpower. The United States had regarded the region as its legitimate sphere of interest for well over a century, and the famous Monroe Doctrine (enunciated by President Monroe in 1823 when he warned European powers that any expansion in Latin America would be regarded as dangerous to US interests) still provided the basis for Washington's special concern for its southern neighbours.

During the Second World War relations between the United States and Latin America proved strong. In an effort to combat Nazi infiltration into the region, President Roosevelt had acted as an extremely friendly neighbour and had successfully avoided any dangerous instability in Central and South America through a series of non-intervention pacts he signed with countries in the region. The Alliance for Progress was an extension of this tradition. The Kennedys, in sharp contrast to their successors, thought that the United States' self-interest was best served by friendly liberal democracies in Latin America, rather than pliant but vulnerable dictatorships (although the Kennedys were not idealistic enough to prefer a Communist regime over a pliant tyrant).

'I think I might have gotten more involved in Latin America myself ... in the second term, anyway,' Robert Kennedy said in 1964, although between 1961 and 1963 he had already been fairly heavily involved – in the Trujillo episode, in the immediate aftermath of the Bay of Pigs invasion and, most famously, in the Cuban missile crisis.[23]

In the days after the Bay of Pigs operation, it was Robert Kennedy who took charge of getting the prisoners taken by Castro back to the United States and organized the paying of various ransoms. This, although a delicate job, was not a crucial one in terms of power or world security. However, there is some evidence to show that his actions on the initiative were unilateral and had not been cleared with the President (again, this is not to suggest that JFK disapproved of the plans, but merely serves to indicate the extent of Robert Kennedy's licence on foreign policy). As Arthur Schlesinger records, the Attorney General

> proposed an exchange of $28 million worth of agricultural products for the prisoners. This was peculiarly his initiative. On the evening of 5 April [1962], I noted in my journal, "the President called me at 7 o'clock to find out what the Food-for-Prisoners deal is all about. This is an operation which ... is strongly backed by Bobby ... We had all assumed that the President knew about it, but apparently no-one had told him."[24]

Within months of the Bay of Pigs disaster, the Kennedy administration set about re-establishing American credentials in the region, with a meeting at Punta del Este in Uruguay, which formally established the Alliance for Progress. Robert Kennedy's involvement in the Alliance later provided him with his first grounds for attacking the Johnson administration and during his Senate years presented him with an opportunity bettered only by Vietnam to distance himself from the new President and suggest that Johnson had betrayed the ideals of the Kennedy administration.

The Alliance for Progress reflected the Kennedys' ideas for a liberal alternative to Communism which, if it could not be achieved through the electoral process, could be helped along with counter-insurgency techniques. It was a series of trade agreements and objectives in which the participants recognized the need for democratic reform. US military aid to countries which shared these objectives of reform would be increased, while military aid to repressive regimes would be cut.

By the end of his career Robert Kennedy's position on Latin American affairs had shifted considerably from the early days, and many of his ideas in 1967 and 1968 were to prove years ahead of their time, but in 1961 he believed that the Communist threat could be countered by an immediate alleviation of poverty and the promise of democratic elections. These were not ignoble ideas in themselves, but getting Latin American dictatorships to agree to elections proved difficult, for in the end the dictators knew that, if faced with a choice between supporting them or risking a Communist overthrow, Washington would give its backing to the anti-Communist, regardless of his government's record on poverty or human rights. Moreover, the Alliance for Progress over-estimated the strength of the middle classes in Latin America, and the policy soon collapsed into one of counter-insurgency.

Che Guevara called the initiative 'an alliance of one millionaire and twenty beggars', and it was inevitable that such a Washington-led proposal would be weighted heavily towards US interests.[25] However, the Kennedy administration believed that stable democracies in the region were in America's best interests, and for a while it appeared as though the Alliance could bring about significant improvements in standards of living for many Latin Americans. During the Kennedy administration, the 2:1 proportion of military to humanitarian aid to the region was reversed, so that by 1963 twice as much humanitarian aid was being sent as military aid, a trend which would not be carried on during the Johnson years.[26]

By March 1964 the new Johnson appointee as Assistant Secretary for Latin America, Thomas Mann, was already telling a meeting of US ambassadors to the region that they should not continue in their criticisms of human rights in the countries where they worked. President Kennedy's policies, he said, showed how fruitless it was to impose democracy on Latin America, and he urged greater emphasis on national security interests.[27]

An early test of the Alliance came with the assassination of Trujillo. After the overthrow of the dictator (with or without US complicity), the

Kennedy administration was convinced that it had to ensure prompt elections for its policy to maintain credibility. In December 1962 Juan Bosch, a left-wing reformer, was duly elected in the first free election in the Dominican Republic for 30 years. The election's success relied on substantial US political and economic involvement in the process and proved a good advertisement for JFK's policy for the region.

When Washington received reports from the US ambassador in the summer of 1962 that the 'government has lost control of the streets to the Communists', who threatened to disrupt the elections, the President asked Robert Kennedy to organize a special counter-insurgency unit to sort out the problem.[28] The Attorney General immediately dispatched to Santo Domingo two American policemen who had been trained at one of the counter-insurgency schools, and order was restored. 'The same [happened] in Venezuela,' Robert Kennedy remembered two years later. 'They sent three fellows down to Venezuela [to restore order]. It's incredible what just a few people can do.'[29]

The Dominican situation, far from being a model for other Latin American countries to follow, however, soon exposed important flaws in the Alliance for Progress. Newly-elected President Bosch was seen by some communists in his country as an American puppet, installed for the benefit of the Kennedy administration. To combat the threat of armed insurrection, Bosch had to call on Washington for more and more military aid, which in turn fortified allegations of pro-Americanism. This spiral of military aid from Washington provoking criticism of Bosch, which resulted in yet more military aid from Washington, went on until he was overthrown in a coup in September 1963. Bosch asked the Kennedy administration via John Bartlow Martin, US Ambassador in Santa Domingo, for military help to prevent the coup. 'I transmitted the request and got an answer saying that they wouldn't send one except to prevent a Communist takeover,' said the ambassador, 'they wouldn't send it to prop up Bosch'.[30] Elsewhere the Alliance had more positive results. In some places it improved conditions for many people, and even Castro declared in 1963 that 'it was a good idea ... a very intelligent strategy'.[31]

Although Robert Kennedy was highly influential in US actions in the region during his brother's administration, he visited Latin America only for 24 hours during the whole of his brother's presidency, when he was sent at the end of 1962 to bolster the Alliance on a trip to Brazil. It was, of course, Cuba which attracted his attention during these years, and his foreign policy reputation during his period in the Senate was largely based on his involvement in the missile crisis of October 1962.

It is indicative of Robert Kennedy's real and perceived influence on foreign policy matters in the Kennedy administration that most studies on the subject afford him as much credit, or blame, for US actions during the missile crisis as they do the President. Khrushchev, reflecting on the crisis afterwards, recalled that the Americans 'had, on the whole, been open and candid with us, especially Robert Kennedy'.[32] Harold Macmillan said in 1969 that 'the way Bobby and his brother played [their] hand was absolutely masterly'.[33]

Given his extraordinary lack of foreign policy experience, and the limits of his official post as Attorney General, Robert Kennedy's serious involvement in the crisis is truly remarkable. Nevertheless, by the time of the crisis in October 1962, he had already cultivated an unconventional channel of communication with the Soviet government. In mid-1961 a New York journalist introduced him to Georgi Bolshakov, who worked for the Soviet embassy's public relations department. Robert Kennedy later described Bolshakov as 'Khrushchev's representative' and claimed that the Soviet leader used to send messages to the US President through Bolshakov, who would pass them on via the Attorney General.[34] 'Most of the major matters dealing with the Soviet Union and the United States were discussed and arrangements made between Georgi Bolshakov and myself', said Robert Kennedy in 1964. 'I met with him about whether the [Vienna summit] meeting should take place, whether the President wanted to meet Khrushchev ... When they were concerned about Berlin, he would come to me and talk about that ...'[35]

Such message-carrying duties were all part of the network of communications which governments build up during the course of diplomatic negotiations, but this one gave Robert Kennedy highly privileged access to the most secret information, some of which presumably was only ever known by Bolshakov, Khrushchev, President Kennedy and the Attorney General. 'I don't know why they [the Soviets] wanted to proceed in that fashion, but they didn't want to go through their ambassador [Mikhail Menshikov] evidently,' Robert Kennedy noted.[36]

By the time of the missile crisis, Robert Kennedy had enjoyed over a year of fortnightly meetings with Bolshakov, and so was much more familiar with the way Khrushchev conducted business than many experts on Soviet relations who relied on official State Department channels for their information. 'The State Department didn't like having him [meet with me] much because this involved circumventing them, I suppose', admitted Kennedy.[37]

Although New York Senator Kenneth Keating (Republican) had claimed for weeks before the official discovery of the missiles that President Kennedy was closing his eyes to their existence, his charges were initially regarded by the White House as part of normal mid-term electioneering. Among Robert Kennedy's initial reactions to the discovery was a fear that it would look bad domestically.[38] (Keating was later Kennedy's opponent for the New York Senate election in 1964.)

President Kennedy was first shown evidence of Soviet missiles in Cuba as he sat on his bed in his dressing gown, reading the papers on the morning of 16 October 1962. His initial reaction was to call the Attorney General, who was informed at 9 a.m. Later that day, Secretary of State Dean Rusk, Secretary of Defense Bob McNamara and the Chiefs of Staff were informed of what the US spy planes had located. Roughly the same group which was later briefed in the cabinet room met almost continuously over the next twelve days to analyse the problem. Robert Kennedy was already first among equals in the group, which came to be called ExComm (the Executive Committee of the National Security Council). It was the Attorney General who oversaw the committee's deliberations and whose personal recommendations were eventually accepted by the President as the best policy proposals.

Both John and Robert Kennedy were initially keen to explore the idea of invading Cuba. During the two ExComm meetings held on 16 October, Robert Kennedy said little, although in the first he pointed out to the President that an invasion was one of the options and asked General Maxwell Taylor, Chairman of the Joint Chiefs of Staff, how long an invasion would take to carry out.[39] In the second, the Attorney General opposed the idea of a surgical air strike and endorsed an invasion. A tape of the meeting reveals that Robert Kennedy wondered 'whether it wouldn't be the argument, if you're going to get into it [Cuba] at all, whether we should just get into it and get it over with and say that, uh, take our losses'. Then he suggested that 'there is some other way we can get involved in this through Guantanamo Bay or something, or whether there's some ship that, you know, sinks the Maine again [US battleship that blew up off Havana in 1898] or something' (i.e. engineer an incident which could be used as a pretext for invading Cuba).[40]

No immediate decision was taken, however, and over the next few days Robert Kennedy strongly suggested that a 'quarantine' or blockade should be undertaken rather than an air strike. In arguing against a strike on the Cuban missile bases, Robert Kennedy appealed to the moral conscience of the group. 'For 175 years we have not been that kind of country. A sneak attack was not in our traditions', said Kennedy (although of course it was).[41]

Robert Kennedy's next decisive intervention in the crisis was his suggestion to the President to ignore an aggressively worded letter sent by Khrushchev and respond to another one received some hours earlier and also sent by the Soviet premier. The first letter asked that President Kennedy promise not to invade Cuba, in return for which the Soviets would remove their missiles. The second was more formally worded and demanded that NATO missiles based in Turkey be removed before any solution could be found.

Until the time of Robert Kennedy's death, the official US version of events was that the Attorney General's inspired idea to ignore the second letter had saved the day without a loss of face for the Americans. Dissatisfied with the official State Department response to the correspondence, Robert Kennedy criticized its hard-line approach and, at the President's suggestion, personally drafted an alternative response which offered to the Soviets a guarantee not to invade Cuba. It was this letter, apparently, which convinced the Soviets that they were being offered a reasonable deal and were not likely to squeeze any more concessions out of the administration.

In fact, Robert Kennedy recorded the true version a few months before he died in his account of the incident, *13 Days*, when he reveals that he struck a deal with the Soviets based on the terms of the second letter, without NATO, the US Congress or even his ExComm colleagues knowing about it.[42] The details of the solution were apparently known only to Robert Kennedy and the President. *13 Days*, which was published posthumously, reveals that Robert Kennedy met with the Soviet Ambassador (by this time Anatoly Dobrynin) and agreed that the NATO Jupiter missiles would be removed. Douglas Dillon, Secretary of the Treasury and ExComm member, later noted that 'I was there, and I don't recall the ExComm telling Bobby Kennedy anything very specific about what he should say to Dobrynin. He got his last-minute and final instructions from the President and only from the President. There would be no written record of this.'[43] The ExComm was not even briefed about the Robert Kennedy–Dobrynin encounter the next day.

Dobrynin reported that 'Robert Kennedy looked exhausted. One could see from his eyes that he had not slept for days. He himself said he had not been home for six days and nights. "The President is in a grave situation," Robert Kennedy said, "and he does not know how to get out of it. We are under very severe stress. In fact we are under pressure from our military to use force against Cuba."'[44] As Robert Kennedy remembered it, he told Dobrynin that 'it was our judgement that, within a short time after this crisis was over, those [NATO] missiles would be gone', and they were.[45] Arthur Schlesinger, while heaping laurels on Robert Kennedy for his intelligence in dealing with the crisis, describes the deal struck with Dobrynin as 'a singular exercise in secret diplomacy'.[46] The difference between the earlier version of how the situation was resolved and the fuller, posthumous one is crucial when studying Robert Kennedy's Senate career and presidential chances.

Much of his reputation as a tough, decisive politician rested on the belief that he and his brother had not given way over the Cuban missile crisis, had stood eyeball to eyeball with the Soviets and had not flinched. In fact, Secretary of State Dean Rusk later criticized Robert Kennedy for being too emotional during the episode. 'This was the first major crisis he had ever lived through. Fortunately, that emotional aspect was not the controlling mood of President Kennedy. He was as calm as an iceberg throughout this situation. The difference in the emotional overtone between Bobby and John was very important to me.'[47] The CIA photo expert who showed Robert Kennedy the U2 pictures of the missiles in Cuba also remembered the Attorney General's agitated state. 'He walked around the room like a boxer between rounds, thumbing his nose and uttering epithets.'[48]

Nevertheless, it was the reputation as a steely adviser to the President which survived, and Robert Kennedy was never required to prove his anti-Communist credentials during his Senate career. The tough image made his suggestions of negotiations over Vietnam, and offers of blood plasma supplies to the Viet Cong, more credible to the public than if they had come from someone who was regarded as soft on Communism.

The truth was, of course, that the Kennedys had struck a deal with the Soviets and had given away more than had originally been admitted to. None of this was known to his New York constituents, however, during Robert Kennedy's Senate career.

The low-income, white, urban and mid-western whites who were attracted to him during the presidential primaries did not know it either, and such issues were traditionally very important to them. Many Polish-Americans, for example, might have been surprised to learn that he had struck secret bargains with the Soviets. None of this would have been so important, of course, had not Kennedy's appeal in the 1968 presidential primaries rested so heavily on his tough-guy image which attracted the ethnic whites. In this sense at least, his much-vaunted 'poverty coalition' between poor whites and blacks was founded on a misperception.

During his early days in the Senate, before his break with the White House over Vietnam, Robert Kennedy's reputation in international affairs rested largely on his dealings with Cuba and other Latin American countries. However, he had gained virtually all of his knowledge of the region at second hand. He had been sent on various missions elsewhere overseas, however, and he was establishing himself in the world community as an international trouble-shooter for President Kennedy. His first official trip abroad for his brother came in August 1961, when he visited President Felix Houphouët-Boigny of the Ivory Coast. Houphouët-Boigny had been to Washington earlier in the year and was dissatisfied with the treatment he had received from the State Department. It was left to Robert Kennedy to patch things up and make the August trip for the Ivoiriens' first anniversary of independence celebrations.

Other trips followed, including a sweep of Asia which took up the whole of February 1962. One of the fourteen countries that Kennedy visited was Japan, where the US ambassador noted that when he needed advice or help in a hurry he would in future call the Attorney General instead of going through the State Department. The main purpose of the 1962 mission was to force the Dutch and Indonesians to negotiate over Indonesian independence. Kennedy believed his trip was successful: 'Nobody had visited Indonesia. I went to offset what was happening there ... I did get [Sukarno] to agree to sit down with the Dutch ... They avoided a war.'[49]

By mid-administration, Robert Kennedy was almost functioning as a mini-State Department, negotiating in secret with Khrushchev's representative, acting as an alternative channel for ambassadors to reach the President and bringing peace to the parts other officials had failed to reach.

Significantly, too, during that fourteen-nation trip in February, he stopped briefly in Saigon. 'We are going to win in Vietnam. We will remain here until we do win,' he told the crowd at the airport.[50]

Part II – The Politics of Dissent

At the end of his brother's administration Robert Kennedy had considerable experience of foreign policy. The career options he seriously considered after President Kennedy's assassination all involved foreign affairs. In 1964 President Johnson offered him the post of US Ambassador to the UN, and, although he declined it, he mentioned that he was prepared to be Ambassador to Saigon. Johnson was not keen on this, however, and so Kennedy opted for the Senate – not out of a burning desire to represent the people of New York, but, as he confided in 1964, because as a Senator he would be in a stronger position to criticize Johnson's foreign policy. '... he's not doing anything for the Alliance for Progress ... he's not paying proper attention to Panama or Brazil ... If I was in the United States Senate, I would have raised a fuss about [US military intervention in] Panama', he said.[1]

Once elected, Senator Kennedy did not have to wait long before an opportunity to attack President Johnson's handling of affairs in Latin America presented itself. The situation in the Dominican Republic had worsened since the overthrow of Bosch in September 1963. Following the coup, the Kennedy administration had cut off all military aid to the new right-wing regime, but this policy was soon reversed by President Johnson. The unpopular authoritarian government on the Caribbean island, backed by the military, found itself the target of an uprising in April 1965. Johnson, alarmed at the prospect of a Communist takeover, ordered 22,000 US troops into the country to restore order. He had not consulted with the Organization of American States, and his action provided Kennedy with ammunition for his first open assault on the President.

Ironically enough, it was during a debate on Vietnam that Kennedy first broke with the administration over the Dominican Republic. On 6 May 1965, he rose to speak on a request from Johnson that more money be made available for the war in Vietnam. After agreeing to vote for the request (although warning that it should not be seen as a blank cheque by the administration), Kennedy used his time on the Senate floor to bring up the Dominican situation. 'Our determination to stop Communist revolution in the hemisphere must not be construed as opposition to popular uprisings against injustice and oppression just because the targets of such popular uprisings say they are Communist-inspired or Communist-led, or even because known Communists take part in them,' he declared.[2]

Stone's Weekly picked up on the significance of the speech with characteristic perception. 'Taken in connection with Teddy Kennedy's leadership in the fight against Johnson on poll taxes, we have here the possible nucleus of a liberal opposition to Johnson,' wrote Stone the week after the speech.[3] He was to prove a regular and incisive critic of Kennedy in the following years, and he often used his influential newsletter to prod the Senator towards a more forthright stand against the Vietnam War.[4]

Later in 1965 Kennedy visited Latin America for his first substantial political trip to the region. In keeping with his habit of ignoring State

Department procedure, he visited the universities and labour gatherings he had been warned against. In Chile he met Communists in a mine and declared: 'If I worked in this mine I'd be a Communist too.'[5] Elsewhere, in Argentina, Brazil and Peru, he witnessed the demise of the Alliance for Progress ideal of putting America on the side of social revolution. Johnson had not maintained the former policy of encouraging reform, and it had been replaced with the old line of anti-Communism at any cost. At the end of his first year in the Senate, Kennedy appeared on *Meet the Press* and warned that 'if all we do ... is to associate ourselves with those forces which are against subversion and against Communism and have rather a negative policy, then I think it is self-defeating.'[6]

The reversion to the old policy of the primacy of national security considerations was made complete within a year or so of Johnson taking office and was reflected in a piece in *Le Monde* in March 1966, which warned that LBJ's policy of siding with the dictators 'spelled the end of Kennedyism'.[7] Within months of this article appearing, Kennedy made an all-out attack on what he regarded as a betrayal of the Alliance for Progress principles. It should be remembered that when he made the speech, in May 1966, he had already broken with the administration's policy on Vietnam by urging negotiations with the North Vietnamese. This break, which had come in February, generated considerable press attention, and by comparison the declaration on Latin America caused only minor ripples.

What precipitated Kennedy's outburst on the Latin American question was Johnson's decision in January 1966 to appoint Lincoln Gordon as his Assistant Secretary of State for Inter-American Affairs. Gordon, a former Ambassador to Brazil, had at one time advocated the overthrow of the progressive Brazilian government by its military.[8] In remarks to the Senate on 9–10 May, in what Senator Wayne Morse of Oregon lauded as 'the most important speech that has been made on Latin American problems ... in the country since President Kennedy initiated the Alliance for Progress', Kennedy restated the original aims of the plan and pointed out where they were not being pursued.[9] 'If we had dealt with Cuba and Batista in the fifties we would not have to worry about Castro,' he said.[10] He went on to criticize the State Department for withholding aid from Peru when the Peruvian government was in dispute with a US oil company.[11] Kennedy pointed out that no expropriation had taken place and that the President of Peru was simply looking for a better tax deal from the oil companies working in his country.

The Senator also pointed out similar cases in Argentina and attacked hold-ups in aid disbursement where, 'for approximately two years, both in Peru and Argentina, important aid projects under the Alliance for Progress were held up because the private US companies were not able to reach agreement with the representatives of the governments of Argentina and Peru'.[12]

It was, of course, Kennedy's first break with Johnson over Vietnam which really caused a furore. On the assumption that Kennedy was keen to distance himself from the administration wherever appropriate, and thereby begin to establish an independent political base from which to launch a bid for the presidency, a break with Johnson over Vietnam was a logical step. However, at this time, early 1966, the country was overwhelmingly in support of winning the war, and Kennedy was saddled with the further burden of having advocated that exact policy himself during his brother's administration, as witnessed for example by his ringing declarations of US intent to stay and defeat the enemy during his trip to Saigon in 1962.[13] He did not oppose the Gulf of Tonkin Resolution of August 1964, which gave Johnson almost unlimited powers to pursue his war aims, and as late as May 1965 was asking that magazine articles which emphasized the heroism of US troops in combat with the Viet Cong be inserted in the *Congressional Record*.[14]

By the end of 1965, however, there was no mistaking that Johnson was prepared to increase substantially America's involvement in the war. In the last six months of that year he had increased the number of US troops in Vietnam from 75,000 in July to 185,000 in December. When Kennedy made his speech in 1966, American bombing, which had been halted since Christmas Eve, 1965, had just resumed.

The build-up to Senator Kennedy's first major statement on Vietnam suggests that he was interested in staking out an identifiable political patch for himself which would be independent of the administration, but would not alienate mainstream Democrats who would ultimately determine his presidential aspirations. This dilemma never left Kennedy, of course, and dogged him right up to end of his career. The tension between independence and disloyalty was a difficult one with which to deal, and he never really mastered it. He had tested the water some months earlier, when in October 1965 he proposed that blood plasma be given to the enemy as a humanitarian gesture.[15] The suggestion was used throughout the next three years to associate him with appeasement, with a small degree of success.[16]

Undeterred, he decided to align himself with those dissenting on the war. This was not easy, however, for despite all his experience in foreign affairs, he was still a very junior Senator and had not been selected to sit on the glamorous Foreign Relations Committee, chaired by Democratic Senator William Fulbright of Arkansas.[17] He stood frustrated at the back of the hearings into the war conducted by the Foreign Relations Committee in the first two weeks of February 1966, astutely associating himself with the proceedings in the minds of the press and public without actually being part of them. His aides remember how he 'several times went to the hearing room and stood among the listening spectators'.[18] The hearings were shown live on television, but Kennedy preferred to attend in person and so publicly associate himself with the debate in this way.

Kennedy's statement, when it came, made an enormous impact. He began by laying claim to the tradition of Abraham Lincoln, who 'was reviled for opposing the war of 1848', and, in a gesture to his father's record, mentioned those who had advocated fuller debate before the Second World War.[19] Then he spoke out against the resumption of the bombing and finally spelled out his ideas for peace. He attempted to set out terms for negotiation with the Communists in Vietnam. 'If negotiation is our aim, as we have so clearly said it is, we must seek a middle ground. A negotiated settlement means that each side must concede matters that are important in order to preserve positions that are essential ... we must be willing to face the uncertainties of election, and the possibility of an eventual vote on reunification.'[20]

Although nowhere in his speech did Kennedy mention the word 'coalition', most commentators agreed he was advocating just that. I. F. Stone could not contain his enthusiasm for the break, welcoming the speech as 'a political event of the first magnitude' and publishing a special edition of his weekly to include Kennedy's remarks in full.[21] The rest of the press also regarded the speech as a highly significant statement, and many influential columnists took their cue. Walter Lippmann in the *Washington Post* enthused: 'It has remained for Senator Kennedy to raise the decisive question about a negotiated settlement ... a negotiated settlement of the war in South Vietnam will have to be negotiated by the South Vietnamese, and our policy should be to refrain from vetoing it'.[22]

The *New York Times* chose to regard the statement as a helpful suggestion for the administration rather than an attack on it: 'Senator Kennedy's proposal ... is less a criticism of the President's policies than an invaluable contribution to the decision-making process';[23] while the *Washington Star* reported Vice-President Hubert Humphrey's reaction to the statement, where he likened allowing Communists to join a coalition government to 'putting a fox in the chicken coop'.[24]

Other administration officials were also unenthusiastic. McGeorge Bundy, President Johnson's principal White House adviser on foreign affairs, described Kennedy's statement as 'neither useful nor helpful'.[25] Under-Secretary of State George Ball denounced the proposals to negotiate with Communists with a view to power-sharing as 'unacceptable'. However, all of the senior Johnson officials who opposed the idea had been in favour of coalition when President Kennedy sought peace in Laos in 1961 on that very basis.[26] Among the participants in the National Security Council meeting which advocated bringing Communists into the Laos government were Vice-President Johnson, Secretary of State Rusk, Ball and Bundy. All of them went along with President Kennedy's efforts to establish a popular front in Laos.

In Britain the *New Statesman* likened Kennedy's February statement to a 'ministerial resignation'.[27] In a piece headlined 'Kennedy ends the consensus', it proclaimed: 'Kennedy has, in one stroke, made the unthinkable thinkable: getting out of Vietnam ... Kennedy has made opposition to the war ... politically possible'; while the *Spectator* recorded that Kennedy, in making his speech, had 'chosen internal exile'.[28]

In an interview with *US News and World Report* two weeks after the speech, Kennedy sought to clarify his position. 'One of the facts of life ... is that the Communists ... will play some role in the Government of a negotiated settlement ... They've been around a long time and they have considerable support in the villages ... [South Vietnamese premier] General Ky has said he has complete control over only 25% of the population at the present time.'[29]

Senate doves welcomed the statement. Wayne Morse, a long-standing critic of the war, expressed 'enthusiastic support for the general policy expressed by the junior Senator from New York', while Claiborne Pell played down the differences between what Kennedy was proposing and the administration's policy, claiming that these were 'slight'.[30] Pell did credit Kennedy with having established 'the irreducible minimums on each side and [having] highlighted the areas where negotiation could be conducted'.[31]

Kennedy had indeed, in the words of the *New Statesman*, made the unthinkable thinkable – he had put a coalition solution on the political agenda, as only few politicians could have. When Eugene McCarthy had advanced the same idea some weeks before, the Minnesotan noted ruefully that it had been considered so 'far out' that nobody noticed. It would not be the last time for McCarthy to be so upstaged.[32]

Journalists sympathetic to Kennedy's ideas even sought out former

Hungarian Prime Minister Ferenc Nagy, who had headed the coalition government in that country at the end of the Second World War. Although Nagy was overthrown by Communists who formed part of that coalition, he came in on Kennedy's side during the national debate. 'A coalition ... of the participating political parties or groups is not dependent at all on domestic popular support but on the help of the outside great powers which are behind them politically,' he offered.[33] That Nagy's thoughts on such a topic were considered so relevant by some elements of the American press gives some indication of how Vietnam was regarded in the overall context of the Cold War, and thought of as easily comparable to the Hungarian situation of twenty years before.

Kennedy, meanwhile, wished to be seen as part of a general movement unhappy about the conduct of the war but did not want to go as far as publicly joining its leaders. He was careful only to make a speech and not call for his proposal to be debated as a Senate resolution, which would have caused a more serious split with the White House. In the following month he did not vote for a motion which called for the repeal of the Gulf of Tonkin Resolution (Eugene McCarthy did). In April he warned of further escalation, and in July voted for a bill introduced by Senator Fulbright to put three members of the Senate Foreign Relations Committee on the Armed Services Committee (which was formerly charged with overseeing CIA activities).[34] Although the bill failed, it provided some indication of Kennedy's continuing dovishness on the war.

The second half of 1966 appears to have been a most indecisive time for Kennedy. No doubt distracted by a trip to Africa, mid-term elections and the need to tiptoe around internecine political struggles in New York, his public comments on the war were relatively rare. It was a time, too, when he was being mooted by I. F. Stone and others as a vice-presidential possibility for Johnson in the 1968 election, and he was certainly reluctant to go any further than his February statement in attacking the administration's foreign policy.[35] In early 1967 he seems to have decided that the most prudent course was a decisive, final break with Johnson over Vietnam, but for the remainder of 1966 he frustrated doves with his apparent reluctance to address the war. Andrew Kopkind in the *New Statesman* noted in July of that year that 'opposition to the war is generally expressed in testimonials of faith in Senator Robert Kennedy. In his turn, he responds with inscrutable smiles and delphic comments ... He did not sign [a motion critical of the administration's Vietnam policy] with the 18 doves – for no very good reason, except that he was late getting into the Senate chamber.'[36]

Murray Kempton in *The Spectator*, meanwhile, thought it sensed a subtle bid for the vice-presidency in 1968. A June Gallup poll had shown Johnson's popularity rating slip to below 50% for the first time since he became President, and a month later another poll in California suggested that Kennedy was preferred to Johnson by a margin of 2:1. 'The chances are that he [LBJ] will come to 1968 badly in need of a new face ... under the circumstances, it would be by no means surprising if he dismissed the loyal Mr Humphrey and accepted the distrusted Senator Kennedy as his vice-presidential candidate', predicted Kempton in *The Spectator*.[37] 'This would be the most unpleasant dose imaginable for him ... but there is almost nothing he would not do to make safe an election', it concluded, in an oblique reference to Johnson's reported distortion of ballot returns in Texas in his elections to the Senate.

Ruminations about Kennedy's long-term political ambitions seem to have been all the rage that summer. *The Spectator* went as far as to publish a 3,000-word article by Kempton in September, mapping out the Senator's various options in some detail.[38] It concluded that the chances of Johnson asking Kennedy to join the ticket were 'dubious', and the chances of Kennedy accepting such an offer 'uncertain'. Kennedy seems to have been uncertain about many political decisions that year, and wisely appears to have been keeping as many options open for as long as possible. If the February speech had opened the door to his championing a significant anti-Vietnam movement which might sweep him to the presidency in 1972, or even before, he had been careful not to push the door so forcefully that it would close any possibility of a reconciliation with Johnson should he decide to make a gambit for the vice-presidency in 1968.

Kennedy's reluctance to show his hand was no doubt frustrating for those, like I. F. Stone, who wanted him to throw in his lot with the doves and make an irrevocable break. 'While others dodge the draft, Bobby dodges the war,' Stone charged in his issue of 24 October 1966. 'Kennedy in the US Senate has at his disposal a forum second only to that of the Presidency. But he hasn't said a word about the war in the Senate since last February ... He even achieved the feat of delivering a speech in New York on 11 October without mentioning Vietnam!'[39] Stone also thought the vice-presidency theory credible. In September he had noted that Kennedy 'has said very little about the war in months ... [he is] being careful not to burn his bridges with the White House and make such a development [the vice-presidential nomination] impossible.'[40]

Kennedy was not given to unnecessary bridge-burning. He knew better than most what it took to become President and, if we assume that objective was always an important one for him, he could not afford to make any more enemies than he needed to. Besides, if he had thrown in his hand with the anti-war protesters and become an all-out dove, what sort of movement would he be heading, and could he steer it towards a presidential victory?

The full implications of the war had still not hit home to most Americans by 1966. At the end of the year, it would be revealed that, for the first time, US casualties outnumbered those of the South Vietnamese in the conflict. But even that was not enough to persuade most Americans that the war could not, or should not, be won. In 1966, there were 4179 Americans killed in action in Vietnam (up from 1130 in 1965), compared with 3242 from the South Vietnamese Army.[41] Media reports of the war were still overwhelmingly pro-administration at this time, while the anti-war movement remained a series of loosely-connected groups with different emphases. Some who were opposed to the war were simply opposed to the way it was being run and believed that a 'Viet-namization' policy (as attempted later by Nixon), whereby the Vietnamese did all the fighting themselves, was the answer. Others questioned America's ability to do the job, others its moral right to be in Vietnam in the first place, and others still questioned the idea of war at all.

It must be stressed that the moral arguments of pacifism, or even of America's right to impose its will on the people of Vietnam, did not figure very prominently in the arguments put forward by the Senate doves during those years – although Kennedy himself in March 1968, in a speech on the Senate floor, wondered aloud about America's moral right to act 'like the God of the Old Testament';[42] and another time made the contentious statement that 'what we are doing to the Vietnamese is not very different than [sic] what Hitler did to the Jews'.[43] Most doves, however, simply wanted to end the war because it was costing too much money and because America was losing it. When Kennedy did criticize the administration's policy on the war, he did it guardedly and via a related subject, usually an American citizen's right to dissent against it. For example, when calls came for historian Eugene Genovese to be dismissed from his university post because he said he hoped the Viet Cong would win, Kennedy defended Genovese's right of free speech.[44] Similarly, Ted Kennedy's criticism of the war concentrated on the issue of refugees rather than the moral question of whether the United States should be fighting it at all.[45]

It was a difficult time for Kennedy, who had so much to lose should he jump the wrong side of the fence on the war. If he went all out against it, like Morse had, he would have become isolated from the mainstream party and have only the anti-war movement (which had certainly not proven itself as an electoral force in 1966) on which to base his run at the presidency. If, on the other hand, he refused to criticize Johnson publicly, he ran the risk of someone outflanking him on the left and stealing much of his natural, radical constituency. Moreover, there was not just the presidency to worry about. He had hardly won New York by a landslide in 1964 and in the early years of his Senate career was still on trial in the eyes of many constituents.

There were convincing reasons for Kennedy to sit tight and wait out the political storm of the late 1960s. Time was on his side – in 1984 he still would be younger than Johnson would be in 1968 – and important advisors, primarily his brother Ted and JFK's closest aide, Ted Sorenson, urged him to wait until the 1972 election before he made his move. His hesitancy grated, however, on staff members like Peter Edelman and Adam Walinsky who knew him to be personally dissatisfied with the conduct of the war. Pressure on him grew steadily during the latter half of 1966 to declare publicly and forcefully against Johnson. When General de Gaulle offered himself as a mediator between Washington and Hanoi in September of that year, Kennedy wrote a letter openly welcoming the French proposals for instant negotiations with a view to power-sharing. In an act typical of his prevarication in those months, he did not send it.[46]

Kennedy held out against the pressure for a long time. In early October his first speech on the war since the February statement welcomed UN Ambassador Arthur Goldberg's suggestions for the Vietnamization of the war. This, according to Stone, put him 'safely back in LBJ's camp'.[47] The statement helped confirm William Shannon's view, published in that month's edition of *Harper's*, that the vice-presidency theory was a strong one. 'With skilful publicity this could be made to appear not as an act of bold usurpation and impatient ambition by Kennedy but a reluctant rescue mission to prop up an ageing wartime President whose popularity is sagging', he proposed.[48]

As the autumn dragged on, so the pressure on Kennedy mounted. The anti-war movement, however, provided no clear evidence in the November 1966 mid-term elections that it was a force which could unseat an incumbent President. The Senator remained in two minds. Privately, there was no question that he was opposed to continuing military involvement, but he told colleagues that to oppose the war more openly would only result in increased bombing, as Johnson would prove the independence of his policy by doing the exact opposite of what Kennedy proposed.

While he stalled, the war ground on in a peculiarly futile fashion. American inexperience in fighting against guerrillas was exposed as never before. Johnson persevered with the disastrous 'strategic hamlet' policy, whereby people were removed from land their families had owned for generations and put into hamlets where they could be protected from the Viet Cong. Unfortunately for Johnson, many locals believed American troops to be more of a menace than the Viet Cong, and the United States never looked likely to win the battle for hearts and minds. A basic misunderstanding of local needs and preferences punctuated American policy towards those it protected. When the Communists destroyed much of the South's rice harvest in the mid-1960s, the United States rushed in California and Louisiana rice, only to find that the Vietnamese hated American rice so much that they used it instead of dirt to fill their sandbags.

It was during this summer of hesitancy that Kennedy decided to travel to Africa. Whatever he eventually did in the short term, a successful, high-profile foreign trip would do his chances of being offered the vice-presidency, or challenging for the presidency itself, no harm at all. America was becoming more and more unpopular throughout the world (a fact which Kennedy did not fail to mention on his return), and the goodwill which President Kennedy had elicited was being steadily eroded. Moreover, nothing emphasized the difference between Kennedy and Johnson more sharply than the sight of the young Senator being mobbed by crowds in the Third World, while the President was besieged by anti-war protests at home and abroad.

Holding to the Kennedy administration theme of being on the side of the people during their revolutions, Senator Kennedy made for South Africa in June 1966. The trip, which also included visits to Tanzania, Kenya and Ethiopia, produced a few good speeches from Kennedy and some excellent publicity. His interest in Africa dated back to the 1961 mission to the Ivory Coast, and he had learned a lot since his first speech on the continent when, addressing an Ivoirien audience, he had described President Houphouët-Boigny as 'the George Washington of your country', presumably imagining that the President could envisage no higher honour.[49]

Interestingly, Robert Kennedy's only altercation with President Kennedy over foreign policy had concerned Africa. He had argued against the United States building the Volta Dam in Ghana. The dam was in danger of being taken over by Ghanaian leader Kwame Nkrumah, who, the Attorney General argued, was 'going Communist'.[50] Robert Kennedy insisted that the money ($96 million) should be spent on America's real friends in the region, such as Houphouët-Boigny. In the end, President Kennedy's position prevailed, although he and the Attorney General 'had some spirited arguments about it', as Robert Kennedy remembered in 1964.[51]

After President Kennedy's death, Robert Kennedy appeared genuinely concerned that Johnson was not paying enough attention to African matters. 'I've had a major effort in the last four months to try to get somebody to do something about Zanzibar', he complained at the end of 1964.[52] Presumably stung into action by Kennedy's impending trip, Johnson made his only presidential speech on Africa the week before Kennedy left for Cape Town.

By 1966 the winds of change had almost swept right through the continent, with only a few countries left operating under minority rule. South Africa, with its brutal apartheid system but relatively sophisticated and liberal press, seemed an obvious place to generate the sort of attention Kennedy needed. The trip duly confirmed his image as a world statesman and a man of the people. President Kennedy had halted loans to the South African government and forbidden any weapons deals with the Pretoria regime in protest at its policies, and Robert Kennedy's credibility with the majority population was swiftly cemented with a visit to 'banned' Nobel Peace Prize winner Zulu chief Albert Luthuli. The South African Prime Minister Hendrik Verwoerd declined to meet Kennedy or permit other ministers to do so.

Kennedy was among the first international figures to attack the South African government on its own soil and he became an instant hero in the townships for doing so.[53]

Thanks to the developed media network in the country, Kennedy's trip to South Africa made headlines across the world in a way which his stops in the other African nations could not. Although he was treated like a head of state by Nyerere in Tanzania, Kenyatta in Kenya and Haile Selassie in Ethiopia, their poor press facilities did not generate the same impact as the South African leg.

The 1966 trip also developed the idea of Kennedy as more than a one-issue wonder, disagreeing with Johnson on nothing but Vietnam. Part of Kennedy's problem at this time was his need to mark out his own political territory. If he opposed Johnson solely on the war, and the war ended, his political career would be finished. While he tried to develop a new philosophy to deal with racial problems on the domestic scene, he also had to attempt to carve out an alternative approach to foreign policy. By the end of 1966, his mind apparently made up to break with Johnson rather than wait for the offer of the vice-presidency, Kennedy embarked on a sophisticated strategy geared to project himself as a worthy and experienced heir to Johnson, familiar with international events and more popular with foreign publics and governments than the President.

It was time for a decision. By December attacks on Kennedy's silence were reaching a crescendo, with Stone accusing him of 'sounding like Hubert [Humphrey]'.[54] At this time, too, his image was being damaged by a long-running battle with William Manchester over the author's account of the Dallas assassination, *The Death of a President*.[55] Although Kennedy tried to stop extracts of the book from appearing on the grounds that they did not respect Jacqueline Kennedy's privacy, others thought that the most offensive passages were those which threatened his relations with Johnson. Some of the manuscript, it appears, included evidence from Kennedy aides complaining about President Johnson's lack of sensitivity towards President Kennedy's family and colleagues in the manner he took over at the White House.

If Kennedy was at all serious about the chances of a vice-presidential nomination, he could not afford such revelations to be made public. Moreover, when the nature of the passages became common knowledge in any case, with drafts of the book circulating in New York and elsewhere, he was put under increasing pressure to make a decisive break with the administration.

Kennedy chose to make another speech on Vietnam in March 1967, one which could be construed only as an all-out attack on the President's policies. For maximum impact, he gradually built up to the announcement with a well-publicized trip to Europe, which reinforced the idea that he was more in touch with attitudes in foreign capitals than was Johnson. In January he left for London, where he met with Prime Minister Harold Wilson and discussed the possibility of British entry into the European Community. He was afforded the sort of welcome not usually extended to American senators, as most European politicians recognized they were probably dealing with a future President.

In Paris, Kennedy was told that a Communist government in South Vietnam was inevitable. De Gaulle warned him that the United States could not prevail against the forces of history which were at work in Vietnam. In Rome, Italian President Giuseppe Saragat told him that

Johnson appeared to be neglecting his allies. In his State of the Union address to Congress two weeks before, the Italian premier noted, Johnson's speech had included 50 lines on Latin America, twenty on Africa and only one brief mention of Europe.[56]

The primary message that Kennedy brought home was clear: Johnson was out of touch with the rest of the world, unlike Kennedy, whose top-level discussions with the leading European powers had helped convince him that the war was wrong. Another message with which Kennedy returned was not so clear. The confusion arose over a peculiar incident in Paris, when during discussions with an official from the French foreign ministry terms of negotiation with the North Vietnamese had been mentioned. The US Ambassador to France, who was present at the meeting, thought Kennedy had been the target of a subtle 'peace feeler' and relayed this information to the State Department.[57] The feeler was so subtle, apparently, that the Senator did not pick it up at all and was surprised at the fuss it caused. When news leaked that Kennedy might have been the recipient of such a signal, Johnson was furious, believing Kennedy to have used the message to enhance his own prestige.

An acrimonious meeting took place on 6 February 1967 between the President and Kennedy on the latter's return to the United States. 'I think the leak came from someone in your State Department', Kennedy is reported to have said. 'It's not my State Department, it's your State Department', Johnson is supposed to have shouted back, meaning, presumably, that it was staffed by Kennedy sympathizers who were more in agreement with the Senator than the President.[58] This was a remarkable attitude for Johnson to adopt, since it not only confirmed the extent of Kennedy's influence but also rested on the belief that Kennedy was a favourite in the Department, which he clearly had never been.

The meeting carried on, with Kennedy advising the President to stop the bombing and begin negotiations. His patience tested, Johnson eventually warned Kennedy that he would 'destroy you and every one of your dove friends in six months. You'll be dead politically in six months.' Kennedy stormed out angrily, according to his aides.[59] Unsurprisingly, the vice-presidency was not mentioned by either side.

The stage was set for Kennedy's break, and on 2 March he delivered his second major speech on Vietnam, separating him irrevocably from the LBJ administration. As always, the speech was only as effective as the publicity it generated. Johnson went to extraordinary lengths to divert attention away from it. As Kennedy aides Milton Gwirtzman and William Vanden Heuvel recall:

On the day of the speech ... Johnson made two unscheduled speeches in Washington, held an unscheduled news conference to announce that Russian Premier Kosygin had agreed to talks on reducing the stockpile of nuclear weapons, announced he was inviting all the nation's governors to the White House, had Senator Henry Jackson of Washington read on the floor of the Senate a predated letter from him, explaining why the bombing was necessary, and confirmed the rumour that his daughter Lucy was pregnant.[60]

Despite Johnson's exertions, Kennedy's speech made a huge media impact the next day. He proposed a unilateral bombing halt and an announcement that the United States would be 'ready to negotiate within a week'. The negotiations, he suggested, could be secured by both sides agreeing not substantially to extend the war while talks were being conducted. He also recommended a gradual withdrawal of US and North Vietnamese troops, who would be replaced by an inter-national peace-keeping force, which would also guarantee free elections in which the Viet Cong would participate.

Before he made his speech Kennedy consulted with Tom Hayden and Staughton Lynd, two radical anti-war activists who had recently returned from Hanoi, but his proposal was essentially a restatement of the orthodox dove line.[61] No-one in the Senate at this time was calling for a unilateral withdrawal of American troops, and the country was still overwhelmingly in support of winning the war. In a Gallup poll published the week before Kennedy made his speech, only 24% of the public said they favoured a halt in the bombing, and by May of that year most college students questioned by Gallup said they considered themselves hawks on Vietnam.[62]

The press reaction to the speech, although extensive, was less enthusiastic than it had been about Kennedy's declaration in February 1966. Commentators were now more wary of his intentions in breaking with Johnson, and many agreed with *The Spectator*, which noted that Kennedy had 'a way of speaking and then lapsing into long silences'.[63] A fortnight before, the magazine had described him as 'a concealed and sporadic enemy [of the President]: he emerges every six months or so openly to express an otherwise muted discontent.'[64]

Few publications applauded the bridge-burning exercise, and although the *New Statesman* conceded that 'the impact of the speech was to separate Kennedy, perhaps once and for all, from the Johnson admin-istration' it also noted that he had been careful to deliver his speech when the Senate debate on the war had ended, so avoiding having his remarks associated with the other Senate doves.[65] Inevitably, *Stone's Weekly* tackled him over this tactic and accused him of refusing to lead the opposition, while putting speeches on the record 'to look good afterwards', as he had done in 1966.[66]

Kennedy's dilemma was over: he had finally set himself apart from the President, even if he was not ready to join the dove team. The break, as he had expected, made him very unpopular in the country, and his Gallup national approval rating dropped eleven points that month (from 48 to 37). That figure would, of course, rise in the coming year, as he had also predicted. In effect, Kennedy was now running for President, although he had not decided in which election. He probably saw 1972 as the only real possibility, but he needed to be ready in case Johnson looked like faltering before then.

The remainder of 1967 was taken up with swipes at the administration's inattention to problems elsewhere in the world, reinforcing Kennedy's image as a politician with a comprehensive foreign policy, in contrast to the President, who appeared increasingly preoccupied with a small country in Asia. To emphasize his broad range of policy alternatives for the world at large, Kennedy brought out a book that year which was to act as a manifesto for his presidential campaign in 1968. *To Seek a Newer World* was essentially a rehash of his major Senate speeches, but more than three-quarters of it was taken up with foreign policy matters: where the Alliance for Progress was betrayed; how to negotiate over Vietnam; the prospects for an overture to China; nuclear disarmament; and so on.[67]

One curious act which was not mentioned in any of the Kennedy biographies was his decision to promote a bill in May 1967 aimed at increasing penalties on those who desecrated the US flag. In the context of all his declarations about free speech, and his defence of academics encouraging the Viet Cong to victory, this decision does seem out of character. Nevertheless, as the *Congressional Record* duly shows, on 3 May 1967, Kennedy co-sponsored Senate Bill 1626 with Senator Alan Bible of Nevada to 'amend section 3 of title 4, US Code of Conduct, which prohibits the desecration or improper use of the flag of the USA by any person within the District of Columbia, so as to make such prohibitions applicable throughout the USA, to increase the penalties prescribed in such section with respect to desecration of the flag, and for other purposes'.[68]

Of much more importance, though, were Kennedy's now rampant assaults on the administration. He attacked proposals to cut funding for the Alliance for Progress and outlined some sensible proposals for the rejuvenation of Latin American economies, many of which, such as that relating to a Third World country's protection of its foreign exchange earnings, are now considered standard practice. Kennedy criticized the Johnson administration's aid budget, for example, noting that at the time, the USA sent $1 billion in aid a year to Latin America, of which $400 million was earmarked for developmental projects. The rest went on surplus-food shipments and businesslike project loans from the US Export-Import Bank. Kennedy proposed a higher aid budget, so more money could be spent on developmental projects.[69] It was many years before the private capital ideas he had propounded were tried out on a large scale, both in the United States and in Europe.

By mid-1967, now liberated from any compunction regarding criticizing his President, Kennedy described the intervention in the Dominican Republic as 'a smarting wound'.[70] He hammered at the necessity for the United States to join the side of revolution and proclaimed that there could 'be no preservation of the status quo in Latin America'.[71] His ideas for the region did not involve any reduction of US interest in the affairs of Latin American countries, which would be maintained through a series of 'partnerships', like that which existed between California and Chile. (California sent technical experts and industrial advisers to Chile in an attempt to improve living conditions in the South American country.)

Kennedy proposed a major increase in development aid to the region in the following years, including a doubling of capital aid from $1 billion a year. The new level, he pointed out, was the annual equivalent of the cost of the Vietnam War for two weeks.[72] His agricultural reforms proposed the creation of internal markets, the lowering of trade barriers and crop diversity. He urged greater help from the International Monetary Fund.[73] He warned against economies dominated by single commodities, which were at the mercy of world prices, and noted that in Brazil for example, 54% of export earnings came from coffee.[74] Many of the problems which he raised seem obvious today, but few were seriously addressing these questions at the time. At a 1967 conference in Punta del Este in Uruguay, birthplace of the Alliance for Progress, the participating governments could not settle on a trading agreement between the United States and its southern partners. Kennedy suggested that the United States was the problem. 'We sought guarantees for US investments and lower tariffs on US sales to Latin America; they sought more favourable treatment for Latin American exports, both of commodities and manufactured goods, to the United States, and had no further desire to protect our economic interests in their countries', he told the Senate.[75]

US companies feared nationalization by unstable governments, and so would not make long-term commitments to the countries in which they operated. 'The most difficult problem facing US business is expropriation,' wrote Kennedy.[76] Investments by major US companies were often short-term and made only on the understanding that the companies retained total control of these international operations (this short-term profit motive was also evident in many US companies' attitude to ghetto investment, when they feared similar problems of sabotage, a volatile workforce, and physical violence against their managers). However, Kennedy argued (with some considerable insight, as would be revealed in the following decades in Latin America and Africa) that for American companies to gain real security in their investments they had to be willing to surrender control of them to the local authorities. What Kennedy advocated was US companies giving up 51% of their shares in a foreign venture to local shareholders. In this way, the success of a company's project would be in the interest of the local authority and therefore more secure. In Mexico this arrangement was already being tried with notable success. However, it took years before many US companies would willingly surrender majority shareholdings abroad.

Kennedy also continued his long-standing criticism of ('his') State Department, claiming that US withdrawal of aid from unco-operative countries was 'not a policy, but the failure of policy'.[77] Moreover, in these 1967 remarks on the Latin American situation, he recognized the existence of a nationalistic Communism, as opposed to one orchestrated by Peking or Moscow – hardly an earth-shattering discovery, but one which many of his Senate colleagues would never make.

We are assured by close colleagues like Senator George McGovern and advisor Arthur Schlesinger that Kennedy experienced a 'growth' in many areas of belief after his brother's death.[78] On civil rights and Vietnam he 'matured' and moved to the left. However, his policies on Latin America, while less trumpeted, bore the marks of genuinely new thinking and were among the most far-sighted he advocated during his Senate years. Latin America was not a burning issue during the 1968 election, of course, which was fought on the issues (as far as it was fought on any issues) of Vietnam, crime, permissiveness and racial tension. The Hispanics who voted for Kennedy in such impressive numbers did so largely as a result of his interest in them as migrant workers and ghetto inhabitants, not because of the new business regulations he was proposing for Central and South America. Similarly, his overwhelming support in the black community had less to do with what he had said in South Africa than what he said in Bedford Stuyvesant. Even the Vietnam War, apparently, did not figure very highly as an issue in black areas, although most black leaders had come out against it: the conflict diverted funds from the War on Poverty, and blacks suffered the highest proportion of casualties in combat.

Having staked out his independence from Johnson, without distancing himself from the party machine (many members of which, like Mayor Daley of Chicago, were quietly voicing concern about the conduct of the war in late 1967), Kennedy began to seek advice on whether a coalition of blacks, anti-war activists and those otherwise disaffected by Johnson's leadership would be strong enough to pull off a presidential election victory. 'Ted Sorenson came to me', recalled anti-war Senator George McGovern, 'acting apparently under Bob's instructions and said: "You and other people are urging Bob to go ... is there support for him? If there is, you should try to establish that fact. You should call some of the people you know." So I called a number of Governors and Senators in my area, and I couldn't find one person who thought he ought to go! ... I reported back that I couldn't find any."' [80]

Securing the party's nomination would be difficult enough. At the 1968 convention, about 20% of delegates would come from southern states, where Kennedy was hardly a folk hero. Another 30% would be dominated by labour interests, where the Johnson–Humphrey team was especially strong and where Kennedy was still resented for his hounding of former Teamsters boss Jimmy Hoffa. The remaining half of the delegates would come from the rest of the country, some directly as a result of primaries, others from closed deals arranged by local party officials. The south and the unions remained dominantly hawkish, and the rest of the country still favoured staying and winning in Vietnam, although support was dwindling. In the second half of 1967 a significant shift in attitude to the war began to take shape which, within a year, left the electorate notably more dovish than it had ever been before. Nevertheless, both the Republican and Democratic Parties produced presidential candidates for the November 1968 election who proposed fighting on in Vietnam, even though about half the country wanted an immediate negotiated halt to hostilities.

This change in public opinion came too late for Kennedy to jump into the presidential race in time to plan his campaign very effectively. Media reporting of the war began to take a more critical tack in 1967, and rules on draft deferments were tightened up in October 1967, making it much harder for students to evade being enlisted. This undoubtedly brought the war home to many families for the first time and encouraged a fresh wave of protest from a previously unpoliticized middle class. Unsurprisingly, too, campus opposition to the war grew stronger during that semester, and in November 50,000 people staged a march on the Pentagon to protest against the war.

Mounting casualty figures no doubt played a major part in moulding public opinion. One hundred and twelve Americans were killed in action in 1964, 1,130 in 1965, 4,179 in 1966 and 7,482 in 1967. At the end of 1964 there were 23,000 American troops involved in the conflict. By the end of 1967 the number had risen to 525,000.[81]

Other reasons have also been suggested for the shift in US opinion at this time. Respected television journalist Walter Cronkite visited the war zone at the beginning of 1968 and on his return broke with the established network tradition of newscaster neutrality by criticizing the conflict directly on his show. At the end of January 1968, the Tet Offensive struck heavy psychological blows against the USA which had underestimated the enemy's strength. It has been suggested, too, that the Vietnam War was the first to be fought on television, and that when Americans witnessed the general horror of war beamed into their homes on a nightly basis they lost the stomach to continue the fight. Television ownership certainly increased dramatically during these years: while in 1960 45 million American homes boasted a television set, by 1968 that number had reached 75 million (a quarter of the sets receiving colour).[82]

Whatever the direct effects of watching the war on television, a definite mood swing against the administration's policies began in late 1967. (Whether television reporting had much to do with this is in fact debatable, but the US authorities were careful in later conflicts to deny reporters the sort of access to combat zones they had enjoyed in Vietnam.) In November of that year, too, Nixon pulled ahead of Johnson in opinion polls for the first time. The administration was clearly in trouble, and the more unpopular it, and its war, became, the more pundits looked towards Kennedy for any sign of movement. Typically, he hesitated.

In June he had introduced Johnson at a New York political dinner with the definition of greatness as contained in Webster's Dictionary. In a fawning introduction of the President, punctuated by the noise of 1,400 anti-war protesters outside the hall, Kennedy noted how Johnson 'has poured out all his own strength to renew the great strength of the country ... he has sought consensus, but has never shrunk from controversy ... he has gained huge popularity but never hesitated to spend it on what he thought important. In 1964 he won the greatest popular victory in modern times, and with our help he will do so again in 1968', he gushed.[83] It is hard to see what Kennedy was angling for in acting in such a way – it could have been that he wanted to prove before party hacks that there was no unbridgeable gulf between himself and the White House, or that, no matter what, he would not threaten party unity; or it simply could have been that one of his speechwriters (in this case Ted Sorenson) went a little over the top in preparing a few routine remarks.

Whatever the reason, such gestures, coupled with Kennedy's unwill-ingness to go for the jugular during these months, forced anti-war activists to search around for a more reliable champion. New York lawyer (and later Congressman) Al Lowenstein began a 'Dump Johnson' movement in late 1967. Lowenstein represented various political organizations on the left (he was a former president of the National Student Association and in 1967 a vice-chairman of the liberal ADA), and headed the search for an anti-Johnson Democrat to stand for President.[84] He approached Kennedy and asked him to run. When Kennedy refused, they talked about other possible candidates. Lowenstein suggested retired Army General James M. Gavin. 'If you can get him', Kennedy told Lowenstein, 'you're really in the ball game'.[85] Gavin, however, turned out to be a registered Republican, and so Lowenstein tried to persuade economist J. K. Galbraith to stand in the 1968 election on an anti-war platform. Galbraith, an Ambassador to India in the Kennedy administration, was keen, but a birth certificate showing him to have been born in Canada ruled out his candidacy on constitutional grounds. Another attempt, this time to persuade dovish Senator Fulbright to run, failed, as did approaches to Martin Luther King and child psychologist Dr Benjamin Spock.

Kennedy still refused to enter the race, although he was contemplating it. At a series of confidential meetings held in October and November 1967, top advisers met to discuss the possibility of his toppling Johnson. Most, including his brother Ted, opposed the idea, although a Harris opinion poll in October showed him beating Johnson 52-32.

In such a situation Kennedy was almost forced to run by public opinion. If he defied common belief and held out until 1972, he risked being blamed for extending the war when he could have won the presidency and stopped it. If that scenario were played out, much of his national constituency might turn against him in the following four years. So as to monitor the situation he cancelled a proposed trip to Eastern Europe in late 1967 (which would have done his standing with

Polish-Americans no harm at all). No doubt the Polish government, and the US embassy in Warsaw, were relieved. During his trip to the country in 1964, Kennedy had annoyed the authorities so much with his emotional appeals to crowds that 'he got the embassy so mad it could hardly sputter,' recalled the ambassador.[86]

At the end of November 1967 Robert McNamara 'resigned' as Secretary of Defense. His removal scotched all realistic hopes that a negotiated settlement of the war was near, and further convinced Kennedy that Johnson was unlikely to pull out of Vietnam.[87] Ted Kennedy, meanwhile, went to the war zone to witness the refugee situation. On his return, he confirmed the reports that Robert Kennedy had been receiving for some months: that the administration was playing down the civilian casualties and exaggerating its efficiency in subduing the enemy.[88]

The former Attorney General began to get moral about the issue. On the television show *Face the Nation* at the end of November, he went beyond the usual criticism of the way the war was being run, and the high casualties, and questioned the right of the United States to be there in the first place:

> We're going in there and we're killing South Vietnamese, we're killing children, we're killing women, we're killing innocent people ... because [the Communists are] 12,000 miles away and they might get to be 11,000 miles away. Do we have the right here in the United States to say that we're going to kill tens of thousands, make millions of people, as we have ... refugees, kill women and children? I very seriously question whether we have that right ... Those of us who stay here in the United States, we must feel it when we use napalm, when a village is destroyed and civilians are killed. This is also our responsibility ...[89]

Far more eloquent now than he had been in Los Angeles in February, during a televised debate on Vietnam with California Governor Ronald Reagan, who had forced him on to the defensive and easily won the contest, Kennedy almost appeared ready to join the campaign fray.[90] Calmer counsel prevailed, however, and he refused a final plea on 27 September from Lowenstein to declare his candidacy. After then unsuccessfully approaching South Dakota Senator George McGovern, who also turned him down, Lowenstein sought out Senator Eugene McCarthy from Minnesota who, to general surprise, accepted (see Chapter 5). McCarthy formally declared his candidacy on 30 November and ensured that some of the Democratic primaries, at least, would be dominated by the Vietnam issue.

McCarthy's narrow loss to Johnson in the New Hampshire primary jolted Democrats around the country and suggested that the President was more vulnerable than almost all the experts had predicted. (See Chapter 5 for primary election results.)

Kennedy's long silence in the second half of 1966 had forced many to conclude that he was a cynical opportunist, and his delay in entering the presidential race only confirmed this view. A full three and a half months after McCarthy had declared (and thereby 'split the party' – a reason Kennedy always put forward himself for not running), he eventually threw his hat into the ring.

What probably tipped the scales, apart from various family members urging him on, and an increasingly embarrassing position which, he believed, meant that McCarthy was taking over much of the constituency which was rightfully his, was the Tet Offensive. At the end of January 1968 the North Vietnamese army and the Viet Cong guerrillas launched a large-scale operation against US troops throughout South Vietnam. Although in strictly military terms a failure which resulted in extraordinarily high casualty figures for the Communists, it was a devastatingly successful psychological coup. It exploded the myth that the United States was about to win the war, as the Viet Cong struck at the most protected American enclaves – including the US embassy in Saigon, which they captured for several hours – proving that the US army was failing dismally to subjugate the Communists.

The Tet Offensive (so named because it took place during the Vietnamese religious holiday of Tet) also increased US public resistance to the war, although a Gallup poll taken just before the offensive showed 70% of the public in favour of the bombing.[91] 'Half a million American soldiers, with 700,000 Vietnamese allies, with total command of the air, total command of the sea, backed by huge resources and the most modern weapons, are unable to secure even a single city from the attacks of an enemy whose total strength is about 250,000', Kennedy told an audience in Chicago on 8 February.[92]

If he was not to lose his status as the most important anti-war figure in the country, Kennedy would have to act, and he did. During his trip to Chicago, Mayor Daley mentioned to him the possibility of setting up a presidential commission to review the war.

Kennedy pursued the commission idea, meeting with the new Secretary of Defense, Clark Clifford, in mid-March to discuss the proposal. Conflicting reports of the meeting make it impossible to know for sure what was said, but it appears as though Kennedy offered not to enter the presidential race if a serious effort was made to set up a commission to review the war.

The commission idea could never have worked, of course, as no President would accept the usurpation of his power in such a way. However, Kennedy probably went through the motions of proposing it anyway to make clear to party bosses that he had gone the extra mile and really had been left with no alternative other than to go for the nomination. Moreover, the most serious proponent of the commission idea was Mayor Daley, with whom Kennedy could not afford to fall out if he were to have a serious chance of the nomination. 'Daley's the ball game', he noted to an aide during the campaign.[93]

Inevitably, the commission idea was rejected by Johnson. The President's decision to ignore the findings of another commission, into the race riots of the previous summer, also spurred Kennedy towards announcing his candidacy. The Kerner Commission Report, published at the end of February, cited white racism as a major cause of the disturbances and, together with the failure of US foreign policy, provided Kennedy with reason enough to join the race.

Nevertheless when he declared his candidacy, most of the country was still probably hawkish, although the impetus was definitely moving towards the doves. Media comment against the war was just beginning to accelerate, and major atrocities against Vietnamese civilians were still not public knowledge at this time. In fact, at exactly the moment Kennedy was declaring his candidacy in Washington on 16 March, 1968, the My Lai massacre was taking place in Vietnam, when US troops from Charlie Company murdered hundreds of innocent civilians. That Saturday morning, as GIs raped, murdered and mutilated some 400 defenceless Vietnamese, Kennedy was announcing his candidacy to end the war. 'I run because I am convinced that this country is on a perilous course ... For the reality of recent events in Vietnam has been glossed over with illusions', he proclaimed.[94]

Earlier that week Kennedy had hit on the morality theme again in his strongest speech yet on Vietnam. 'Are we like the God of the Old Testament that we can decide here in Washington, DC, what cities, what towns, what hamlets in Vietnam are going to be destroyed?' he had demanded in the Senate.[95] His public comments on the war in the next few weeks were often even more emotional. Kennedy's best chance of capturing the nomination, thought his campaign team, was to concentrate on his public appeal. In this way, the thinking went, he would not only generate valuable votes in the primaries he entered, but also persuade party bosses (who held the key to many more convention delegates) that he was the likeliest candidate to win in November.

'We're going to do it a new way – in the streets,' predicted Senate aide Adam Walinsky.[96] Student audiences would convey this idea best, as they were often wildly enthusiastic about Kennedy and identified with his 'pop star' image. Consequently many of Kennedy's speeches were made at college campuses so that television viewers could witness how popular the candidate was (black audiences were often just as emotionally charged as students, but such images sent the wrong sort of signals to television watchers and so Kennedy tried to avoid addressing them in a similar way).

To hype up a student crowd, of course, Kennedy concentrated his attacks on the Vietnam War, which by now was very unpopular on campuses. 'Can we ordain to ourselves the awful majesty of God – to decide what cities and villages are to be destroyed, who will live and who will die, and who will join the refugees wandering in a desert of our own creation?' he asked at Kansas State University.[97] Most of his major addresses in the first days after he announced his candidacy were to these sorts of audiences who, according to various reports, were 'wild', 'uncontrollable' or simply 'frenzied'. In California he spoke to what reporter Jules Witcover described as 'a mob scene that in size, frenzy and physical threat of stampede rivalled anything that De Mille ever had committed to film'.[98]

Kennedy hammered on at his emotional Vietnam theme. 'Our brave young men dying in the swamps of Southeast Asia. Which of them might have written a poem? Which of them might have cured cancer? Which of them might have played in a World Series or given us the gift of laughter from the stage or helped build a bridge or a university? Which of them would have taught a child to read?'[99] In Los Angeles ('before one more screaming crowd' as Arthur Schlesinger remembered it[100]) he accused Johnson of calling on 'the darker impulses of the American spirit'.[101] Even sympathetic journalists were uncomfortable with the emotive attacks, and some press reports described the Senator as a demagogue. Kennedy was making an overt attempt to cash in on the emotion surrounding his name, but defended his actions by suggesting that the system left him with no alternative. 'I have to win through the people. Otherwise I'm not going to win,' he explained to the *New York Post*.[102]

Kennedy's first primary contest was in Indiana, however, which was among the most conservative above the Mason–Dixon line. Wallace had

done very well there in 1964, winning 30% of the vote in the Democratic primary, and Kennedy had to modify his approach for the contest,
scheduled for 7 May. After Johnson's sensational withdrawal from the
race on 31 March, Kennedy was left to slug it out with McCarthy in the
rest of the primaries with no substantial differences between them over
the main issue of Vietnam. But in Indiana a 'favourite son' candidate was
standing. Governor Roger Branigan represented the powerful local
Democratic Party machine, and by beating him Kennedy could show
the Daley camp that his organization was just as powerful as theirs.
With Johnson out, Branigan's candidacy was interpreted as an effort for
Vice-President Humphrey, who had announced his candidacy in the
days after Johnson's withdrawal.

However, with the main primary contests now between McCarthy
and Kennedy, the war receded as an issue and became secondary to that
of race. The 'ghetto problem' was brought into focus even more sharply
four days after Johnson's announcement that he was no longer a candidate, when Martin Luther King was assassinated in Memphis. The killing
sparked off a wave of violent reaction in nearly every major US city and
put the whole question of racial violence at the top of the political agenda.

Kennedy's win in Indiana (see Chapter 5) was fairly impressive, given
his lack of local party support. The *New Republic* noted that 'of the top
100 Democrats in the state who backed John F. Kennedy in the 1960
primary, only one ... went with Robert Kennedy this year. Of some 200
top elected officials, such as mayors and legislators, only three had
announced for Kennedy ten days before the primary.'[103]

Foreign policy featured well down the list of most voters' concerns in
Indiana. Kennedy concentrated on the 'law and order' issue, and where
he did mention international affairs it was, as one reporter noted, to
'remind his listeners that he knew how to take a "firm line" against the
Communists, having learned this during the Cuban missile crisis'.[104]
That this line had not been quite as firm as Kennedy was claiming was,
of course, not discovered until after his death, but it probably did not
make a crucial difference anyway, as most voters tended to judge
Kennedy largely on the basis of image.

So despite all his soul-searching on the Vietnam War, despite the
months of inner turmoil on when, and how, best to criticize the administration's policies on Vietnam, when it finally came down to what mattered,
i.e. votes in primaries, the issue was not the most important one.

Kennedy beat McCarthy in Nebraska, South Dakota and California.[105]
He lost to McCarthy in Oregon where, interestingly, the racial problem

was not significant and the campaign focused slightly more on Vietnam. In California the contest between Kennedy and McCarthy predictably concentrated on domestic issues, although the war and one or two other, more minor, foreign policy issues did surface sporadically during the campaign.

Nevertheless foreign affairs were cited repeatedly by Kennedy during the campaign to emphasize his suitability for office. It was remarkable that after four years as Attorney General, and three and a half years as a New York Senator, Kennedy's major qualifications for the presidency lay in his experience of international events. During a rather stilted debate on television with McCarthy on 1 June for example, Kennedy took several opportunities to remind viewers of his broad responsibilities in foreign policy during the Kennedy administration. 'While I was a member of the National Security Council for three and a half years, I was involved in some of those matters during that period of time in connection with Latin America and in connection with Africa, with the test ban treaty, and I suppose the most critical crisis that has ever been faced by mankind, the Cuban missile crisis in October 1962', he recalled.[106]

A few days previously, Kennedy had stressed the importance of the war as an issue in the campaign and warned that if neither himself nor McCarthy arrived at the convention with a high enough number of delegates Humphrey would be nominated, which would mean that 'there will be no candidate [in November] who has opposed the course of the war in Vietnam'.[107]

During the televised debate a questioner referred to a proposal made by Kennedy that week that the United States send 50 Phantom military aircraft to Israel and asked McCarthy if he agreed. McCarthy said he did, and the issue was passed over quickly as a minor one on which the candidates did not disagree. Four days later, Kennedy gave his victory speech in the California primary, which he had won by just under 4% of the vote. He did not realize – ever – that the gap had been so tight, as the full returns did not come in for some time and showed McCarthy to have done much better than had been predicted earlier.

Kennedy rounded off his remarks with a reminder that 'American troops and American Marines [are] carrying the major burden of [the Vietnamese] conflict'.[108] Then he left the platform and was assassinated by a Palestinian supposedly motivated by his victim's support for Israel. Kennedy – however disturbed the reasoning of his assassin – was apparently killed over an issue of foreign policy.

Although he never held any ambassadorship, had never worked in the State Department and had never been based in any country other than his own, Robert Kennedy had made a significant contribution to the development of US foreign policy. He had come a long way in a decade (in 1956 he had voted for Eisenhower), and his political contribution is generally remembered for his advice during the Cuban missile crisis and his opposition to the Vietnam War.

In 1985 Eugene McCarthy noted that the deal which finally ended the Vietnam War was based on proposals put forward during the Democratic Convention of 1968. 'Kissinger negotiated the deal and said he based it on the Democratic plank of 1968. That plank was a Kennedy plank – it was the one suggested by Bobby Kennedy's people and adopted at the convention.'[109]

Chapter Five

The Presidential Campaign

'On to Chicago and let's win there ...' – RFK, 5 June 1968

Exactly when Kennedy decided to run for President is unclear. He had hovered near the brink of declaring himself a candidate for much of 1967. By January 1968 he was ready to go, and then suddenly pulled back from an announcement, momentarily frightened that it would be a reckless and harmful decision.

In many ways, of course, he had been running as an undeclared candidate ever since he entered the Senate in January 1965. Some Democrats believed he should have been a presidential candidate even before that, and during the 1964 primaries he won write-in votes in six states, including more than 19% of the Massachusetts primary vote. However, he never seriously considered challenging Johnson for the presidency that year, although of course he was initially disappointed not to be offered the vice-presidency. But by the 1966 mid-term elections, Kennedy had begun to grant favours to candidates whose support he would need if he did decide to run in 1968.

He was particularly popular with candidates whose campaigns had financial problems. As the *Wall Street Journal* of 17 October 1966, explained: 'When a Kennedy comes for a fund-raising affair, not only do tickets sell fast but the local party keeps practically all the proceeds. When Mr Johnson or Mr Humphrey comes for a fund-raiser, anywhere from 50% to 100% of the proceeds usually must go to the Democratic National Committee in Washington.'[1]

Kennedy made a series of appearances both for those with safe seats and no-hopers that autumn and took the opportunity to impress party bosses with the enthusiasm he could generate among voters. With an eye on courting the sort of constituency he would focus on during his own campaign, he made a series of appearances in Polish-American districts of Chicago and joined a motorcade through the city with the all-important Mayor Daley, whose support would be crucial to any Kennedy bid for the presidency.

Daley was, above all, a symbol of the old politics. Perhaps the last old-style boss, his fiefdom spread out from Cook County to encompass Chicago and much of Illinois. Democrats around the country looked to Daley for guidance – if the Chicago boss gave his imprimatur to a candidate, party members nationally would follow. In the 1960 election, when John Kennedy was deciding who to pick as his running mate, Daley's preference was considered. Robert Kennedy made it clear to Senator Henry Jackson that should he want the vice-presidential ticket, '[Jackson] would have to convince leaders like Mayor Daley of Chicago ... that he can help the ticket the most'.[2] The chief king-maker in the Democratic Party, Daley had been highly influential in securing John Kennedy's victory in 1960.[3] While Daley had supported John Kennedy, however, he was less enthusiastic about Robert. For a start, Daley was a hawk on the war. He was also fiercely loyal to the Democratic Party, and would not advocate an open split with the incumbent President. However, he refused to come out against Kennedy, preferring to see how strongly Kennedy did in the primaries, and had agreed not to make a commitment to any candidate until June.[4]

Speculation during 1966 that Kennedy might make an assault on the White House two years later was fired by a series of opinion polls showing Kennedy a popular alternative to Johnson. A Gallup poll in March that year suggested Kennedy would be preferred to Nixon by 54% to 41% of all voters, and a Harris poll in September had him leading President Johnson by 47% to 41% among Democrats and by 39% to 37% among all voters.[5]

Such statistics were bound to provide fuel for media commentary on Kennedy's chances for 1968, and several pieces appeared towards the end of 1966 exploring the prospects of his taking on Johnson during the 1968 primaries. Most agreed that it would be unlikely that Kennedy would announce in 1968 and that he would rather wait until 1972, when Johnson would not be standing for re-election and the other likely candidate, Hubert Humphrey, would be regarded as out of touch by many of the younger generation. Helen Hill Miller in the *New Republic* of 15 October, 1966, noted that it was 'foolish to talk about Robert Kennedy in '68' but outlined how he might be forced into the race if the war in Vietnam continued and the President's popularity remained in decline.[6] *The Nation* of 14 November suggested that a Kennedy bid in 1968 was 'improbable, but hardly impossible' and predicted that the Senator would wait until 1972.[7]

Kennedy's problem was that neither 1968 nor 1972 was the optimum year for him to run for President. In 1968 he would have been a Senator for less than four years and would not have developed his alternative coalition sufficiently to be sure of a strong campaign. Moreover, it would mean taking on the incumbent President who hated him personally and risk splitting the Democratic Party. If the war suddenly ended, Kennedy would have been deprived of his most important issue.

By waiting until 1972, however, there was a danger that someone else might begin to attract Kennedy's new-found national constituency. A less cautious Democrat might even run against Johnson in 1968 and win. The 1970 gubernatorial elections could throw up a young, liberal candidate who might usurp Kennedy's place as the new radical hope. Kennedy had already voiced worries about New York Republican Mayor Lindsay, and in any case 1972 was a long way off and Kennedy's popularity might wane in the intervening years.

In many ways Kennedy was like an Olympic athlete who peaks off-year. The ideal time for him to run for President would have been around 1970, when, of course, there was no presidential election, and when he would be running for re-election to the Senate. He was left with the choice of running too early or leaving it too late.

The dilemma dogged him throughout 1966 and 1967, and advisers offered conflicting opinions right up until he announced in mid-March 1968. One of the first to suggest he run was Senate aide Adam Walinsky, who outlined the case in a memo to the Senator the day after the November 1966 mid-term elections. 'Johnson is a lame duck', proposed Walinsky, and over the next year the rest of Kennedy's Senate staff joined in the effort to persuade him to run in 1968.[8]

During 1967, however, nearly everyone else in the Kennedy entourage, including most of JFK's former advisers (and principally his brother, Ted) urged caution, believing that Johnson was unbeatable and that Kennedy could spoil his chances for 1972 if he pushed too quickly. In March 1967 Hugh Sidey noted in *Life* magazine that 'the last thing Kennedy wants to do is run in '68'.[9] In fact, Kennedy probably quite fancied the idea of campaigning in 1968, but it was not a question of personal like or dislike. Kennedy, characteristically, would run only if he thought he could win and kept himself out of the race until he was convinced he could obtain the nomination.

In October an estimated 50,000 anti-war protesters demonstrated outside the Pentagon, and the peace movement was gaining such momentum that early the same month a group of Kennedy's advisers met to explore the possibility of his joining the race in 1968 after all.[10] The advisors included Ted Kennedy and former JFK intimates Ted Sorenson, Pierre Salinger, Arthur Schlesinger Jr., and Kenneth O'Donnell. Most were still against it (although, incredibly, the prospect that Johnson might offer Kennedy the vice-presidency the following year was still discussed as a serious possibility).[11]

At the end of October more and more politicians were urging Kennedy to run. In a response to a question at Berkeley, Senator Eugene McCarthy declared that 'times arise in politics when an individual like Bobby Kennedy has no right to calculate that things will be better for him personally if he waits until 1972'.[12] Early indications also showed that the anti-war movement might enjoy more political muscle than had previously been expected. In November the Peace and Freedom Party (PFP) managed to register 71,000 people and have its name included on the California primary ballots.

When McCarthy accepted Al Lowenstein's invitation at the end of 1967 to be a focus for the anti-war movement, Kennedy was immediately cornered. A McCarthy effort, if only partially successful, threatened to attract the constituency of dissent Kennedy had so assiduously cultivated in the previous years. If McCarthy's candidacy failed badly, on the other hand, it would strengthen Johnson's grip on the party and would suggest that the anti-war liberals were incapable of electoral success.

McCarthy was a successful and influential Senator: he had been mooted as a possible running-mate for Johnson had LBJ won the nomination in 1960, and he was very nearly offered the position in 1964. That year he was re-elected to the Senate by the biggest majority ever achieved by a Democrat in Minnesota and he enjoyed membership of two of the most important Senate committees, Finance and Foreign Relations.

McCarthy announced his presidential bid at the end of November. The first primary was scheduled for 12 March, in New Hampshire. Meanwhile, Kennedy dithered. He believed that the organization he was trying to build was not ready to propel him to the White House. At the end of 1967, although very popular throughout the country, he could count on the support of very few labour leaders and very few party bosses. Both would be needed to win the nomination in 1968. The party had not fully emerged from the days when a few key Democrats in a few key states could all but decide on the nominee. In Illinois, of course, Daley still ruled from Chicago. In California, too, there were the remnants of the old machine (although Jesse Unruh from that state was, at least, on Kennedy's side). In Ohio, New York, Pennsylvania and Texas – the other states which sent more than a hundred delegates to the 1968 convention – Kennedy would have to rely on local heavyweights to provide delegate votes. Of the fourteen state primaries scheduled, only seven – New Hampshire, Wisconsin, Indiana, Nebraska, Oregon, South Dakota and California – were regarded as having any real significance. In only three of those, Wisconsin, Oregon and California, were the delegates bound as a result of the popular vote.[13]

In January 1968 Ted Kennedy returned from Vietnam and reported on the refugee problem at first hand. However, along with most advisers, Ted still counselled that Robert Kennedy should not enter the campaign and should bide his time until 1972.[14]

Nevertheless, Ted's report about the state of things in Vietnam seriously tempted Kennedy to announce in late January. His supporters – some of them politically very valuable – were beginning to leave him to join the McCarthy campaign. Despite working for McCarthy, Lowenstein was still urging Kennedy to run. In a stormy meeting between the two in January, Kennedy cited the usual reasons for his determination to stay out – it was too difficult to win, it would spoil his chances for 1972, it would disrupt party unity, etc. 'The people who think that the honour and future of this country are at stake don't give a shit what Mayor Daley and Chairman X and Governor Y think. We're going ahead and we're going to win, and it's a shame you're not with us because you could have been president,' countered Lowenstein.[15] Kennedy was impressed by such arguments and almost decided to join the race.

Then, just as he was on the brink of declaring, the North Koreans seized the American ship *Pueblo*. Immediately, President Johnson called up 14,000 reserves and, briefly, the public were with him. The incident reminded Kennedy how such small events, completely outside his control, could determine the popularity of the President and, therefore, the success of his own campaign. A week later, however, the Tet Offensive caused Kennedy to change his mind again. As already discussed, this initiative by the North Vietnamese army and the Viet Cong was a devastating psychological blow for those Americans who were convinced that they were winning the war, and as news of the offensive reached the United States public opinion began to swing away from the administration and towards the peace protesters.

On 8 February, while reports from Vietnam were beginning to recognize the significance of the North Vietnamese attacks, Kennedy breakfasted with Richard Daley in Chicago. He hovered once again on the brink of announcing, but Daley persuaded him to stall while the idea of a special commission on the war was explored.[16]

Kennedy held off, but pressure was growing for him to announce. The Tet Offensive had generated substantial unease among the public, and McCarthy appeared likely to capitalize on the mounting disquiet. On top of the Vietnam issue, Kennedy was outraged at the White House's reaction to the Kerner Commission's report into inner-city riots, published on 29 February. The Commission criticized some of the Johnson administration's Great Society programmes and made important recommendations to the President to avert more violence. However, the report was received by administration officials with stony silence. 'He's not going to do anything about the war, and now he's not going to do anything about the cities either!' complained Kennedy.[17]

Meanwhile McCarthy was making the most of public dissatisfaction. He began campaigning in New Hampshire at the end of January from exactly the same spot where John Kennedy had begun his campaign for the presidency eight years earlier. Speaking next to a bust of the late President on 25 January, McCarthy began the first of just fifteen days he would spend campaigning in the state. The New Hampshire results shocked the most experienced political analysts. McCarthy did not actually beat the President but, like the Tet attacks, he caused enough damage to inflict a massive psychological blow on the administration. Johnson took 49.4% of the vote, but McCarthy won an astounding 42.2% and picked up twenty of the 24 delegates.[18]

Kennedy's mind was all but made up. He was waiting only for the proposal on the war commission to be formally rejected and then he could go.

At about 5 p.m. on Thursday, 14 March (the day after the New Hampshire results were declared), Secretary of Defense Clark Clifford called the Senator's office and relayed the President's formal rejection of the idea. Kennedy was now free to run without being charged with failing to explore all other options to end the war. It was the last in a series of hurdles in his own mind that he had to overcome to announce his candidacy. 'That night I decided to run for president,' he recalled, although in reality it had been a protracted process of weighing up advantages and disadvantages over months and probably years.[19]

Some close advisers, including President Kennedy's former press secretary, Pierre Salinger, were not aware just how close Kennedy was to running, and only at this point knew of his immediate plans to announce. So 'last-minute' had the final decision been, in fact, that *The Listener* magazine dated 14 March was being sold in Britain containing an interview with Kennedy on why he would definitely not be a candidate.[20]

To qualify for the California primary, Kennedy had formally to open his campaign by Monday, 18 March. For media purposes, however, Saturday was obviously the best choice, as his declaration would be the biggest news for the widely read Sunday papers and would guarantee him an interview on one of the popular weekend political programmes. Moreover, Sunday was St Patrick's Day, and the newly announced candidate could expect large-scale media coverage if he joined the march in New York.

So at 10 a.m. on Saturday, 16 March, Kennedy walked into the same Senate caucus room where he had interrogated Jimmy Hoffa in the 1950s and where his brother had announced his presidential candidacy on 2 January, 1960. With the same opening line used by John Kennedy that day, the Senator declared: 'I am announcing today my candidacy for the Presidency of the United States' and, in a blatant and hopeless attempt to deflect attention away from his personal feud with the President, continued: 'I do not run for the Presidency merely to oppose any man but to propose new policies.'[21] He then went on to outline why he felt it necessary to run – because of the war and the rioting in the cities – and he praised McCarthy's 'remarkable' campaign.

Kennedy's first major decision as candidate would be which primaries to enter. He confirmed at the time of his announcement that he would be standing in California (4 June), and that state law required he also be on the ballot in Nebraska (14 May) and Oregon (28 May). However, to win the nomination Kennedy would have to convince the party bosses that he was the most electable candidate to put up against the Republicans in November. To do this, he would have to enter and win most, if not all, the available primaries. More importantly, he would have to demonstrate that he could win votes from crucial areas which might otherwise go Republican and that he would elicit massive support from traditional Democratic voters. Although Kennedy's popularity among black voters was anticipated, he would have to show that he could gain those votes without alienating whites, especially blue-collar whites, who might otherwise be attracted to a candidate like Nixon. Moreover, many Democrats who would vote in the primaries depended on local Democratic control of their state for their jobs. The patronage system was still a powerful force, and party regulars would be hoping to nominate a presidential candidate who would improve their chances of success in local elections come November. Some elected officials had the power to dispense jobs, and so the potential recipients of those jobs would have a vested interest in seeing an attractive candidate appointed. As many voters would associate local candidates with the party's national candidates, it was important that the national candidates could prove they would be very popular. Were Kennedy to come across as too liberal, for example, or too soft on crime, he might ruin the hopes of a number of local Democratic politicians running for office from Congress to local city hall. The Chicago political machine, for instance, was structured by a collection of 50 wards run by aldermen who had powers to appoint jobs and even collect taxes.[22] 'Each ward committeeman controls about 500 jobs … Overall, the apparatus controls about 35,000 jobs', marvelled one English journalist in 1968.[23]

In Kennedy's case the doubts arose about his ability to attract votes from the white working class. His position on the war was not especially helpful to securing support from this traditionally patriotic group, and neither was his identification with black aspirations. Although he was running at a time of relative economic prosperity, racial tensions in northern cities were coming to dominate the domestic political agenda, as low-income whites voiced their fears about increased violence and 'preferential treatment' for blacks, whose neighbourhoods in their view appeared to be enjoying federal investment as a reward for rioting.

It was crucial that Kennedy should make an impressive showing among blue-collar whites if Mayor Daley and his acolytes were to be convinced. An excellent test of Kennedy's pulling-power with this group would be in Indiana, the first primary he would enter, to be held on 7 May. Indiana was known as a hard-line state on racial matters. Despite its northern location, it had traditionally afforded the Ku-Klux Klan a remarkable level of support. In the mid-1920s it was calculated that most members of its state legislature were supported by the Klan. In more recent times Alabama Governor George Wallace had become a hero among its low-income white population, winning 30% of the vote in the 1964 presidential primary. The state also had a long military tradition, was home of the headquarters of the American Legion, and in the spring of 1968 had no real anti-Vietnam War movement.

It did, however, have some compensations for Kennedy. A write-in campaign organized against his wishes by hard-core supporters had won him 5% of the 1964 primary, and if he could win here, in a state with such a tough reputation, it would go a long way to persuading the hard-bitten party bosses that he was a serious candidate. Also, there were several large pockets of black voters. In 1967 Richard Hatcher became only the second black person ever elected mayor of a major US city when he narrowly beat party machine candidate John Krupa by 1,300 votes to win in Gary, Indiana (Carl Stokes had become the first a few months before, when he became mayor in Cleveland, Ohio). Kennedy had asked aide Dick Tuck to go to Gary and help Hatcher during the election, and so in 1968 he had not only a political IOU from the mayor but also an aide with expertise of the city's electorate.

Kennedy's initial task was to win the Indiana primary convincingly, and win it with a significant number of blue-collar votes from white districts. Much of his campaign concentrated on this effort, and his staff were quick to highlight any evidence that he was popular in these areas. For years, much of the Robert Kennedy legend has relied on the voting figures from Indiana, and they have been used to 'prove' that Kennedy could have brought about some sort of magical coalition between low-income whites and blacks throughout the country. However, this belief its rooted more in the skilful manipulation of Kennedy's spin doctors than in real evidence.

However, he also had certain advantages over McCarthy and his other opponent, Governor Branigan. Kennedy had, after all, been 'head cop' for four years as Attorney General and therefore was a poor target for those hoping to suggest that as a liberal he was soft on crime. Kennedy consistently emphasized his law and order credentials during the Indiana campaign. 'I was the chief law-enforcement officer of this country for four years,' he kept reminding voters in the state.[24]

Kennedy strove hard for the white 'ethnic' vote, as it was called. Many of the whites whom Kennedy was hoping to attract were Irish (although McCarthy, too, was Irish and Catholic), who had regarded President Kennedy as near-saintly and a validation of their cultural origins. Others were Polish. Robert Kennedy had been very enthusiastically received during his trip to Poland after President Kennedy's death and, of course, had a reputation for not compromising with the Soviets from his dealings over the Cuban missile crisis (that this reputation was unfounded was not revealed until after his death).

However, the emphasis on crime and race during the Indiana campaign was not just Kennedy's attempt to shift the agenda on to issues where he would be strong with low-income whites. After President Johnson's dramatic retirement from the race on 31 March, the war temporarily receded as the primary issue between the Democratic candidates. Kennedy and McCarthy were both doves, and so in the days immediately following Johnson's withdrawal, the other major concern – violence in the cities – began to increase in importance. It became dominant when, four days after Johnson's announcement, Martin Luther King was assassinated, provoking riots in almost every major city across the country.

Kennedy was in Indianapolis on the night of King's death and helped to avert violence by speaking in the heart of the city's ghetto. Such gestures confirmed his reputation as someone whom blacks would listen to, and someone who might be able to stop them rioting. Such qualities were important to the working-class whites whom Kennedy was hoping to attract.

There were those, of course, who regarded Kennedy's close relationship with black voters as dangerous, believing that such familiarity could only breed contempt, and that his identification with black pride encouraged the violence. In a poorly timed piece on the eve of Martin Luther King's death, the *Wall Street Journal* suggested that voters might hold Kennedy responsible if the Poor People's Campaign in Washington turned violent: 'Might there not be a sharp reaction against him as the man whose speeches helped stir the rioters?' it asked.[25] In fact, in the following days Kennedy accompanied police through the streets of the capital, helping to defuse tension in the black neighbourhoods.

Officially the presidential campaign was suspended for a week after King's death, but Kennedy's trips to riot-torn Washington, and the emotion his appearance at King's funeral elicited from the black crowds, cemented his image as someone black leaders could do business with. The frenzied crowds, often black, which characterized the television coverage of Kennedy's campaigning reaffirmed his support in this area. During the Indiana primary, it seemed possible that he might be able to pull off the all-important task of gaining votes from large numbers of low-income blacks and whites.

At the end of April, just over a week before the vote, a detailed Gallup poll of the national electorate revealed Kennedy's strengths and limitations.[26] Among voters aged 21 to 29, Kennedy led McCarthy by 41% to 32% (with Humphrey on 16%). Among voters aged 30 to 49, McCarthy led Kennedy 35% to 27%, with Humphrey on 23%. With voters 50 and over, McCarthy held on at 32%, with Kennedy trailing Humphrey by 29% to 25%. The study also revealed that McCarthy was more popular with those who had been to college, leading him to remark that 'the better-educated people vote for us', but that Catholics preferred Kennedy to the former seminarian McCarthy by 36% to 30% (although McCarthy did better among Protestants, beating Kennedy 33% to 26%).

Perhaps the most important statistic in the study, however, was Kennedy's lead over McCarthy and Humphrey among labour-union families. Kennedy was narrowly ahead of McCarthy by 31% to 29%, with Humphrey, who was popular with union bosses, on 27%. This constituency was one of Kennedy's prime targets for his coalition, of course. He needed the votes of union members, in the face of the best efforts of many employers and union officials to oppose him.

The union hierarchy in Indiana made an impressive effort to prevent Kennedy from winning votes among blue-collar whites. The Committee on Public Education (COPE), the political wing of the AFL-CIO, had 270,000 leaflets distributed to industrial workers in the closing weeks of the campaign which appealed to their patriotism and ridiculed Kennedy's anti-war position. In language highly reminiscent of that used by George Wallace (who urged voters to 'Stand Up For America'), the COPE leaflets encouraged them to 'Stand Up For What's Good in America and Be Counted'.[27] COPE activities would also hinder Kennedy in Oregon. A concerted phone campaign there urged 50,000 union members to vote for President Johnson, whose name remained on the ballot even though he was no longer a candidate (Johnson won more than 45,000 votes in the Oregon primary, more than 12% of the total).

Kennedy campaigned hard in the so-called 'white ethnic' areas of Indiana, notably in the southern part of the state and in the suburbs around Gary. He was careful to tone down his youthful aggressive manner which had characterized the early days of his campaign, when he had appeared at universities around the country and generated emotional reactions from students. For Indiana, he had cut his hair, avoided the excesses of emotional appeals – which had led several journalists to charge him with demagoguery – and emphasized how he would cut government expenditure to pay for social programmes. Interestingly, the spending cuts he cited most often were in research for supersonic travel and space exploration, both of which had been proposals enthusiastically supported by President Kennedy. In a similarly conservative vein, he stressed the money-saving aspects of his urban renewal proposals, calling for 'a greater partnership between government and private enterprise to make our cities live again'.[28] The *New York Times* noted how his fiscal plans 'fit perfectly with [those] advocated by Republican leaders in the House of Representatives'.[29]

In the last week of the primary campaign, Kennedy's pitch for the blue-collar vote appeared to be paying off. More importantly, it was seen to be paying off. Winning these votes was only half of Kennedy's battle. He also had to convince party bosses like Daley that his votes had come from this constituency and that he could repeat the effect nationwide come November. What was important to Kennedy was not only the result but also the way it was reported to the rest of America. Thus in the days before the election Kennedy aides stressed the importance of the blue-collar vote to journalists, and the theme was taken up in several media outlets.

In the sort of coverage Kennedy could only pray for, the *New York Times* noted on the day of the election that 'In the areas surrounding Gary, Mr Kennedy has found substantial support in the white working-class wards that went heavily to George Wallace in 1964. Some of those voters indicated to reporters that although Mr Kennedy had the negro vote they looked upon him as a tough Irishman with whom they could identify.'[30]

On the night before the election, Kennedy's campaign ran a half-hour television commercial emphasizing law and order and local control over government programmes – both high-priority issues for blue-collar whites. In order actually to win the election, Kennedy had only to rely on a heavy black turn-out and an average response from the white wards. However, such a result would not have been in the best interests of his long-term plan to be hailed as the new champion of the white working class.

The total number of those voting in the primary was expected to be about 600,000. Kennedy could rely on almost all of the black vote in the state, which was 135,000, or about 45% of the total he needed to win an overall majority. The *New York Times* reported that 'nearly half the votes Senator Kennedy hopes to win in this primary could be cast by negroes. If this happens, it may be the first time any politician has won an important state election from this kind of power base ...'[31] However, Kennedy could not afford to be seen to have relied heavily on the black vote, which could not be so easily repeated elsewhere in the country. He did win the primary with 328,000 votes in an extremely high turn-out of over 775,000 Democrats. However, with his huge slice of the black vote (NBC reported him taking over 90% of it), Kennedy's claim to be the first choice of blue-collar whites was not that convincing, even though many newspapers (and, later, Kennedy biographers) promoted the idea that he had achieved some sort of class-based coalition and had united poor blacks and poor whites to challenge the political hierarchy.

Kennedy won with 42% to Branigan's 30%, with McCarthy on 27%. It was the early media analyses of the results, however, which were crucial in shaping the perception of what had happened. The idea that Kennedy had secured a coalition of poor blacks and whites immediately took root and has lived on in nearly all of the work done on Kennedy since his death.

The *New York Times* correspondent relayed how

> Senator Kennedy also did well with blue-collar whites in the industrial areas and with rural whites. He carried the seven largest counties in the state, where George Wallace polled his largest vote in the primary of 1964. Thus in Lake County, which contains Gary and where both negroes and blue-collar whites live, Senator Kennedy polled 57,842 votes to 42,902 for McCarthy and 23,290 for Branigan. He carried most of the tier counties in the southern part of the state, which are peopled by a number of white southern migrants and where the Ku-Klux Klan was strong in the 1920s and made his strongest showing 'in Lake County, near Chicago'.[32]

Daley could hardly fail to be impressed by such a triumph on his own doorstep.

Several commentators followed the line Kennedy was hoping for and pushed the idea that he had done magnificently well among the working-class whites. Television correspondent Charles Quinn remembered 'all these whites, all these blue-collar people and ethnic people who supported Kennedy'.[33] A British television programme, *This Week*, covered Kennedy in Indiana and stressed how well he was doing with low-income whites.[34] After Kennedy's death, Paul Cowan wrote in the *Village Voice* that he was 'the last liberal politician who could communicate with white working-class America',[35] and author Robert Coles repeated the idea that Kennedy 'could do the miraculous: attract the support of ... desperate blacks ... and ... working-class white people'.[36]

In his biography of Kennedy, Jack Newfield recounts how 'Kennedy carried white backlash counties like Hammond, Gary, South Bend, East Chicago' in the Indiana primary.[37] In another Kennedy memoir, David Halberstam supported the myth, suggesting that 'The Poles in Gary came through, two to one ... a fine gift for the omnipresent Mayor Daley',[38] and Jules Witcover, in his book about the Kennedy campaign *85 Days*, claims that 'Precinct breakdowns showed [Kennedy won] more than the usual number of blue-collar whites for a Democrat in the backlash neighbourhoods.'[39]

The misconception still survives. On 15 May, 1992, Sidney Blumenthal wrote in the *New Republic* that 'Reforging the black–white coalition that briefly cohered in support of Robert Kennedy's candidacy has remained an evanescent Democratic dream'.[40] The truth, however, was that Kennedy had depended on blacks for nearly half of the votes he took to win the Indiana primary, and that support from the 'white backlash' areas was not impressive at all. Kennedy did win industrial centres such as Gary, but largely on the strength of his black support. McCarthy won the white suburbs which had gone for Wallace four years before. Without the huge black support, Kennedy would have run about even with Branigan.

The misconception about Kennedy's victory in the white neighbourhoods originates with a column written by Rowland Evans and Robert Novak the day after the primary, which interpreted the result as Kennedy having won 90% in black precincts and 'running two to one ahead in some Polish precincts'.[41] In fact, Kennedy lost 59 out of the 70 white precincts in Gary. The mistake is pointed out by Kennedy aides Milton Gwirtzman and William Vanden Heuvel in their biography of Kennedy, and they concede that 'the Kennedy campaign organization believed the misconception and encouraged it'.[42] Kennedy himself also believed it and made a point of thanking the blue-collar whites in his victory speech on the evening of the primary. Later that night he told Larry O'Brien: 'I've proved I can really be a leader of a broad spectrum. I can be a bridge between blacks and whites without stepping back from my positions.'[43]

Moreover, not only did Kennedy not do as well among blue-collar whites as he and many others originally believed: there is evidence to suggest that he may have fared even worse in other states. In addition to his popularity with the particularly influential Polish community in Indiana (based in part on his reputed anti-Communism), Kennedy held a special appeal for some industrial workers in the state, without which his meagre vote among whites would have been even worse. Although elsewhere in the country his poor relations with labour officials would have been a disadvantage, in some quarters of Indiana they were something of a bonus. The International Brotherhood of Teamsters (IBT) harboured considerable hostility for Kennedy, but the IBT had a history of extremely poor relations with truckers in Indiana, which may well have worked to Kennedy's advantage.

Although Indiana steel-haulers were officially a part of the IBT, Teamsters boss Jimmy Hoffa had done little to advance their cause, believing that these 'owner-operators' were not proper teamsters. This attitude had led to a long-running feud between Hoffa and the steel-haulers. The year before Kennedy entered the Indiana primary, a new agreement had been worked out between the employers and Hoffa which – while very beneficial for most drivers – had not done much for the steel-haulers. Steel-hauler Bill Kusley led a wildcat strike in Indiana in June 1967 which was opposed by the IBT.[44] Violence between Hoffa's IBT and the newly formed Fraternal Association of Steel Haulers (FASH) broke out in the following weeks, and in August Kusley's strikers began to picket the Teamsters offices in Indiana in an overt show of defiance.

More violence ensued, and although the strike was called off in late 1967, the residual bad feeling between FASH and the IBT carried on for some years. Exactly how much Kennedy benefited from the anti-Hoffa feeling in the state is difficult to quantify, but Hoffa biographer Walter Sheridan was sent by Kennedy to Indiana to maximize support among industrial workers. In fact, an early casualty of Kennedy's investigations during the McClellan hearings had been the corrupt (Democratic) mayor of Gary, who was indicted as a result of Kennedy's enquiries. Presumably Kennedy cashed in on some residual popularity gained from ousting a criminal politician the decade before. Blue-collar whites around the rest of the country might not have been so well disposed towards him. (The IBT in Indiana backed Governor Branigan during the primary.)

Nevertheless, whatever the true interpretation of the Indiana primary, Kennedy had won the battle to create an impression of himself as someone who could win the votes of poor whites. What was genuinely impressive, however, was the extent to which blacks supported him. He not only won about 90% of the Indiana black vote but on the same day swept the primary in Washington, DC, by 62% to Humphrey's 37%. The capital's overwhelmingly black population favoured Kennedy by a huge margin, despite Humphrey's impressive civil rights record. Kennedy's slate in Washington, DC, even included black radical Colin Carew.

Although John Kennedy had done well among blacks, who had supported him in some crucial states and held the balance of votes in his 1960 victories in Chicago, Michigan and Pennsylvania, Robert Kennedy was far more popular with non-white voters. In fact, only 68% of non-white voters went for John Kennedy in 1960. In a poll featured in *New York Magazine* in July 1968, 92% of Harlem residents said that the death of their Senator affected them as much, if not more, than the death of President Kennedy. McCarthy saw 'no need to stir up the blacks and minorities. They were Bobby's people and I saw no point in wasting time campaigning there.'[45]

Another area where Kennedy bettered his brother's appeal was in the state of Nebraska, which held the next primary after Indiana. Although the vast rural area of Nebraska was hardly natural territory for Kennedy, it offered him the opportunity to keep the momentum from Indiana going and, as his opponents hardly bothered to put up a fight in the state, to notch up an impressive margin of victory.

John Kennedy's electoral experience in Nebraska eight years earlier had been disastrous, losing to Nixon by 62% to 38% (only the 36% from Mississippi had been worse). During the 1960 election Robert Kennedy had complained to JFK's campaign manager in Nebraska, Rip Horton, about his poor level of organization: Kennedy made sure the mistakes were not repeated in 1968. He also enjoyed one or two practical advantages his brother never had. Phil Sorenson (brother of JFK adviser Ted) had been lieutenant-governor of the state for two years, and in 1966 had won the gubernatorial primary (though he lost the general election). His state-wide organization was still intact, and Kennedy made thorough use of it.

While McCarthy made just one visit to the state, and the Humphrey campaign relied on the union machine to get out the vote, Kennedy made numerous appearances throughout Nebraska and won the primary by 52% to McCarthy's 31% (with combined Humphrey and Johnson votes totalling 13%). Kennedy's staff were keen to interpret the result as more evidence of his stunning success among poorer whites, and he did win most of the counties with concentrations of Poles and Germans.[46] Another statistic the Kennedy campaign was keen to push was that he had won in 24 of the 25 counties where he had waged a personal campaign (and lost the other – at the University of Nebraska – by two votes). The implication was that Kennedy could break down the hostility many felt towards him by appearing in person and that he was becoming an increasingly attractive candidate. Once again, however, he had relied on support from the black community for his winning margin. The concentration of blacks around Omaha had favoured him by over 85%. Nevertheless, Kennedy felt sufficiently lifted by the result to make an outright appeal to McCarthy supporters to switch to himself as the most hopeful anti-administration candidate.

Kennedy had hoped to finish off McCarthy as a serious candidate by the time of the Oregon primary, scheduled for 28 May, but McCarthy's 31% in Nebraska had kept him in touch and he was hoping for a decent result in Oregon in the following week to propel him into the most important primary so far, that in California. Kennedy, on the other hand, faced problems in Oregon. It had no real black voting base on which he could draw, and his claims to be the champion of the white working class risked exposure. For all his professionalism, too, Kennedy made some basic errors in Oregon. He appointed Congresswoman Edith Green to run his campaign, largely because she had run John Kennedy's successful primary there in 1960, but Green was not a popular figure in the state in 1968, as Kennedy's intelligence network should have gathered. Kennedy also refused an offer to debate with McCarthy on television in the belief that such exposure could only benefit his rival. This refusal made Kennedy look arrogant and helped sway many of the don't-knows away from him.

Kennedy also began to speak unguardedly to the press. He told a reporter on 21 May that 'if I get beaten in any primary, I am not a very viable candidate'.[47] The pressure was on Kennedy to keep winning – he had to demonstrate to the party bosses his claims to be a super-candidate, winning everything he entered. (Much of the Kennedy legend was based on this principle. In 27 previous political elections, no Kennedy had ever lost.) However, Kennedy had one eye on the California primary, and did not ensure that his campaign was organized as it should have been. The war was unpopular in Oregon, but voters preferred McCarthy's phlegmatic style to Kennedy's aggression. Gun registration was also an important issue for some voters in the state, who resented any infringement of their constitutional right to bear arms.[48]

On this, McCarthy had a slight edge over Kennedy. While Kennedy favoured federal registration and federal enforcement, McCarthy was less insistent and was happy to let individual states take responsibility for enforcing gun controls. In 1967 Kennedy had voted to cut federal funding for the National Board for the Protection of Rifle Practice. McCarthy had voted against the cut. Also, in an unlucky break for Kennedy, the revelation that while Attorney General he had authorized the tap on Martin Luther King's telephone broke in the final days of the campaign, resurrecting his old ruthless image.

On the eve of the Oregon vote, a Quayle opinion poll showed Kennedy holding a slight lead over McCarthy, by 34% to 32%. The early returns the next day were good, too. One Polish journalist even filed a story to Europe (presumably his last) confirming that Kennedy had won.[49] In reality, Kennedy had been beaten convincingly, by 45% to 39%, and his injudicious remark about not being a viable candidate if he lost duly reappeared to haunt him. Fortunately for him, however, attention swiftly moved on towards the California primary, which offered the largest number of delegate votes so far (174, compared with 63 from Indiana, 35 from Oregon, 30 from Nebraska and 23 from Washington, DC). South Dakota (26 votes) also held its primary the same day as California. Although there would be other primaries to follow, in a sense California marked the biggest prize for Kennedy. Its reputation as a sort of mini-America, containing roughly all of the country's facets in microcosm, meant it was the perfect place for Kennedy to demonstrate his voter-appeal. If he won convincingly, it would probably spell the end of McCarthy's campaign and leave a clear contest between himself and Humphrey. Defeat in California, however, would almost certainly mean the end of Kennedy's chances of securing the nomination.

Kennedy's campaign in California tested his new coalition to its limits, as New Leftist Tom Hayden joined in the effort with Daniel Patrick Moynihan, who was to end up in the Nixon administration. Kennedy's mixture of new and old politics soon ran into trouble, however, over his delegate slate, which had been assembled by old-style politician Jesse Unruh. The Peace and Freedom Party, which had surprised many conventional politicians by registering enough signatures to get on the primary ballot, attacked the slate of delegates standing for Kennedy as a largely cynical collection of professionals who did not represent the anti-war activists he claimed to lead. In fact, many had been ready to stand as delegates for President Johnson until they were signalled to switch by Unruh. The PFP produced a pamphlet damaging to Kennedy within the anti-war movement called 'Hookers for Kennedy' which exposed much of the delegate slate for what it was: a collection of Unruh's political cronies used to carving out political deals in the traditional way.[50]

Not included in this attack on the Kennedy delegates were Cesar Chavez, leader of the Mexican-American National Farm Workers' Association, and Paul Schrade, state chief of the radical United Auto Workers' Union.[51] Also on the slate from the new politics was State Senator Mervyn Dymally, a black with militant links, and Tom Bradley, a leading black liberal (later mayor of Los Angeles). However, these figures were joined by individuals such as Representative Bob Movetti, who had been in favour of the war until just before the election and had sponsored an anti-riot bill which was regarded as hostile to blacks.

There were other problems, too. Many Californian professional politicians resented the Kennedy machine for imposing one of its own – Pierre Salinger – on the state as a senatorial candidate during the 1964 elections. Salinger had lost, and although the remnants of his organization were helpful to the Kennedy campaign his candidacy still grated on local Democrats. Despite these difficulties, Kennedy's personal performance in California was excellent. He campaigned to the point of exhaustion, drawing impressive crowds wherever he went, and rectified his previous mistake of not debating with McCarthy. In contrast to Oregon, there were plenty of centres where Kennedy could count on huge support. There were large black areas in Watts and around San Francisco. He could also rely on support from the state's large Hispanic community. His earlier identification with Cesar Chavez's struggle for union recognition made him a more attractive candidate to Hispanics than McCarthy, who had opposed migrant workers' rights under the minimum wage law. As usual, McCarthy's strengths lay in the white suburbs around urban centres, and he was aided by at least $50,000 from Humphrey's supporters, which was given with the Vice-President's blessing to stop the Kennedy bandwagon.[52]

However, it was Kennedy's much-vaunted 'personal campaigning' which captured the media's imagination. One reporter noted:

> Outside the oldest building in Los Angeles, in the little plaza in front of the eighteenth-century mission church ... worshippers were holding up babies to see their champion, and hanging from the branches of liveoaks. In Watts they were standing on the roofs of automobiles, denting them with their weight, and at Griffith Park in Hollywood they were perched on the floodlight pylons, sixty feet above the heads of the crowd.[53]

Once again, however, Kennedy had to do more than impress journalists with his popularity among blacks. He made a special effort with low-income whites and with the sizeable and influential Jewish vote: on 18 June New York would hold the largest primary, sending 190 delegates to the convention, and an impressive showing among Jewish voters in California would also provide a significant boost to the New York campaign. There was the usual danger, too, that by cosying up to black interests Kennedy would put off the more conservative whites, and he began to avoid main streets in Watts where his motorcade would attract hordes of young blacks and give rise to television images which would frighten whites.

During the final days of the campaign, Kennedy and McCarthy finally met for what proved to be an indecisive and disappointing debate. The discussion was aired live on television on Saturday, 1 June (the day Sirhan Sirhan bought his gun) but the contest was bland, with Kennedy repeatedly stressing his White House experience – whether it was relevant to the question or not. Kennedy scored a minor point when he forced an admission that one of McCarthy's advertisements had misrepresented him, claiming that he was involved in the 1965 decision to put US troops in the Dominican Republic (when of course he had left the administration by then and had opposed the intervention from his Senate seat). Nevertheless, it was a small point and certainly no knock-out blow.

More significant, however, was Kennedy's obvious pitch to white concerns about black housing. Confident that the black vote was his for keeps, Kennedy could afford to make extravagant bids for support in white suburbs. When the debate turned to urban renewal, Kennedy contrasted his own plans for ghetto regeneration with McCarthy's more orthodox ideas on inner-city dispersal to the suburbs. 'When you say you are going to take 10,000 black people and move them into Orange County [a staunchly white backlash area] ... you take them out where 40% of them don't have any jobs at all,' said Kennedy.[54] The effect was to terrify Orange County viewers, implying that McCarthy was about to inundate them with ghetto blacks. It was a cheap shot from Kennedy and one which exposed his preoccupation with diverting white votes away from McCarthy. (It also prompted California Governor Ronald Reagan to note that Kennedy was 'talking more and more like me'.)[55]

Kennedy, of course, was among the first to recognize what a crucial influence television coverage can have on an election. As his brother's campaign manager, he had encouraged John Kennedy to meet Nixon for the legendary debates in 1960. For those debates, 87% of American had easy access to a television set, a number which grew steadily through the 1960s, so that by 1970 the figure had risen to 95%.[56] Television had developed rapidly in those ten years and new levels of technology brought with them new demands on the candidates.

The stilted campaign debates were now only one feature of the television coverage of the campaign. Political media specialists believed that for optimum impact a candidate should be featured on the nightly news programmes, and so Kennedy conducted a sophisticated campaign aimed at maximum television news exposure.[57] At that time California was divided into three television areas, centred around San Francisco, Los Angeles and San Diego. Hitherto, candidates had circulated from day to day among the three areas, sometimes managing to hit two areas in the same day by making an appearance in, say, Los Angeles in the morning before trekking to San Francisco for an early evening event. However, because of the advances made in jet travel, and his wealth, Kennedy could make appearances in all three areas during the same day, which he often did, and so obtained coverage on all three local news stations in the state.

Kennedy's problem, however, was that the coverage was generally one-paced, in that it showed him doing much the same sort of thing –

being surrounded by black (or Mexican) faces. Such pictures made good, if repetitive, television but also gave the impression that Kennedy's candidacy relied on the emotional reaction of crowds rather than thoughtful debate.

McCarthy, on the other hand, used the medium even more subtly than Kennedy. Knowing that he was not much of a crowd-puller, McCarthy surrendered exposure on the nightly news in favour of appearances on daytime chat-shows. These suited his calm, witty and relaxed style and were generally longer than the quick news clips Kennedy was working so hard to achieve. Typically, McCarthy would appear for fifteen or twenty minutes on a chat-show, discussing the state of the nation in a measured and reasonable manner, while Kennedy would appear for two minutes later on in the evening being crushed by youngsters swarming around his car in a ghetto.[58]

The Kennedy staff realized what was happening but could do little to prevent it. They encouraged television stations to go into Kennedy's headquarters and record an interview with him, but then he would go off to a rally or some other crowd-based event, and, when the television station came to choose which footage to use that night, the crowd scenes were usually preferred, as they made better television.

In the end, Kennedy's win was a victory for his new coalition. The final totals were 1,472,166 (46%) for Kennedy and 1,322,608 (42%) for McCarthy. As Kennedy's staff later conceded, the winning margin

> had been fashioned in Los Angeles, among the negroes and Mexican-Americans who turned out in very high numbers for a primary. McCarthy carried the suburban areas around Los Angeles and San Francisco and those metropolitan areas, like San Diego, which tend to be more conservative and have a specially high proportion of white voters who moved to California from the South or Southwest.[59]

The strong appeal to blacks and Mexican-Americans won Kennedy this primary, and not any fusion of poor whites and blacks. By working with the new Mexican-American organizations, led by Chavez, Kennedy had circumvented the old political route of party machinery and had drawn out black voters in huge numbers. Some Mexican-American precincts gave him 100% of the ballot.

'In the counties of the Central Valley, the Mexican-American vote stimulated by Chavez had given Kennedy majorities, but in all the other ranching, agricultural and sparsely settled areas of the state he did

poorly', admitted his campaign organizers.[60] By working with unortho-
dox political 'bosses' like Chavez and 'Black Jesus', a local community
leader in Oakland, Kennedy applied the old rules to the new game.
Some of these figures from his coalition of new politics could still be
used like old ward managers, turning out the vote for the appointed
candidate. 'In Mexican districts that morning [of the primary], in house
after house, workers came around saying very simply: "Cesar says this
is the day to vote for Robert Kennedy." It was the biggest turnout in
their history. They voted roughly 15-1 over McCarthy', noted one
journalist.[61] One area where Kennedy had succeeded with whites,
however, was with the Jewish vote, and thanks to concerted efforts in the
last weeks of the campaign he had drawn about level with McCarthy –
a good omen for what might have transpired in New York.

An equally encouraging result came from the South Dakota primary,
which Kennedy won with surprising ease, beating McCarthy by 50% to
20%. What was especially gratifying, however, was that Humphrey
managed only 30% (it was actually still Johnson's name which appeared
on the ballot, but a vote for LBJ was recognized as support for his Vice-
President). Humphrey was born in South Dakota, and should have
appealed strongly to its farming communities.

Had Kennedy lived, however, it is unlikely that the California result
would have knocked McCarthy out of the race. McCarthy had finished
a strong second and may have fancied his chances of beating Kennedy in
New York. In fact, McCarthy went on to win in New York on 18 June,
taking 63 delegates (30 still went for Kennedy, even though he was dead,
in the hope that another candidate might emerge behind whom they
could rally).

If Kennedy had gone on to win the nomination, it is likely that he
would have done so, not on the strength of blue-collar white support,
but on massive turnouts from black and Mexican-American areas. This
sort of power base might have frightened the party power-brokers, but
Kennedy's staff may have been able to keep the real nature of his
coalition hidden and exaggerated instead his popularity with white
ethnics to make the constituency appear more palatable.

Of course, most of the delegates at the convention would come from
states without primaries, and while Kennedy was busy demonstrating
his voter appeal, Humphrey was quietly picking up delegate promises
from around the country. Ultimately, however, the party would probably
have gone for the candidate which it believed was most electable. The
1968 nomination was largely decided by the party professionals and

Kennedy aide Richard Goodwin recalls the conversation he had with the Senator after the first California returns were in and just before Kennedy left his suite in the Ambassador Hotel to make his victory speech.

According to Goodwin, Kennedy believed that too many delegates not subject to primary results were controlled by governors and other establishment political leaders beholden to Johnson and Humphrey, and he put his own chances of securing the nomination at 50-50.[62] Nevertheless, others on his staff were confident after the California result that they had the potential to win enough delegates. Figures drawn up by Kennedy's aides and shown to the Senator on the evening of the California primary estimated his delegate strength – either firmly committed or 'preferring' him – at 524 delegates, out of a total of 1,312 needed to win.[63]

McCarthy, at that point, had 204 delegates either committed to him or preferring him for the first ballot. Humphrey, on the other hand, already had 994, with only 872 left undecided. It would have been a tall order for Kennedy, but if he could have pulled off a victory in New York (where he certainly would have been favourite) he may have managed it. His organizers predicted that by the time of the convention they would have most of McCarthy's delegates and were aiming at a total of 1,432 to Humphrey's 1,153. Despite McCarthy's declaration in 1985 that 'I was prepared to give my delegates over to Ted on the second ballot, but I wouldn't have done it for Bobby',[64] McCarthy's campaign manager Jeremy Larner conceded that at the Chicago convention 'it was commonly accepted that no delegate count on earth could have stopped Ted's brother from taking the nomination'.[65]

There is only a limited point in guessing what would have happened at the convention, or in the general election in November, but had Kennedy won the nomination it appears likely that he would have been a stronger candidate than Humphrey and beaten Nixon fairly easily. Of course, the results from November 1968 are complicated by Wallace's candidacy as an independent, and Kennedy supporters' claims that he would have taken significant numbers of Wallace votes had he lived. In July that year, the *Village Voice* suggested that 'many of them [Wallace supporters] planned to vote for Kennedy this year ... but now that Kennedy is dead they are nearly lost to the Democrats'.[66] However, the hard evidence for supposing that Kennedy was the first choice of many Wallace voters remains fairly thin. For example, Lake County went to Humphrey in November anyway (by 47% to Nixon's 36% and Wallace's 16%), and so a Kennedy nomination might not have been very beneficial in attracting white ethnic support.

Wallace did cost the Democrats victory, however. If Kennedy (or any other candidate) had done only marginally better than Humphrey in a small number of states, it would have been enough to swing the election. Nixon beat Humphrey by 301 electoral votes to 191, and by a popular vote of 43.4% to 42.7%, with Wallace winning 46 electoral votes and taking 13.5% of the popular vote. If the states where Wallace held the balance and Nixon won by less than 3% had gone to Humphrey, the Democrats would have won with an electoral college majority of 275 to 261.

In California, Humphrey lost the presidential election vote by 47.8% to 44.7%, or by 223,346 votes. Nationally, there were about 6,000,000 voting age Hispanics, and over 10,000,000 blacks of voting age, both with high concentrations in California (6.2% of the Californian voting age population in 1968 was black). It would only have taken a very small increase in the Democratic vote to have won nationally in 1968, and Kennedy might have been able to inspire a larger Hispanic and black turnout in November than had Humphrey.[67]

According to a study of black voting patterns in presidential elections, 'in 1968, black voter turnout was down in the north and west from 72% to 65% (although it was up in the South 44% to 52%, partly due to the Voting Rights Act of 1964). The overall black voter turnout was down 1% in 1968.'[68] Another study suggests that 'had non-whites outside the South come to the polls in 1968 as they had in 1964, Hubert Humphrey would have received a greater popular vote than Richard Nixon ... the low turnout implied a boycott of the Democratic candidate by blacks ... factors such as ... the Vietnam War ... the deaths of Martin Luther King and Robert Kennedy appeared to mark a loss of faith by the [black] electorate in institutional solutions'.[69]

Kennedy's alternative power base would have relied on generating a huge turnout among black and Hispanic voters. This power base may just have been sufficiently strong, in electoral terms, to present the presidency to Robert Kennedy (or even to his brother Ted). However, no other candidate – not even Jesse Jackson – has managed to reproduce the sort of enthusiasm Kennedy enjoyed among blacks and Hispanics. Had he won, the Democratic Party would have realigned behind this new coalition which Kennedy had pulled together in little more than a thousand days as Senator.

Chapter Six

The Assassination

Quite apart from Jimmy Hoffa and the Californian ranchers, there were plenty of others who had sufficient motive to kill Robert Kennedy. The pro-Vietnam military hawks gained from his death, the anti-Kennedy elements in the FBI gained, the Ku-Klux Klan gained, those worried that the truth about Dallas would emerge gained (as a Robert Kennedy presidency might have explored the conspiracy theories with more vigour than other administrations) and the traditional labour organizations gained. Abroad, it could be claimed that Cuba, the Soviet Union, Saigon and Pretoria all gained. The list is endless. On the other hand, there need not have been any political motive at all for Kennedy's assassination. Although Sirhan Sirhan, convicted of the murder, eventually said he did it for Palestine, many suggest he concocted the story to cover his lack of motive (to make his actions seem more rational in court).

As a Senator from New York, Kennedy was obliged to take an interest in the Israeli question, but it was not an overriding concern and he was certainly not especially associated with the Israeli cause. Whatever the motive, fewer were surprised by Robert Kennedy's assassination than by his brother's five years earlier. He had often mentioned the possibility of an early death. Talking in 1966 about his presidential prospects in 1972, he said: 'Six years is so far away; tomorrow is so far away. I don't even know if I'll be alive in six years.'[1] In March 1968 he told CBS that 'you have one time around and you don't know what's going to be in existence in six months or a year ... so I am impatient to make a contribution'.[2]

Of course, a few weeks later he told Walter Fauntroy at Martin Luther King's funeral that he believed 'there are guns between me and the White House'.[3] On the night of King's death, someone asked him if the murder brought back memories of Dallas. 'Well, that,' he said. 'But it makes me wonder what they might do to me, too.'[4] The spectre of Dallas never left him, and he was familiar with the most graphic details of the killing. As Jacqueline Kennedy had been too distraught in the months after the murder to deal with the many requests for access to information on the assassination, it fell to Robert Kennedy to 'approve the arrangements by which the X-rays, clothing and other evidence of the events in Dallas were to be made available to specialists'.[5] Moreover, Kennedy routinely received threatening letters at his Washington office (as has his brother Ted for 30 years), and some were considered serious enough to make the FBI issue receptionists in Kennedy's office with lists and photographs of people known to be dangerous.[6] Once he entered the presidential race, the volume of these letters increased. Jacqueline Kennedy became worried that 'If he becomes president they'll do to him what they did to Jack.'[7]

During the campaign, there were several reports of people with guns. Campaign aide Fred Dutton remembered an incident in Lansing, Michigan, when someone saw a gunman on a rooftop opposite Kennedy's hotel: 'I went into the bedroom where Bob was, and I didn't say any-thing to him because we always tried to be as low-key as we could. I pulled the blinds shut, but Bob knew immediately what was going on. He said "I don't want that. Don't do that. I'm not going to start ducking or run"' said Dutton.[8] When Kennedy left the hotel, he had his driver pull up in front of the hotel, got out of the car (much to the conster-nation of local police) and plunged into the crowd, shaking hands. On another occasion, journalist Joe Mohbat asked him if he ever considered the possibility of assassination. Kennedy replied that he thought about the danger a lot, but added: 'If I'm ever elected president, I'm never going to ride in one of those bubble-top cars.'[9]

During the first weeks of his presidential campaign, in April, the plane carrying Kennedy and the press corps experienced difficulties taking off and almost ran off the runway. As the pilot geared up for another attempt, Kennedy told reporters that 'in all modesty, if we don't make it this time, you fellows are going to be in the small print'.[10] In the following month Kennedy told French writer Romain Gary that 'there will be an attempt on my life sooner or later. Not so much for political reasons, but through contagion, through emulation' and he told campaign aide John Stewart: 'If it's going to happen, it's going to happen.'[11] One foreign journalist thought there was 'something darkly Irish about his submission [to this fate]' but Kennedy really had little choice.[12] Either he could retreat from public life in the hope that a lower profile would make him a less attractive target, or stay in the public eye and ride his luck. How far this fatalism affected his political career – whether it influenced his decision to jump into the 1968 race instead of waiting until 1972, for example, is unclear. There was always the possibility that he would be assassinated, but his entry into the campaign – and King's murder three weeks later – brought the issue into sharper focus. During the California primary, one San Francisco magazine advised its readers not to vote for Kennedy 'because they're going to kill him, and you don't want to waste your vote on a dead man'.[13]

The apparent inevitability of the murder made it no less shocking. Kennedy was shot at the Ambassador Hotel in Los Angeles hours after he had won the California primary of 4 June. He finished his victory speech to several hundred campaign workers gathered in the ballroom just past midnight, and in the first minutes of 5 June he left the ballroom stage to give a press conference. He took a short cut to avoid the crush, and he was walking through a crowded kitchen pantry when he was hit by three bullets.

'I was walking backwards, watching Bobby, and this man was right directly to my right. And he fired. He obviously knew how to handle a pistol. He was standing there with his arms straight out: bam! bam! bam! … like that, which is the way a pistol shooter, a guy who learns to shoot a pistol on a range, lines a gun,' said journalist Pete Hamill.[14]

'The staring little man in the kitchen had taken a .22 revolver from underneath his yellow jacket … and taken aim; Kennedy had seen him, screamed "No!" and half-glanced for a space against the wall, anywhere, to escape. He had been shot still smiling', reported John Pilger.[15]

There were at least 76 people in the small pantry, and five of them – other than Kennedy – had bullet wounds, two of them to the head. Paul Schrade, Kennedy supporter and regional director of the UAW, was shot in the head.[16] He and the others who had been hit all survived. Only Kennedy did not.

Sirhan was immediately grabbed by several people who had seen him step out in front of the Senator, take aim and shoot at Kennedy. Mayhem ensued, with Sirhan being grabbed but still apparently having control of his gun. It was eventually wrenched from his hand in a violent struggle with several campaign aides.

Kennedy, meanwhile, had slumped to the floor, bleeding from the neck, head and shoulder.[17] Kennedy's shirt was opened and his fingers clasped a rosary which had been put on his chest. The ambulance arrived, and its crew put Kennedy on to a stretcher. The Senator moaned 'Don't lift me, don't lift me,' according to ambulanceman Max Behrman, but he was carried into the ambulance and, with Ethel by his side, was rushed to the Central Receiving Hospital, where doctors initially thought he was dead.[18] When a heartbeat was found, he was transferred to the Good Samaritan Hospital, which had more sophisticated facilities to treat his injuries.

Sirhan, meanwhile, had been arrested and taken into police custody. Almost immediately the Senator's security arrangements were being questioned: how could a man with a gun slip into the hotel and get near enough to shoot Kennedy?

To promote his image of accessibility, Kennedy had asked that there be no obvious security presence in the hotel and had specifically insisted that uniformed security – either police or private guards – not be used. However, the Ambassador did have its own security guards on duty throughout the evening, and one of them was actually holding Kennedy's arm when the shooting took place. Evidence about the full extent of security that night is contradictory.

Journalists Alistair Cooke and John Pilger were both covering events in the hotel, but they offer very different impressions of security. Cooke recalled that 'Guards and cops blocked the entrance to the ballroom, and passport and birth certificate and, I believe, a personal recommendation from Senator Kennedy could not have got you in. My own press credentials were quite useless ...'[19] Pilger, on the other hand, reported that

> Press tags were given to almost anybody who wanted them; reporters drifting over from the souring McCarthy celebration at the Beverly Hilton picked up their "accreditation" without having to say who they were ... there was virtually no "security". A few hotel guards tried to question people as they streamed into the ballroom but, overwhelmed by the exuberance of the crowd, they soon gave up ...[20]

Eyewitness Martin Patrusky, a waiter at the hotel, claimed that the man who shot Kennedy was 'wearing a blue press badge'.[21] Accounts of the shooting itself are also highly conflicting. There was no real consensus, for example, on the distance between Sirhan and Kennedy when the shots were fired. Although the forensic evidence suggested that the gun barrel had to be between one and three inches from Kennedy's ear when it was fired, no eyewitness put Sirhan's gun closer than two feet from the Senator.

Thane Cesar, the guard who had Kennedy's arm during the shooting, recalled it was difficult to make out what was really going on because of the bright fluorescent strips on the pantry ceiling: 'Mainly because of the lights being in your eyes, you couldn't see nothing back there.'[22]

Three witnesses said they saw someone other than Sirhan with a gun in the pantry. Lisa Urso told author Philip Melanson she saw someone blond, in a grey suit, 'by Kennedy' who pulled a gun.[23] Another said she saw a tall man draw and fire some kind of handgun. Don Schulman was interviewed on radio immediately after the shooting and described an exchange of fire between the gunman and a security guard. 'The man who stepped out fired three times at Kennedy ... hit him all three times ... and the security guard then fired back ...'[24]

Thane Cesar himself told police that he drew his gun in reaction to Sirhan's shots but says he did not fire. The controversy over how many guns were fired in the pantry would not be so significant if strong evidence did not exist suggesting that more bullets were recovered from the scene than could have been fired by Sirhan's gun.

Sirhan's .22 revolver was capable of holding eight bullets. Nine bullets, therefore, would mean two guns and thus a conspiracy. In its enthusiasm to quash any suggestion of conspiracy, the Los Angeles Police Department was insistent that the amount of damage done to people and property in the pantry could all have been caused by Sirhan's eight bullets.

The question of the number of bullets is further complicated by police photographs taken at the scene which show two bullets in a pantry door-frame. Neither of these bullets is among the eight accounted for in the LAPD explanation, and they are therefore 'extra bullets'. The LAPD later changed its mind about these bullets and claimed they were nails.[25]

If there were more than eight bullets, Sirhan must have had an accomplice (unless by a bizarre coincidence two people attempted separate assassination attempts on Kennedy at exactly the same time). From the very beginning of the investigation, people said they saw Sirhan with a woman in the hotel that night, the famous 'girl in the polka-dot dress'. (When he was interviewed under hypnosis in his cell in 1968, Sirhan's reply to the question 'Who was with you when you shot Kennedy?' was 'Girl the girl the girl ...') Eleven separate witnesses said they saw her in Sirhan's company, but she was never traced.[26]

The police were left with one official suspect, safely in custody. Kennedy fought off death for another 24 hours, but his condition was always weak. Ethel and Ted Kennedy discussed the funeral arrange-ments at the hospital while he was still alive and decided that the service should be in New York's St Patrick's Cathedral and burial next to President Kennedy at Arlington Cemetery, outside Washington, DC.

The east coast of America was waking up to the news of Kennedy's shooting on the morning of 5 June. The time difference meant that

Kennedy's constituents in New York, and his colleagues in Washington, first heard about the assassination attempt from early-morning news bulletins.

The Senate did not sit on Wednesday, 5 June, but in the House of Representatives congressmen offered their immediate reactions. Representative Gerald Ford from Michigan, who had been a member of the Warren Commission, and who would later become US President, noted that 'in the light of what transpired at the time of the assassination of President Kennedy [the murder of Lee Harvey Oswald by Jack Ruby while under police protection], the suspect reportedly in custody must be zealously protected while the most thorough investigation and prosecution of this tragedy are undertaken and carried forward'.[27]

The Kennedy shooting dominated the early business of the House, which had begun at 11 a.m. Washington time, when news bulletins suggested Kennedy might still live, and Representative Helstoski reported to the House that the Senator had survived surgery without any apparent brain damage. Others began to guess at Sirhan's motive. 'The young man being held by police has stated he hates wealthy people and hated Senator Kennedy because he was rich. Obviously this young assassin has a sick mind', offered Representative Pucinski.[28]

The quest for Sirhan's motive would not prove so simple, however, and speculation about why he would want to shoot Kennedy ranged from the traditional 'lone nut' theory, which had Sirhan acting on impulse to achieve fame, to the notion that he did it to strike a blow for Arab freedom by killing Kennedy on the first anniversary of the Six-Day War against Israel.

The discovery of a notebook at Sirhan's house further fuelled theories about his motives. The notebook, which is often erroneously referred to as 'Sirhan's diary', is a collection of scrawly, unusual sentences, described by experts as 'automatic writing', like that written under hypnosis. On one page, dated 'May 18 9.45 a.m. – 68', Sirhan writes: 'My determination to eliminate R. F. K. is becoming more the more of an unshakable obsession' and repeats the phrase 'R. F. K. must be assassinated' a dozen times. The entry finished with 'Robert F. Kennedy must be assassinated before June 5 68 Robert F. Kennedy must be assassinated I have never heard please pay to the order of of of of of of of of of of of this or that 8000000 please pay to the order of.'[29]

The spiral-bound notebook has writing on 48 of its pages, of which Kennedy is mentioned on two. Despite Sirhan's later claims to have acted out of outrage at Kennedy's support for Israel, there are no mentions whatsoever of Middle Eastern politics, Israel or Palestine. There are seventeen pages which have references to money.[30] Nevertheless, Sirhan's history as a Palestinian immigrant whose family had suffered under the Israelis led many to believe Sirhan's reasons were obvious. Sirhan had seen his brother killed by an Israeli truck and had witnessed the agony of Arabs as they lay dying from Israeli bomb attacks.

The motive was one which Sirhan sought to amplify in the weeks and months after his arrest, and he suggested he was particularly incensed by Kennedy's support for a proposed sale of 50 US Phantom military aircraft to Israel. John Weidnar, manager of a Pasadena health food shop where Sirhan had previously worked, told *The Times* that Sirhan 'had a lot of complexes, mainly related to Israel'.[31]

However, as several investigators have suggested, Sirhan's political motive appears to have been worked out little by little as his trial approached, and did not surface until a considerable time after his arrest.[32] He did not, for instance, shout out any political slogans as he shot Kennedy in the pantry. Neither did he take the opportunity to publicize his cause by offering himself as an Arab hero when questioned by the police or his attorneys. It was not until later that he decided on the image of an Arab hero to make himself appear sane to the jury at his trial.[33]

The most popular theory about Kennedy's death is that Sirhan was somehow hypnotized into murdering the Senator. He is highly prone to hypnosis and has undergone numerous tests in prison in attempts to encourage him to recall the shooting. The main point of contention on the hypnosis theory is whether it is possible to hypnotize somebody to do something he really does not want to do, and then somehow programme him into forgetting that he has done it or that he was ordered to do it. Some hypnosis experts claim that, no matter how sophisticated the technique, a hypnotized subject would remember being hypnotized after he came out of his 'trance' and that Sirhan cannot remember being hypnotized at all.

However, from the descriptions given by those who first saw and spoke to Sirhan after the shooting, he does appear to have been in some sort of stupor. Alistair Cooke remembers Sirhan with 'a limp head and a face totally dazed'.[34] The chief psychiatrist on Sirhan's defence team, Dr Bernard Diamond, recalled that 'it was immediately apparent that Sirhan had been programmed ... he showed this phenomenon of automatic writing, which can only be done when one is pretty well trained'.[35]

Moreover, for those who believe that there could have been some CIA involvement in the killing, there is the evidence that the agency had experimented with hypno-killers as early as the 1950s, and the idea was already being put to use elsewhere in the world.[36]

The questions remain: if Sirhan was programmed, who programmed him, and if Sirhan alone did not shoot Kennedy, who else was involved? Sirhan, apparently, had been stalking Kennedy for some time before 5 June. On 20 May a man resembling Sirhan's description (and accompanied by a woman) tried to force his way into a restaurant where Kennedy was eating.[37] Four days later, a psychology professor and his wife spotted a man they later identified as Sirhan at a Kennedy rally. On 2 June Sirhan was at a Kennedy function at the Ambassador Hotel itself.

Two days afterwards he returned and apparently shot Kennedy. However, even the mechanics of the shooting itself do not make a lot of sense. Sirhan – for whatever reason – had apparently little interest in escaping after the murder. He chose to shoot Kennedy in a crowded place at close range in full view of scores of people. He chose a small, easily hidden gun to carry out the hit, but the .22 is also a very weak revolver. Of the six people believed hit by its bullets, five survived. For an assassin bent on killing Kennedy, choosing such a small calibre of gun was taking a gamble.

Moreover, if the conspiracy theory is to be accepted, it would appear that Sirhan's co-assassin would have to be very close to Kennedy (close enough to have put a gun to within three inches of Kennedy's right ear). To get into such a position, the co-assassin would be taking a substantial personal risk, knowing that Sirhan was about to fire eight bullets in the general direction of Kennedy. (Firing a bullet into the area just behind the ear, where Kennedy was shot is, incidentally, a method of assassination favoured by military intelligence around the world.)[38]

The security guard Thane Cesar was just behind Kennedy's right side when the shooting began. He admits that he did have a gun on him that night, but despite several attempts no one has been able to prove his complicity in the crime. The secrets of the assassination remain buried in Sirhan's mind, and, although eminent psychiatrists have offered to help him unlock them through hypnosis, it is not necessarily in his interests to reveal more about the murder than is already known and the offers have not been taken up.

Sirhan himself was shocked when he realized what he had done. 'My, my my childhood, family, church, prayers … the Bible and all this … [Sirhan was raised a Christian] "Thou shalt not kill" … and here I go and splatter this guy's brain out. It's just not me', he told prosecution psychiatrist Dr Seymour Pollack in 1985.[39]

cultural/social impacts

On the day after the shooting Sirhan's mother sent Ethel Kennedy a telegram saying: 'It hurt us very bad what has happened ... I want them to know that I am really crying for them all.'[40]

The country tried to come to terms with the death. Someone placed a bouquet of flowers on Kennedy's desk in the Senate. A New York television station suspended programmes and for several hours just transmitted a card bearing the word 'SHAME'. Others called for tighter laws on gun control.

Meanwhile, as tributes poured in from cities across the world, the US army was preparing for the worst. 'The country is preparing for what could be called a state of siege,' one reporter noted on 8 June. 'The Army's Directorate for Civil Disturbances Planning and Operations has been in a state of alert since yesterday morning, the California National Guard has 26,800 men ready for deployment in the streets, and 10,000 regular troops are standing by outside Washington.'[41] It was widely believed in army and police circles that Kennedy's death could provoke the sort of violence which had broken out after the assassination of Martin Luther King two months before.

In Washington, DC, all police leave was cancelled. The city's black mayor, Walter Washington, explained that the police were 'trying to be at the ready'.[42] The Pentagon announced it was taking 'certain prudent actions' in case Kennedy's death provoked a new outburst of rioting. 'The action consists in ensuring that contingency plans, in which troops are detailed for duty in civil disturbances in various parts of the country, are all in order', said a Pentagon spokesman.[43]

The riots never materialized. Perhaps blacks did not feel the same anger about Kennedy's death as they did about King's. After the violent orgy which followed King's murder, the cities may have been too tired for any more rioting. In some senses, too, the circumstances of Kennedy's death were less likely to incite a mob response. While most Americans heard of King's death in the evening or night of 4 April, news of Kennedy's shooting broke at breakfast-time in the urban centres of the east. Moreover, Kennedy had not been killed immediately, and early reports suggested he might survive.

News from the Los Angeles hospital gradually became less optimistic, and the announcement of death, when it eventually came just before 2 a.m. California time on 6 June, arrived as no great shock: many Americans had spent the previous day expecting it. Moreover, the immediate capture of Sirhan no doubt restricted the sort of frustration felt after King's death, where the (perceived) murderer had escaped (and would not be apprehended until 8 June, the day of Kennedy's funeral).

The most serious recorded outbreak of violence was in Chicago, when police arrested a young black, nineteen-year-old Aaron Myers, and charged him with the murder of Abder Rayyan, a middle-aged Jordanian grocer, who had been shot dead in his shop on the night of Saturday, 8 June. After the shooting, police suggested that the murder might have been 'an act of revenge for Mr Kennedy, as the suspect in LA is also Jordanian'.[44]

Kennedy's body had been flown back to New York, and his casket placed in St Patrick's Cathedral. People waited in queues for up to ten hours to enter the cathedral and file past the coffin. There were, noted a journalist, 'a disproportionate number of Negroes' waiting to pay their respects.[45]

The funeral, inevitably, was riven with petty politics. Local and national politicians were desperate for tickets and for passes to the train which would take the funeral party from New York to Washington for the burial. (Kennedy's old adversary, Alabama Governor George Wallace, asked for three tickets. He was refused.) Just before the funeral began, the Secret Service picked up a man with a gun in his briefcase, who turned out to be Gary De Dell, a Kennedy aide from his upstate New York office. De Dell had forgotten he had a gun in the case.

The funeral entourage left St Patrick's and headed for Penn Station for the train to Washington. Thousands of mourners lined the track between the two cities. Some saluted, others waved American flags, others still held up holy pictures. Children put coins or flowers on the track to be crushed by the train and kept as souvenirs. Secret Serviceman Kellerman kept guard on the right side of the locomotive. He had been in the car with John F. Kennedy in Dealey Plaza when the President was assassinated.

The train reached Washington several hours late. It was already dark as the procession made its way by road through the capital to Arlington, pausing outside the Justice Department, which Kennedy had run while Attorney General, outside the Senate Office buildings, and by the Lincoln Memorial.

When the Poor People's March, originally suggested by Kennedy to King, had arrived in Washington some weeks before, it set up camp next to the memorial in a shanty village known as Resurrection City, and Kennedy aides thought it appropriate that the procession should make a stop here. The Poor People's camp was lit by thousands of candles as Kennedy's coffin passed by. Rev. Frederick Kirkpatrick, an organizer of

Resurrection City, remembered: 'When the cortège passed ... a lot of people raised their hands. A soul brother. Soul force. So that when they raised their hands with the fist clenched, it meant that they were in cahoots. They took him as a soul brother! Right. Blue-eyed soul brother we used to call him.'[46]

The coffin was brought up the hill at Arlington, prayers were said and Kennedy was laid in a grave near his brother. President Johnson ordered immediate secret service protection for the remaining presidential candidates. The April riots were still fresh in the public memory, and social analysts tried to explain the breakdown in law and order on America's violent tradition, on the growth of television and on the decline of family values. Violence became the dominant political issue – the turbulence which rocked the country's cities after the King assassination was genuinely frightening for many Americans, and posed a serious physical threat. Kennedy's assassination added to the belief that things were getting out of control, that the social fabric was rupturing, that citizens everywhere could become victims. On his way home from Kennedy's burial, the Senator's chauffeur, Lee Morrow, was mugged by seven youths, hit in the face with a stick and robbed of his wallet (which contained three petrol credit cards in the name of Robert F. Kennedy).[47]

The apparent lurch into lawlessness confounded the public and bewildered social commentators. After the Kennedy assassination, newspapers across the country found it difficult to grasp the dimensions of the new lawlessness and struggled to make sense of the violence. Many quoted the Senator's speech on the death of Martin Luther King: 'We've had difficult times in the past. We will have difficult times in the future. It is not the end of violence; it is not the end of lawlessness; it is not the end of disorder. But the vast majority of white people and the vast majority of black people in this country want to live together ... and want justice for all human beings who abide in our land.'[48]

For others, though, Kennedy's death was part of a pattern. It signalled the end of hope for many political activists and came as a bitter blow so soon after the death of King.

Walter Fauntroy remembers: 'After Bobby Kennedy was assassinated I could almost feel the difference in the Poor People's Campaign Camp in Washington ... as people said, "Well, it's over. Every time a leader steps up who we feel addresses our needs, they shoot him." By that time, you'd had Malcolm X killed, John F. Kennedy killed, Martin Luther King killed, and then Bobby Kennedy ... that was a sort of last straw.'[49]

social

Conclusion

Had he lived, of course, many things might have been different. Tom Hayden wrote in the late 1980s that 'If you believe that [Kennedy would have won the presidency], his death becomes one of the central events of your life. That single event was the death of hope for peace in Vietnam for five, six or seven years, and the death of political hope for many people ...'[1] That might be overstating Kennedy's political contribution, but there is no doubt that an unquantifiable legacy remains. A certain political generation grew up around Kennedy's coalition, the 'burned-out Robert Kennedy workers', as Hayden called them.[2] Tip O'Neill noted that in the immediate aftermath of the Watergate scandal there was significant public pressure on government to open up, and the influence of Robert Kennedy could be detected in the new intake of elected officials.[3]

In the Congressional elections of 1974 and 1976 many new Democrats were elected, promising to clean up Washington and do away with the old vestiges of Congressional privilege and seniority. In many ways these 'Watergate babies' heralded the decline of the old party system. Many were elected without significant machine support and felt no obligation to be loyal to the party. O'Neill – no friend of Kennedy's – 'was struck by how many told me they had no interest in politics until Robert Kennedy's Presidential campaign in 1968. Kennedy was their hero, and he was the one who had turned them on to the possibility of running for office'.[4]

This Congressional generation was faced with many of the same issues which Kennedy tackled in the mid-1960s, such as where Democrats stood on foreign intervention, what new proposals they had to promote racial equality and how they could reorganize the left after the demise of union power.

Kennedy confronted these issues by looking to build an alternative coalition for the Democratic Party. 'He was the first person who had any power who began to try to grope toward a post-New Deal liberalism,' suggests Kennedy Senate aide Peter Edelman.[5]

His success in constructing this coalition was never fully tested, of course. In the presidential primaries, his appeal to some parts of it were measured, but others were not. There is no doubting his strong appeal to urban blacks in California and Indiana. He appeared to be an acceptable candidate for much of the anti-war movement, too, despite his earlier involvement in American participation in Vietnam. There can be no accurate assessment of his appeal to the wider American public, however, to those outside the Democratic Party, to the national electorate. While his success in the primaries may have suggested, for example, that it was possible to get the votes of much of a state's work-force without the imprimatur of their labour unions, it certainly did not prove that it was possible for a Democratic candidate to win the American presidency without the backing of the AFL-CIO.

Yet it would be wrong to judge Kennedy's Senate career solely in the context of his 1968 presidential campaign. His stated aim for running for Congress was so he could attack Johnson's foreign policy.[6] Beginning in February 1966, he launched a series of significant assaults on American policy in Vietnam, and argued the dove case as persuasively as any of his Senate colleagues. But as Tip O'Neill suggests, Kennedy's real legacy could be the generation of politicians he inspired to public service.

Senator Gary Hart of Colorado, who twice ran for the Democratic presidential nomination in the 1980s, judged Kennedy to have been no less than 'a reform prophet of a new world order. Before anyone else, he saw beyond the Cold War, the nuclear arms race, proxy wars, the East–West polarization. Like Vaclav Havel two decades later, he searched for a new way, a "third way" beyond ideological confrontation and toward an agenda of common humanity'.[7]

New York Governor Mario Cuomo offers a similar eulogy: 'The real irony is that the things that Bobby Kennedy believed, said, and died for were things which never had their day. The problem was not that these ideas became part of the fabric of the US and didn't work; the problem was they were never given the opportunity to express themselves.'[8]

It would be an exaggeration to claim that Robert Kennedy was the most influential politician of his generation. His political record appears modest when compared to those of Hubert Humphrey or Richard Nixon, for example. Nevertheless, Kennedy is likely to be rememberd by generations to come as a politician who anticipated some of the crucial issues to confront the world at the end of the twentieth century.

During the campaign for the mid-term elections in November 1994, President Clinton was asked to list what he regarded as priorities for his domestic programme. 'What we have to do is to bring free enterprise to the inner cities ... That's what the empowerment zones are about; that's what those community development banks to low income people are about', he said.[9]

Prophet or not, Kennedy's journey from Cold Warrior to radical liberal was a transformation which took the main body of American liberalism 30 years to complete.

Bibliography

Despite the millions of words written about Kennedy since 1968, his full impact on the development of American liberalism has yet to be fully investigated. Many commentators have found it difficult to separate the substance from the image. All of Kennedy's biographers knew him personally, and so lacked a detachment helpful to objective analysis. Other commentators who have written about him have often been distracted by issues other than straight politics, such as his alleged involvement with Marilyn Monroe and the circumstances surrounding his assassination.

It was Emerson who wrote that 'Each age, it is found, must write its own books; or rather, each generation for the next succeeding. The books of an older period will not fit this.'[1] However, so far the books on Robert Kennedy have all been written by his contemporaries, most of them his friends (Emerson also warns that the 'love of the hero corrupts into worship of his statue').

The books which significantly feature Robert Kennedy can be considered in several loose chronological groups, starting with the series of post-Dallas tributes written about President Kennedy by some of JFK's closest advisers. This clutch of stylish hagiographies includes Arthur Schlesinger's *A Thousand Days: John F. Kennedy in the White House* (Houghton Mifflin, Boston 1965), Ted Sorenson's *Kennedy* (Hodder & Stoughton, New York 1965), and Pierre Salinger's *With Kennedy* (Doubleday, New York 1966).

These early histories, written at the very beginning of Robert Kennedy's Senate career, portray him as the late President's dependable lieutenant, obviously more important to the administration than Lyndon Johnson. 'As for the President,' notes Salinger, 'his closest friend and confidant was his brother, Robert ... It was Bob that JFK turned to in moments of crisis ... His advice to JFK was sound and his judgement good'.[2] Schlesinger is even more emphatic about the Attorney General's relationship with the President, which he describes as 'an extraordinary partnership ... The communication was virtually telepathic and their communion complete ... Especially in foreign affairs, one turned more and more to Bobby.'[3]

Robert Kennedy soon became the subject of biographies in his own right. As early as 1967 William Shannon's *The Heir Apparent* (Macmillan, New York) appeared, followed a year later by Penn Kimball's *Bobby Kennedy and the New Politics* (Prentice-Hall, New Jersey). Both were written while Kennedy was still alive, as was the bulk of Margaret Laing's *Robert Kennedy* (MacDonald, London 1968). Largely sympathetic, they concentrate on Kennedy's chances of eventually winning the presidency, and Shannon's work also presents the idea of Kennedy as an existential politician, a theme which would be taken up with great enthusiasm in the books which appeared after his death.

Although Ted Kennedy had declared in his eulogy at Robert Kennedy's funeral that 'my brother need not be idealized or enlarged in death beyond what he was in life', several biographies appeared in the following year which were generously sympathetic to his memory.[4] Written by journalists friendly with Kennedy, they emphasized his attractive qualities and were weak on criticism. David Halberstam's *The Unfinished Odyssey of Robert Kennedy*, (Barrie & Jenkins, New York 1968), was followed by Jules Witcover's *85 Days* (Quill, New York 1969) and Jack Newfield's *Robert Kennedy: A Memoir* (E. P. Dutton, New York 1969). All were written by young liberal journalists who perceived the Nixon victory as an unmitigated calamity. Kennedy, in exaggerated contrast, is presented as a political saviour.

'The year 1968 marked a breakthrough for the new politics, but only that; the old politics still hung on. Robert Kennedy might have achieved transition; in his absence there was, instead, chaos', mourned Witcover.[5] Newfield was even more desolate: 'From this time forward, things would get worse', he wailed. 'The stone was at the bottom of the hill and we were alone.'[6]

A study of the 1968 election called *American Melodrama* (Viking, New York 1969) by a team of reporters from the London *Times* was more detached and analysed Kennedy's campaign with a colder eye than their American colleagues. Similarly, *On His Own: RFK 1964–68* (Bantam, New York 1970) by two of Kennedy's aides, Milton Gwirtzman and William Vanden Heuvel, largely avoids the excesses of journalism and offers a detailed, if partial, analysis of Kennedy's Senate years.

The earlier emotional works of both the JFK and RFK biographers spawned an equally emotional revisionism in the early 1970s which was every bit as unbalanced as the original accounts. During those years a reaction against government institutions gained considerable force, and journalists of the 1960s were mocked by their colleagues for having been so gullible in believing the hype about Vietnam, the Great Society and the piety of the Kennedys. However, the gullibility was often replaced with cynicism, which did not necessarily make for clearer analysis. Nancy Gager Clinch's *The Kennedy Neurosis* (Grossett & Dunlap, New York 1973) was aimed at President Kennedy's drive for dominance and power, which it explained in largely unconvincing psychoanalytical terms. Henry Fairlie's *The Kennedy Promise* (Eyre Methuen, London 1973) also sought to debunk the legend but its analysis is flawed by an obvious anti-Kennedy bias which accuses the brothers of magnifying the Cuban missile crisis for political gain and for keeping the country in a state of feverish excitement as they led it from one crisis to the next. At least Fairlie did not claim to be a clinical observer of Robert Kennedy's politics, conceding that 'it is difficult to write sensibly of the man' before concluding that 'his achievements were so slight'.[7]

Others were also sceptical about the Kennedy record, and New Left historians began to depict the Kennedy brothers as aggressive Cold Warriors, responsible for Vietnam and the Cuban missile crisis. In David Horowitz's *From Yalta to Vietnam* (Pelican, London 1973), an overview of American foreign policy since the Second World War, John and Robert Kennedy are presented as a couple of jingoistic macho-men. 'Robert Kennedy declared there was no question but that the President would order the use of nuclear weapons to save Berlin,' he noted.[8]

The first hints of a reaction to the revisionism appeared in the following years with Arthur Schlesinger's epic *Robert Kennedy and His Times* (Deutsch, New York 1978). However, Schlesinger's biography is not so much a work of post-revisionism as a seductive restatement of the early assessments of Kennedy as a great liberal hope. Schlesinger's book, it should be remembered, appeared during a Democratic presidency at a time when the Republicans looked to be set for many years in opposition, and it avoids the apocalyptic tone of those written during the first Nixon administration.

A more balanced picture began to emerge, at least in the more serious studies. While the BBC produced a programme in 1980 (*Reputations*) which offered a studied interpretation of Kennedy (even if it did appear to dwell on Eugene McCarthy's bitter analyses), a series of sensational stories began to emerge with increasing frequency in the world's popular press.

Originally fuelled by revelations at the Senate hearings on assassinations in 1977, which suggested that John Kennedy had cavorted with at least one woman close to the Mafia, the press accusations were widened to include Robert Kennedy's relationship with various women, particularly Marilyn Monroe.

Such accusations had actually begun much earlier, during Kennedy's 1964 election to the Senate. Right-wing activist Frank Cappell's *The Strange Death of Marilyn Monroe* (New York, 1964) was published in September that year. It alleges that Kennedy was involved in a Communist conspiracy to kill Monroe to protect his reputation. The charges were not taken seriously at the time, and the book did Kennedy no perceivable harm, but as the line between serious history and popular journalism began to blur in the late 1970s and 1980s the allegations resurfaced in more respectable studies than Cappell's.

There are two main theories which implicate Kennedy with Monroe's death. Both agree that President Kennedy and/or Robert Kennedy were sexually involved with the actress. The first suggests that Monroe, dangerously unbalanced in the summer of 1962, threatened to expose her relationship with the President and that the Attorney General had her killed to keep her quiet. The second contends that Monroe was killed by anti-Kennedy forces, either a CIA/FBI conspiracy, as suggested by Norman Mailer in 1973, or the Mafia, as outlined in Anthony Summers' *Goddess* (Gollancz, London 1985), in the hope that an investigation of her murder would bring to light her past sexual activity with the Kennedys so as to destroy the administration through scandal.

Despite the flimsy evidence, the notion that Robert Kennedy was linked to Monroe's death gained popular currency during the mid-1980s, when the history of the Kennedy family began to be examined as though it was a century-long soap opera. Peter Collier and David Horowitz's *The Kennedys: An American Drama* (Warner, New York 1985) traced the family's rise and fall in generally pedestrian terms, although it reserved venom for its study of Robert Kennedy's children. Doris Kearns Goodwin's *The Fitzgeralds and the Kennedys: An American Saga* (Weidenfeld and Nicolson, London 1987) is in more academic vein, although its investigation ends with the election of John Kennedy to the White House.

At the more serious end of analysis is Alonzo L. Hamby's *Liberalism and its Challengers* (Oxford University Press, 1985), a survey of the American left since the Second World War. Hamby suggests that John and Robert Kennedy were from the same tradition of liberalism, both working outside the system and relying on great personal appeal. However, he repeats the standard myth that Robert Kennedy relied on 'the lower-middle-class blue-collar-ethnics' for support and suggests that Robert Kennedy 'alone could revive the old Roosevelt coalition', when in fact Kennedy was forced to carve out a replacement for the old Roosevelt coalition. Nevertheless, Hamby does recognize that 'the most intense criticism of both [John and Robert Kennedy] appears to have come from believers in ideological formulas as the key to political leadership',[9] a view echoed by Robert Kennedy's daughter Kathleen Townsend in 1988: 'He didn't think that words like liberal and conservative were very appropriate. Maybe that's why liberals were always very uncomfortable with my father.'[10]

More recently, the Robert Kennedy legacy has been re-examined in the context of his brother's presidency. Thomas Reeves' *A Question of Character* (Bloomsbury, London 1991), is a scathing biography of the late President, and it also takes a swipe at his Attorney General, who was 'more intense, ambitious, abrasive and less inclined towards lechery [than John Kennedy]'.[11]

There are also, of course, several books which appeared under Robert Kennedy's name, including *The Enemy Within* (Popular Library, New York 1960). Written as a real-life crime-buster, it concentrates on Kennedy's time on the McClellan Committee. *To Seek a Newer World* was also motivated by obvious political gain, as it sought to highlight the difference between himself and the old-style Democratic Party exemplified by the Johnson administration. When Kennedy ran for President, it was quickly billed as his manifesto, although it was not much more than a collection of Senate speeches.

More interesting are *13 Days*, Kennedy's account of the Cuban missile crisis – and the oral histories he made in the years after the Dallas assassination which were published in 1988. *13 Days* was written in the last months of Kennedy's life and did not appear until after his death, so that his secret deals with the Soviets were not known in his lifetime.

Robert Kennedy: In His Own Words, the edited oral histories, are also remarkably candid. Kennedy makes no pretence at concealing his distaste for Johnson or for certain foreign leaders (including Nehru and Adenauer).[12] The private and frank conversations reveal Kennedy characteristically hesitant about his political future. He is keen that the 'Kennedy wing' of the party should carry on, although he realizes that it is largely up to him to determine exactly what that wing should stand for.[13] His subsequent years as Senator ensured that it became associated with the more radical elements of the party. However, Kennedy's presidential campaign possibly marked the zenith of radical liberalism. His alternative coalition was submerged by the old Democratic orthodoxy which, in turn, was overpowered by the conservatism of the 1970s and 1980s. The notion of liberalism declined so rapidly that by the 1988 election it had become the ideology which dared not speak its name, being referred to in sinister tones as 'the L word'.

The dialectic of liberalism missed a beat with the death of Robert Kennedy in 1968, and the development of radicalism was retarded by the Democratic Party's split into the McGovernite wing and the traditional, labour wing (exemplified by Mondale's candidacy). A Robert Kennedy presidential nomination, successful or not, might have provided the party with the direction it has been lacking since 1964 and given back liberalism its respectability.

Notes

INTRODUCTION

1. Edwin O. Guthman and Jeffrey Shulman (eds), *Robert Kennedy: In His Own Words* (Bantam, New York 1988) p. 414.
2. Murray Kempton, quoted in Jean Stein and George Plimpton, *American Journey: The Times of Robert Kennedy* (Signet, New York 1969) p. 88.
3. Kennedy, *In His Own Words*, pp. 185–95.
4. Kennedy, *In His Own Words*, p. 334.
5. See BBC TV series *The Kennedys*, 1992, Part III, *Robert Kennedy*.
6. Reedy in BBC *The Kennedys*.
7. Kennedy, *In His Own Words*, p. 417.
8. Kennedy interviewed by John Bartlow Martin. See Kennedy, *In His Own Words*, p. 417.
9. Goldwater quoted in Penn Kimball, *Bobby Kennedy and the New Politics* (Prentice-Hall, New Jersey 1968) p. 129.
10. See Max Weber, *On Charisma and Institution Building* (University of Chicago 1968) p. 342.
11. See Arthur Schlesinger, *Robert Kennedy and His Times* (Deutsch, London 1978) p. 675.
12. Kennedy, *In His Own Words*, p. 416.
13. Arthur Waskow in November 1967 edition of *The Nation*.
14. Tom Hayden, quoted in Jules Witcover, *85 Days* (Quill, New York 1988 edition) p. 342.
15. See Barbara Deckard, *The Women's Movement* (Harper and Row, New York 1975) p. 332. The women's movement had a very tough reception from the mainstream and radical left. Stokely Carmichael's infamous phrase that 'the only position for women in SNCC is prone' was largely indicative of reactions in the mid-1960s. Kennedy did not regard the women's movement as politically significant, but he would have been in a fairly strong position to have cultivated links to it had he lived, or had it managed to organize before mid-1968. Although JFK was not as popular with women voters as legend suggests (in 1960 he gained only 49% of the women's vote to Nixon's 51%), he made some effort to respond to women's concerns.

In December 1961 President Kennedy established a presidential commission on the Status of Women. Its report was made public in October 1963, and recommended that the President issue an Executive Order embodying the principle of equal opportunity in employment. The following month, a few days before his death, JFK set up the Interdepartmental Committee on the Status of Women. Robert Kennedy could have made a fairly persuasive case that women's issues had been addressed seriously by JFK's administration. In the months after Robert Kennedy's death the women's movement did begin to make its presence felt politically, and black feminist Shirley Chisholm was elected to Congress in November 1968.

16. Allen Ginsberg, quoted in Stein and Plimpton, *American Journey*, p. 213.
17. Ginsberg in Stein and Plimpton, *American Journey*, p. 213.
18. William Vanden Heuvel and Milton Gwirtzman, *On His Own* (Doubleday, New York 1970) p. 108.
19. Vanden Heuvel and Gwirtzman, *On His Own*, p. 108.
20. Vanden Heuvel and Gwirtzman, *On His Own*, p. 108.
21. Theo Lippman Jr., *Senator Ted Kennedy* (Norton, New York 1976) pp. 93–5.
22. Vanden Heuvel and Gwirtzman, *On His Own*, p. 101.
23. Chavez quoted in BBC TV series *The Kennedys*, October 1992, Part III.
24. Newfield, as quoted by Arthur Waskow, November 1967 edition of *The Nation*.
25. In February 1967, for instance, only 24% of Americans approved of a bombing halt in Vietnam. See Schlesinger, *RFK & His Times*, p. 771. In March 1968, 70% still wanted to continue with the bombing, and 61% regarded themselves as hawks. See G. H. Gallup, *The Gallup Poll: Public Opinions 1935–1971* (New York 1971) p. 32.
26. Kennedy's popularity did not rely, apparently, on his position on Vietnam, and so he had a relatively free hand to choose policy at will without it necessarily adversely affecting his political support. For example, a national Gallup poll of April 1968 quoted in Godfrey Hodgson et al, *An American Melodrama: the Presidential Campaign of 1968* (Viking, New York 1969) p. 166, showed that Kennedy's support was drawn equally from those in favour of, and those opposed to, the war. 'For Robert Kennedy, the issue of the war ... made no measurable difference at all. Among people who approved of Johnson's war policy, he scored 28%. Among those who disapproved, he scored 28%. It was, to say the least, a strange situation for a peace candidate ...'
27. Kennedy, *In His Own Words*, p. 414.
28. Neil Sheehan (ed.) *The Pentagon Papers* (*New York Times* Publications, New York 1971) p. 181. See also *The Best and the Brightest*, by David Halberstam (Random House, New York 1972) p. 336: 'By 1963, as [RFK's] perceptions had developed ... he had a new reputation, as the

best man in government to bring an unconventional idea to. Some of the people working under [Averell] Harriman [Senior statesman and roving ambassador in JFK administration], like Michael Forrestal [White Advisor on Vietnam], and [Roger] Hilsman [Assistant Secretary of State for Far Eastern Affairs] felt themselves encouraged in their doubts [about the war] by Robert Kennedy and felt that he more than anyone else in the upper level of government regarded the war as a war ... where civilians might be paying a particularly hard price ... Perhaps it was symbolic that the first senior official who questioned the overall policy was Robert Kennedy, totally secure in his place in the Administration, and also secure in his credentials as an anti-communist.'

29. Duhl, quoted in Stein and Plimpton, *American Journey*, p. 169.
30. Jack Newfield, *Robert Kennedy: A Memoir* (E. P. Dutton, New York 1969) p. 180.
31. Tom Wicker, quoted in Stein and Plimpton, *American Journey*, p. 266.

1. KENNEDY, POVERTY AND CIVIL RIGHTS

1. Eldridge Cleaver, *Post-Prison Writings* (Jonathan Cape, London 1968) p. 21.
2. *CBS* debate 26 September 1960. JFK opened his remarks in the television debate with Richard Nixon by comparing the crisis over slavery that America faced in the 1860s with that of the Cold War that she faced in 1960. See Richard Nixon, *Six Crises* (Garden City, New York 1962) p. 353.
3. Many blacks remained disenfranchised, of course, until the Voting Rights Act of 1965. Voting statistics from *Crisis* magazine, 1965, p. 29. See also Mark Stern, *Calculating Visions* (Rutgers University Press 1992) pp. 20–39 on JFK's attitude to civil rights during the 1960 campaign. In 1956, Democratic candidate Adlai Stevenson had won 61% of the black vote over Republican Dwight Eisenhower's 39%. In the presidential election of 1964, Lyndon Johnson took 94% of the black vote. See Harold Stanley and Richard Niemi, *Vital Statistics in American Politics* (Congressional Quarterly, July 1990). Also see Kennedy, *In His Own Words*, p. 212.
4. Schlesinger, *RFK & His Times*, pp. 137–69. See also Dan Moldea, *The Hoffa Wars* (Paddington Press, London 1978).
5. Schlesinger, *RFK & His Times*, p. 234. The black best known to John Kennedy at this time was probably George Thomas, who had been his personal butler since the mid-1940s and who served him in the White House. Thomas was described by JFK Press Secretary Pierre Salinger as 'a negro of unfailing good humour'. See Pierre Salinger, *With Kennedy* (Doubleday, New York 1966) p. 124. Three months into the

JFK administration, Robert Kennedy resigned his membership from Washington's Metropolitan Club on the grounds that it refused to serve blacks (Schlesinger, *RFK & His Times*, p. 290).

6. Schlesinger, *RFK & His Times*, pp. 317–27.
7. Boynton v. Virginia, December 1960, Case 364. Weeks before JFK's inauguration, the US Supreme Court ruled that the Interstate Commerce Act forbade discrimination in bus terminals serving interstate carriers. See Donald G. Nieman, *Promises to Keep* (Oxford University Press 1991) p. 74.
8. Kenneth O'Reilly, *Racial Matters: The FBI's Secret File on Black America, 1960–1972* (Free Press, New York 1989) pp. 49–152.
9. In January 1962, the FBI told Robert Kennedy that Martin Luther King had a member of the American Communist Party in his camp. Kennedy told King not to associate with the Communist (Levison). King refused and Kennedy authorised a tap to be placed on Levison's phone. See O'Reilly, *Racial Matters*, pp. 152–92 and Kennedy, *In His Own Words*, pp. 138–44.
10. Thomas C. Reeves, *A Question of Character, A Life of John F. Kennedy* (Bloomsbury, London 1991) pp. 339–40. See also Kennedy, *In His Own Words*, pp. 82–4, and Schlesinger, *RFK & His Times*, p. 299.
11. Robert Kennedy, *The Pursuit of Justice* (Popular Library, New York 1962) p. 108.
12. Walter Jackson, *Gunnar Myrdal and America's Conscience: social engineering and racial liberalism, 1938–1987* (University of North Carolina Press, London 1990) pp. 272–311 and Gunnar Myrdal, *An American Dilemma* (Harper and Row, New York 1962 edition).
13. Michael Harrington, *The Other America* (Macmillan, New York 1962).
14. Daniel P. Moynihan, *Maximum Feasible Misunderstanding* (Free Press, New York 1971) p. 68. Although Moynihan campaigned for RFK during the California primary, they disagreed over urban policy. Moynihan later became RFK's successor as Senator for New York (Democrat) but after the 1968 election worked for Nixon's White House. RFK said of his proposals for urban renewal: 'He knows all the facts, and he's against all the solutions.'
15. Schlesinger, *RFK & His Times*, p. 413.
16. Richard B. Morris (ed.) *Encyclopaedia of American History – Sixth edition* (Harper and Row, New York 1982) pp. 530–1.
17. Moynihan, *Maximum Feasible Misunderstanding*, p. 152.
18. Moynihan, *Maximum Feasible Misunderstanding*, p. 154.
19. Moynihan, *Maximum Feasible Misunderstanding*, p. 178.
20. Lyndon Johnson, *The Vantage Point: Perspectives on the Presidency 1963–69* (Rinehart and Wilson, New York 1971) pp. 508–11.
21. Schlesinger, *RFK & His Times*, p. 638.
22. Schlesinger, *RFK & His Times*, p. 639.
23. Moynihan, *Maximum Feasible Misunderstanding*, p. 68.

24. Richard Polenberg, *One Nation Divisible: class, race and ethnicity in the US since 1936* (Viking, New York 1980) p. 202. See also John E. Schwarz *America's Hidden Success* (Norton, New York 1988), Harold Cruse, *Plural But Equal* (Morrow, New York 1989), Lisbeth B. Schorr and Daniel Schorr *Within Our Reach: Breaking the Cycle of Disadvantage* (Archer, New York 1989) and David T. Ellwood, *Poor Support: Poverty in the American Family* (Basic Books, New York 1988).

25. Moynihan, *Maximum Feasible Misunderstanding*, p. 79.

26. Moynihan, *Maximum Feasible Misunderstanding*, p. 84.

27. Bobby Seale, *Seize the Time* (Hutchinson London 1969) p. 112.

28. Seale, *Seize the Time*, p. 113.

29. Cleaver, *Post-Prison Writings*, p. 21 (this piece, called 'Robert Kennedy's Prison', was written on 10 May 1967). Although Kennedy was never popular with the Black Panther leadership, during his California primary campaign in 1968 Black Panthers reportedly cleared the way for his motorcade to progress through crowds to the ghetto in West Oakland. See Stein and Plimpton, *American Journey*, p. 343.

30. Moynihan, *Maximum Feasible Misunderstanding*, p. 97.

31. Moynihan, *Maximum Feasible Misunderstanding*, p. 111.

32. Moynihan, *Maximum Feasible Misunderstanding*, p. 95.

33. Otto Kerner, *Report of the National Advisory Commission on Civil Disorders* (New York 1968) p. 490.

34. Arnold Schuchter, *White Power, Black Freedom* (Bantam, New York 1986) p. 281.

35. John C. Donovan, *The Politics of Poverty* (New York 1967) pp. 74–78, quoted in Schlesinger, *RFK & His Times*, p. 783.

36. Murray Kempton *The Spectator*, 19 May 1967, p. 577.

37. Robert Kennedy, *To Seek A Newer World* (Bantam, New York 1968) p. 46.

38. Kennedy, *Seek a Newer World*, p. 37.

39. *Congressional Record*, 14 October 1965.

40. *Congressional Record*, 21 January 1966.

41. Murray Kempton, *The Spectator*, 19 May 1967, p. 577.

42. Kennedy, *Seek a Newer World*, p. 40.

43. Kennedy, *Seek a Newer World*, p. 39.

44. *Congressional Record*, 22 February 1967.

45. Kennedy, *Seek a Newer World*, p. 40.

46. Johnson, *Perspectives on the Presidency*, p. 365.

47. Johnson, *Perspectives on the Presidency*, p. 420.

48. Jim Heath, *Decade of Disillusionment* (Indiana University Press 1976) p. 230.

49. Heath, *Decade of Disillusionment*, p. 231.

50. Heath, *Decade of Disillusionment*, p. 235.

51. *Stone's Weekly*, 12 April 1966.

52. *Stone's Weekly*, 19 April 1966. In his 1966 New Year Newsletter to constituents, however, Kennedy had hinted that both objectives might

be pursuable. 'Our most urgent question perhaps is whether we must raise taxes to ensure enough resources for the war in Vietnam and for a progressive program at home.'

53. *Newsweek*, 7 May 1968.
54. Schlesinger, *RFK & His Times*, pp. 786–7.
55. *Newsweek*, 7 May 1968.
56. *Newsweek*, 7 May 1968.
57. Schuchter, *White Power, Black Freedom*, p. 294.
58. Bedford Stuyvesant publicity leaflet, 1991.
59. Peter Walker, *Trust the People* (Collins, London 1987) p. 30.
60. *The Guardian*, 5 May 1992.
61. *The Guardian*, 30 May 1992.
62. Dr Kenneth Clark quoted in Stein and Plimpton, *American Journey*, pp. 141–2: 'There was no sensitivity on the part of Bobby to the basic problems and issues.'
63. Kennedy, *In His Own Words*, pp. 225–6. See also Schlesinger, *RFK & His Times*, pp. 330–3, and note 62 above.
64. Kennedy, *In His Own Words*, pp. 225–6.
65. Kennedy, *In His Own Words*, pp. 225–6.
66. Tom Hayden, quoted in Stein and Plimpton, *American Journey*, p. 221. CORE had been founded during the Second World War at the University of Chicago to protest against northern racism. Between 1961 and 1963 CORE's northern chapters grew more militant, picketing retail chains and banks, and pressing for positive discrimination in employment practices. McKissick, attracted by Nixon's ideas on black capitalism, backed him for re-election in 1972. See Hugh Davis Graham, *The Civil Rights Era* (OUP 1991) pp. 105–7.
67. *Amsterdam News* on 23 March 1963 reported that Kennedy employed Earl Graves, 'said to be the only Afro-American senatorial staff assistant in the country … [he] works in all areas of the Kennedy New York offices … [and] has worked for Kennedy ever since the Senator was elected.' According to the Amsterdam News of 18 May 1968, it was Graves who broke the news of Martin Luther King's assassination to the Senator.
68. *Congressional Record*, 1965–1968 passim. On Kennedy's death, his salary to 6 June was paid to his widow Ethel. While other senators received $15,000 for the first six months of 1968, Mrs Kennedy was given $12,999.99 plus a one-off payment of $30,000.
69. *Congressional Record*, 11 February 1967 Some of the early desegregation protesters who volunteered for sit-ins at lunch counters etc. were so poor that they had to be given money to buy food and drink at the counters to make their point.
70. Malcolm X had been promoting black pride since the late 1950s through the Nation of Islam. Frantz Fanon, writer and activist in the Algerian revolution, attended the first Congress of Black Writers and

Artists in Paris, in 1956, and was best known for his writings on negritude, or black cultural pride. In 1960 he was appointed Ambassador of the Algerian Provisional Government to Ghana.

71. *Congressional Record*, 18 March 1966. Kennedy was uneasy with the Black Power slogan, however, if it implied segregation at the cost of integration. In an interview with the *Christian Science Monitor* on 11 July 1966, he said that 'Black Power could be damaging not only to the civil-rights movement but to the country.'

72. *Congressional Record*, 12 July 1967.

73. Vanden Heuvel and Gwirtzman, *On His Own*, pp. 91–2.

74. Vanden Heuvel and Gwirtzman, *On His Own*, p. 91. Adam Clayton Powell was elected to Congress in 1945, and in 1960 chaired the House Committee on Education and Labor. Accused of corrupt use of public funds he had been censured by House colleagues and had temporarily lost his seat in 1957. Robert Kennedy regarded Powell as lazy and a sloth. 'He [Powell] always exacts a price, a monetary price, for his support,' said Kennedy (*In His Own Words* p. 72). Powell endorsed Eisenhower in 1956 and JFK in 1960.

75. Vanden Heuvel and Gwirtzman, *On His Own*, p. 92.

76. Kennedy, *In His Own Words*, p. 226. Malcolm X, charging that the JFK administration had co-opted the March on Washington, referred to it as the 'Farce on Washington'. He declared that 'white liberals took over the March on Washington, weakened its impact, and changed its course; by changing the participants and the contents, they were able to change the very nature of the march itself.' See Benjamin Goodman (ed.), *The End of White Supremacy: Four Speeches by Malcolm X* (Merlin House, New York 1971) pp. 141–6.

77. Vanden Heuvel and Gwirtzman, *On His Own*, p. 93.

78. *Congressional Record*, 18 March 1967.

79. Personal interview with Eugene McCarthy, May 1985.

80. Personal interview with John Bartlow Martin, June 1985.

81. Schlesinger, *RFK & His Times*, p. 788.

82. Bruce Perry, *Malcolm X* (Station Hill, New York 1991) p. 240.

83. Personal interviews with McCarthy and Martin, May and June 1985.

84. Personal interview with McCarthy, May 1985.

85. Classic studies on charisma include Max Weber, *On Charisma* (see Introduction, note 10); *Politics as Vocation* (Philadelphia 1964); *Sociology of Religion* (Methuen, London 1965); and Richard Tucker, *A Theory of Charismatic Leadership* (Daedalus, London 1968).

86. Weber, *On Charisma*, p. 410. Moreover, in his biography of South African black consciousness leader Steve Biko, Donald Woods notes: 'As a journalist I had interviewed many prominent personalities in various countries, but for me none of them approached the stature of Steve Biko. The one who came the closest to him in "charisma" was Robert Kennedy, with whom I had long discussions both in South

Africa and the United States. But the charisma of Kennedy was born of circumstance, background and events.' See Donald Woods, *Biko* (Paddington Press, London 1978) p. 70.

87. Ernest House, *Jesse Jackson and the Politics of Charisma* (Westview Press, Boulder 1988) p. 320.

88. Personal interview with Walter Fauntroy, March 1985.

89. Personal interview with Fred Dutton, February 1985.

90. See Mary Wilson, *Dream Girl – My Life as a Supreme* (Sidgwick & Jackson, London 1987) p. 217; James Brown, *The Godfather of Soul* (Macmillan, New York 1986) pp. 191 and 195. Motown was keen to sell records to black and white markets in the early 1970s and both black and white artists had hits with *Abraham, Martin and John*, which was written in the months following Robert Kennedy's death. It devotes a verse each to Abraham Lincoln, John Kennedy, Martin Luther King and Bobby Kennedy. Tom Clancy, the DJ who included extracts from speeches of the Kennedys and King, was white.

Although Lincoln is featured in the *Abraham, Martin and John* song, the list is usually restricted to the trinity of King and the two Kennedys. On the twentieth anniversary of the March on Washington, for example, T-shirts were sold at the Lincoln memorial bearing the images of the three, and there is an oblique reference to the three in Don McLean's song *American Pie*, which mentions them as 'the Father, Son and Holy Ghost'. The timing of King's and Robert Kennedy's assassinations – only two months apart – have probably contributed to the popular association. On the tenth anniversary of Robert Kennedy's death, Allard Lowenstein (in 1968 a New Left activist who urged Kennedy to run for the presidency and later a New York Congressman) wrote a piece for the *Washington Star* (5 June 1978) which touched on this. 'Perhaps because Robert Kennedy was the last of the three to die, his death seems the cruellest – bearing the cumulative freight of what had gone before, multiplying the doubt that there was any place for hope in a society where the best spokesmen for hope could not survive … with him went the spirit of a generation.'

91. Henry Hampton and Steve Fayer with Sarah Flyn, *Voices of Freedom: an oral history of the Civil Rights movement* (Bantam, London and New York 1990) p. 706. Jackson's list includes several new names in addition to the basic three, and the inclusion of Medgar Evers and Malcolm X are particularly revealing. Both were assassinated during the mid-1960s, but neither has achieved the stature of King or the Kennedys in popular culture.

92. Personal interview with Eugene McCarthy, May 1985.

93. Personal interview with George McGovern, May 1985.

94. Personal interview with John Bartlow Martin, June 1985.

95. Henry Fairlie, *The Kennedy Promise* (Eyre Methuen, London 1973) p. 356.

96. Cleaver, *Post-Prison Writings*, p. 22.
97. David Garrow, *Bearing the Cross* (Vintage, London 1987) p. 576. On 25 March 1968, King said he would settle for either Kennedy or McCarthy as the Democratic nominee. Kennedy and King were never personally very close, the wiretapping incident no doubt making such contact difficult. However, his widow Coretta Scott King was invited to join Kennedy's funeral train (and was welcomed aboard by Ethel Kennedy with the words 'There's our pal'); at the time of their deaths their political relationship, at least, had improved from Robert Kennedy's days as Attorney General.
98. Roy Wilkins, *Standing Fast* (Penguin, London 1977) p. 330.
99. Personal interview, March 1985.
100. Personal interview, May 1985. All police leave in Washington, DC, was cancelled. *The Times* of 7 June reported that America was preparing 'for what could be called a state of siege': the Pentagon had 26,800 men from the California National Guard 'ready for deployment in the streets' should violence erupt and had readied troops 'detailed for duty in civil disturbances in various parts of the country'. Of course tension had been heightened by the disturbances ignited in the preceding weeks by the King assassination.

    Large-scale violence did not break out anywhere, although police suspected the murder of an Arab shopkeeper in Chicago on 10 June could have been motivated by revenge for Kennedy's death. The nearest the Poor People's Campaign came to an outbreak of hostility was in the rhetoric of campaign leader Hosea Williams, who charged that 'They are trying to kill off all our leaders so that we will be leaderless' (*The Times*, 6 June).
101. Hampton and Fayer, *Voices of Freedom*, p. 487.

2. KENNEDY AND INDUSTRY

1. John Davis quoted in Philip Melanson, *The Robert F. Kennedy Assassination*, (Shapolsky, New York 1991) p. 4.
2. See Schlesinger, *RFK & His Times*, p. 790 on opposition from the American Farm Bureau to migrant workers' rights.
3. Ben Bradlee, *Conversations with Kennedy* (Norton, New York 1975), p. 126.
4. Pierre Salinger, *With Kennedy* (Avon, New York 1966) pp. 46–9. See also Walter Sheridan, *The Rise and Fall of Jimmy Hoffa* (New York 1972), and Schlesinger, *RFK & His Times*, pp. 137–69.
5. O'Rourke soon recovered. By 1964 he was President of Teamster Joint Council 16 in New York City, the largest Teamster organization in the state. Joint Council 16 endorsed RFK for the Senate in 1964. See Sheridan, *Rise & Fall of Jimmy Hoffa*, p. 379.

6. There had been a Trotskyist faction in the Teamsters in the 1930s, when Trotskyism had popular currency among American intellectuals on the left. See also Moldea, *The Hoffa Wars*, p. 26.
7. Moldea, *Hoffa Wars*, pp. 30–5.
8. Moldea, *Hoffa Wars*, p. 84. For Hoffa's draft deferment, see p. 39.
9. Schlesinger, *RFK & His Times*, p. 153. Hoffa freely admitted to Kennedy over dinner in February 1957 that he had arranged the setting up of seven such locals in New York City just before the council election in 1956.
10. Sheridan, *Rise & Fall of Jimmy Hoffa*, p. 134.
11. Moldea, *Hoffa Wars*, p. 59.
12. The anti-communist witchhunts of the early 1950s hit the American labour organisations very badly, some of whom were suspected of being in league with the Soviets. In the American trade union movement, anti-communism came to be regarded by many as a legitimate component of American patriotism, and union leaders like Walter Reuther and Joseph Curran struggled to wrest control from unions with Communist Party links. See John Patrick Diggins, *The Proud Decades* (Norton, New York 1988). pp. 165–80. Also see Schlesinger, *RFK & His Times*, pp. 183–4.
13. Schlesinger, *RFK & His Times*, p. 160.
14. Schlesinger, *RFK & His Times*, p. 139.
15. Schlesinger, *RFK & His Times*, p. 191.
16. Schlesinger, *RFK & His Times*, p. 186. See also Anthony Carew, *Walter Reuther* (Manchester University Press 1993).
17. Kennedy, *In His Own Words*, pp. 228–9: 'I got hold of Walter Reuther. … So then he got together with [CORE director James] Farmer and [Martin Luther] King and got the other leaders of the March together and explained the situation. They all went to Lewis and made Lewis agree to let them edit the speech.'
18. Tom Hayden, *Reunion* (Hamish Hamilton, London 1988) p. 125: 'Walter Reuther … sent a five-thousand dollar check to help us get started' (See Chapter 3, p. 170).
19. Vanden Heuvel and Gwirtzman, *On His Own*, p. 355.
20. Kennedy aide Peter Edelman, quoted in Stein and Plimpton, *American Journey*, p. 313: 'Jack Conway, the labor leader, called me and said, "Walter Reuther and I think it would be a very good idea if your Senator would go out to Delano with the Senate Migratory Labor Subcommittee, which is going to hold hearings out there …" Finally, after about three days, [Kennedy] said, "Well, okay. If Walter Reuther and Jack Conway want me to do it, I suppose I'll do it."'
21. Harrington, quoted in Stein and Plimpton, *American Journey*, p. 312.
22. Edelman, quoted in Stein and Plimpton, *American Journey*, p. 314.
23. *Wall Street Journal*, 12 December 1967.
24. Vanden Heuvel and Gwirtzman, *On His Own*, p. 355.

25. Vanden Heuvel and Gwirtzman, *On His Own*, p. 356.
26. See Schlesinger, *RFK & His Times*, p. 405.
27. Kennedy, *In His Own Words*, p. 204.
28. Vanden Heuvel and Gwirtzman, *On His Own*, pp. 352–5.
29. *Congressional Record*, 8 June 1965, p. 13903.
30. *Congressional Record*, p. 13903.
31. *Congressional Record*, p. 13904.
32. *Congressional Record*, p. 13904.
33. See *Congressional Record*, 12 September 1967, pp. 25127–9. The bills were S.1803 (to strengthen the Labor and Advertising Act of 1966), and S.1565 (to control all illegal transportation of tobacco); three were co-sponsored by Senator Randolph, and were printed as S.2394 (to change the warning on packets), S.2395 (to regulate the broadcasting of tobacco advertising) and S.2396 (to tax cigarettes on the basis of their tar and nicotine content).
34. *Congressional Record*, 12 September 1967, p. 25129. Ted Kennedy carried on the fight against cigarette advertising after RFK's death. In January 1976 he introduced a bill with Senator Gary Hart to establish a new 'health tax' on cigarettes, with the amount on each brand determined by the brand's tar and nicotine content.
35. Kennedy, *In His Own Words*, p. 204.
36. Kennedy, *In His Own Words*, p. 194.
37. *Wall Street Journal* 17 October 1966.
38. *Wall Street Journal* 3 April 1968.
39. Vanden Heuvel and Gwirtzman, *On His Own*, p. 352.
40. Hubert Humphrey, *The Education of a Public Man* (Garden City, New York 1976) p. 324.
41. Kennedy, *In His Own Words*, p. 300.
42. Kennedy, *In His Own Words*, p. 301.
43. Personal interview with John Bartlow Martin, June 1985.
44. *Wall Street Journal*, 3 April 1968.

3. KENNEDY AND THE NEW LEFT

1. Stein and Plimpton, *American Journey*, pp. 212–14.
2. Stanley Hymin, *Youth in Politics* (Basic Books, New York 1972) p. 213.
3. Hymin, *Youth in Politics*, p. 236.
4. Howard Zinn, *SNCC – The New Abolitionists* (Beacon, New York 1965) p. 140.
5. Zinn, *New Abolitionists*, p. 121.
6. Kennedy, *In His Own Words*, p. 93: 'We got the bus, and they got in the bus, and nobody would drive them. So I told the Greyhound, Mr. Greyhound, that he should get a bus driver ...'
7. Schlesinger, *RFK & His Times*, p. 299.

8.   Zinn, *New Abolitionists*, p. 140.
9.   See Stein and Plimpton, *American Journey*, p. 313, and note 17 in 'Kennedy and Industry' chapter.
10. Stokely Carmichael, quoted in Fairlie, *The Kennedy Promise*, p. 356.
11. Hayden, *Reunion*, p. 87. SDS was far more of a New Left grouping than was SNCC, which developed – after Carmichael's election – into a black radical organisation.
12. Hayden, *Reunion*, p. 312.
13. Hayden, *Reunion*, pp. 80–2.
14. Hayden, *Reunion*, p. 86.
15. Hayden, *Reunion*, p. 212.
16. Hayden, *Reunion*, p. 285.
17. Hodgson et al, *An American Melodrama*, p. 555.
18. *Ramparts*, February 1967.
19. *Ramparts*, February 1967.
20. *Ramparts*, February 1967.
21. *Ramparts*, February 1967.
22. *Ramparts*, March 1968.
23. Hayden, *Reunion*, p. 203.
24. Abbie Hoffman, *Revolution for the hell of it* (Dial, New York 1968) p. 240.
25. *Ramparts*, February 1967.
26. Jerry Rubin, *Do It!* (Simon & Schuster, New York 1970) p. 58.
27. Kennedy, *Seek a Newer World*, p. 14.
28. Kennedy, *Seek a Newer World*, p. 15.
29. See Jules Witcover, *85 Days*, p. 153: 'Some of the young Turks in the Kennedy organization, such as speechwriters Walinsky and Greenfield and researcher Edelman, were disturbed at the old-line conservatism creeping into their candidate's pitch [during the Indiana Primary].'
30. Personal interview with Arthur Schlesinger, June 1985.
31. Lynd, quoted in Stein and Plimpton, *American Journey*, p. 220.
32. See Vanden Heuvel and Gwirtzman, *On His Own*, p. 113. 'He had approved these programmes during his brother's administration, although he did not know that some young people had joined [some student organisations] without knowledge of their true sponsorship.'
33. Hymin, *Youth in Politics*, p. 133.
34. Hymin, *Youth in Politics*, p. 234.
35. Hymin, *Youth in Politics*, p. 189.
36. According to Hymin, media interest in McCarthy's campaign took off on the second weekend in January. Many colleges were still on Christmas break, and so an unusually high number of students – still on vacation – walked the streets campaigning for McCarthy. The idea of a 'children's crusade' for McCarthy took root in the media, and dominated much coverage of the campaign.
37. Hayden, *Reunion*, p. 290.
38. Hayden, *Reunion*, p. 290.

39. *The Nation*, November 1966.
40. *The Nation*, November 1966.
41. Newfield, *RFK: A Memoir*, p. 324.
42. Hayden, *Reunion*, p. 267. Also see Schlesinger, *RFK & His Times*, p. 898. Kennedy supporters in the 1968 campaign included Michael Harrington, John Lewis, and Cesar Chavez.
43. Hayden, *Reunion*, p. 290.

4. FOREIGN POLICY

Part I – The White House Experience

1. *Congressional Record*, 21 January 1965, p. 10030.
2. See Schlesinger, *RFK & His Times*, p. 884. After the 1968 Indiana primary Kennedy asked 'why do I have so much trouble with Jews? ... Is it because of my father when he was in England? That was 30 years ago ...'
3. Schlesinger, *RFK & His Times*, p. 74.
4. Kennedy, *In His Own Words*, p. 31.
5. Kennedy, *In His Own Words*, p. 438: 'Generally, in all of these countries [which included Indochina, India and Pakistan], he [JFK] was very critical of Foreign Service representation ... their lack of knowledge, of information about what was going on in their country; their lack of feeling for the people.'
6. Schlesinger, *RFK & His Times*, p. 92.
7. Melvin Gurtov, *The US against the Third World* (Praeger, New York 1974) p. 41.
8. Schlesinger, *RFK & His Times*, p. 562.
9. Mandela was arrested by South African police at a roadblock in August 1962. Reports that a CIA informant had tipped off the South African police appeared after Mandela's release in 1990. See *Atlanta Journal and Constitution*, 10, 12 and 13 June 1990.
10. Roger Louis and Hedley Bull, *The Special Relationship: Anglo-American Relations since 1945* (Oxford University Press, 1986) p. 288.
11. Georgie Anne Geyer, *Guerrilla Prince – Fidel Castro* (Little Brown, New York 1991) p. 240.
12. Kennedy, *In His Own Words*, pp. 33–6: 'It seemed to me,' he remembered in 1964, 'that we had to fill three or four hundred positions by January[1961]. And then after that we had to fill – by April or May – we had to fill another eight hundred or a thousand.'
13. Kennedy, *In His Own Words*, p. 320.
14. Kennedy, *In His Own Words*, p. 32.
15. Kennedy, *In His Own Words*, p. 270.
16. Kennedy, *In His Own Words*, p. 321.

17. Kennedy, *In His Own Words*, p. 326.
18. Schlesinger, *RFK & His Times*, p. 417.
19. Kennedy, *In His Own Words*, p. 249.
20. William V. Shannon, *The Heir Apparent* (Macmillan, New York 1967) pp. 110–4: 'The Vietnam War was the ugly child ... of the Kennedy administration's belief in the efficacy of counter-insurgency techniques against guerrilla warfare. And no-one had been a more devoted proponent of those techniques from 1961 to 1963 than Robert Kennedy ... [Robert] Kennedy became a zealous convert to the doctrines of guerrilla warfare ... Within the government, he was regarded as "Mr Counter-insurgency."'
21. Shannon, *Heir Apparent*, p. 111.
22. David Halberstam, quoted in Stein and Plimpton, *American Journey*, p. 229.
23. Kennedy, *In His Own Words*, p. 297.
24. Schlesinger, *RFK & His Times*, p. 469.
25. Kennedy, *Seek a Newer World*, p. 108.
26. Gurtov, *US against the Third World*, p. 90.
27. Edwin Lieuwen, *Generals versus Presidents* (Praeger, New York 1964) p. 146.
28. Kennedy, *In His Own Words*, p. 257.
29. Kennedy, *In His Own Words*, p. 257.
30. John Bartlow Martin in Kennedy, *In His Own Words*, p. 387.
31. Schlesinger, *RFK & His Times*, p. 577.
32. Khrushchev in Ronald Pope (ed.), *Soviet Views on the Cuban Missile Crisis* (University Press of America 1988) p. 137.
33. Schlesinger, *RFK & His Times*, p. 532.
34. Kennedy, *In His Own Words*, p. 258.
35. Kennedy, *In His Own Words*, p. 258.
36. Kennedy, *In His Own Words*, p. 259.
37. Kennedy, *In His Own Words*, p. 259.
38. Kennedy, *In His Own Words*, p. 37.
39. Mark White, 'Belligerent beginnings', *Journal of Strategic Studies* VI (March 1992) p. 16. White's essay is a splendid study of the initial reactions of the President and his cabinet to the crisis. JFK and RFK, it appears, were among the most aggressive ExComm members that first day, both enthusiastic about military action against the Cubans.
40. White, 'Belligerent beginnings', p. 16.
41. Robert Kennedy, *13 Days* (Pan, New York 1968) p. 90. Robert Kennedy's argument that a surprise attack was against American traditions was obviously nonsense. The nation was founded on a sneak attack carried out by George Washington. Ignoring military protocol, Washington led his troops across the Delaware River on Christmas Day, 1776, and launched an attack on British troops who had camped there for the winter. Attacks on American Indians carrying truce flags were not

uncommon a hundred years later, and during the Second World War British and German fighter pilots were astonished to witness US planes killing enemy air crew who were parachuting to the ground. The shooting of defenceless parachutists defied the European code of conduct and was first introduced by American pilots. Nevertheless, RFK's allusion to some fictitious legacy of moral superiority in military matters appears to have had some impact on the ExComm.

42. Kennedy, *13 Days*.
43. Douglas Dillon in James Blight and David Welch, *On the Brink* (Hill & Wang, New York 1989) p. 66.
44. Dobrynin in James Blight, *The Shattered Crystal Ball* (Rowman and Littlefield, New York 1990) p. 142.
45. Kennedy, *In His Own Words*, p. 31.
46. Schlesinger, *RFK & His Times*, p. 509.
47. Rusk in Blight and Welch, *On the Brink*, p. 180.
48. CIA photo expert, as quoted in BBC TV documentary *CIA*, July 1992.
49. Kennedy, *In His Own Words*, p. 31.
50. Schlesinger, *RFK & His Times*, p. 712.

Part II – The Politics of Dissent

1. Kennedy, *In His Own Words*, p. 390.
2. *Congressional Record*, 6 May 1965, p. 9037.
3. *Stone's Weekly*, 17 May 1965.
4. See especially *Stone's Weekly* in 1965, editions of 17 May, 28 June, 6 September, 18 October, 29 November and 13 December. *Stone's Weekly* in 1966, editions of 7 February, 14 February, 28 February, 7 March, 25 July, 5 September, 3 October, 24 October and 19 December. *Stone's Weekly* in 1967, editions of 30 January, 20 February, 13 March, 27 March and 15 April.
5. Schlesinger, *RFK & His Times*, p. 695.
6. *Stone's Weekly*, 13 December 1965.
7. *Stone's Weekly*, 7 March 1966.
8. *Stone's Weekly*, 18 May 1966.
9. *Congressional Record*, 9 May 1966, p. 10090.
10. *Congressional Record*, 9 May 1966, p. 10091.
11. See Schlesinger, *RFK & His Times*, pp. 639–40. Earlier on 14 December 1963, US Ambassador to Mexico Thomas Mann had been promoted to Assistant Secretary of State for Inter-American Affairs, and also asked to head the Alliance for Progress. 'Not until Tom Mann came back in 1964' said Alphonse de Rosso of Standard Oil of New Jersey 'did the business community feel it was "in" again with the US government ... Mann suspended virtually all aid to Peru in an effort to force the democratic ... government to come to terms with the

International Petroleum Company, a Standard Oil of New Jersey subsidiary.' 'I think [Mann]'s going to be a disastrous appointment', said Kennedy in 1964 (Kennedy, *In His Own Words*, p. 267).

12. *Congressional Record*, 10 May 1966.

13. Gallup Polls from 1965 to 1968 consistently showed public support for the war. In February 1966, 64% of the public regarded themselves as hawks on the war. As late as March 1968, 61% regarded themselves as hawks, and 70% wanted to continue the bombing. See Gallup, *The Gallup Poll: Public Opinion 1935–1971*. For Kennedy's declarations in Saigon, see note 50 above.

14. *Congressional Record*, 6 May 1965, p. 9760.

15. Schlesinger, *RFK & His Times*, p. 732.

16. Barry Goldwater regarded the blood offer as 'closer to treason than academic freedom', and the *New York Daily News* asked Kennedy 'Why not light out for the enemy country and join its armed forces?'. Schlesinger, *RFK & His Times*, pp. 732–3.

17. Fulbright had been mooted as a possible Secretary of State in the JFK White House. Schlesinger said JFK liked Fulbright '... the bite of his language, and the direction of his thinking on foreign affairs' (Schlesinger, *A Thousand Days: John F. Kennedy in the White House*, (Houghton Mifflin, Boston 1965) p. 139). However, Robert Kennedy opposed the Fulbright appointment, considering his segregationist views to be a possible handicap when dealing with emerging Third World countries (See Schlesinger p. 136). Fulbright offered JFK advice on foreign affairs twice during his presidency, and was ignored both times. He counselled against invading the Bay of Pigs, and strongly urged JFK to order an invasion of Cuba when the Soviet missiles were found there.

18. Vanden Heuvel and Gwirtzman, *On His Own*, p. 219.

19. *Congressional Record*, 14 March 1966, p. 5619.

20. *Congressional Record*, 14 March 1966, p. 5619.

21. *Stone's Weekly*, 28 February 1966.

22. *Congressional Record*, 14 March 1966, p. 5620.

23. *Congressional Record*, 14 March 1966, p. 5620.

24. *Congressional Record*, 14 March 1966, p. 5620.

25. *Congressional Record*, 14 March 1966, p. 5620.

26. *Stone's Weekly*, 28 February 1966.

27. *New Statesman*, 25 February 1966.

28. *The Spectator*, 11 March 1966.

29. *Congressional Record*, 15 March 1966, p. 5684.

30. *Congressional Record*, 20 February 1966, p. 3581.

31. *Congressional Record*, 23 February 1966, p. 3881.

32. *Stone's Weekly*, 28 February 1966.

33. *Congressional Record*, 23 February 1966, p. 3881.

34. *Congressional Record*, 19 July 1966. See also *Stone's Weekly*, 25 July 1966.

35. See *Stone's Weekly*, 5 September 1966, *New Statesman*, 18 July 1966 and *The Spectator*, 8 July 1966: all believed the vice-presidency theory was a credible one.

36. Andrew Kopkind in *New Statesman*, 18 July 1966.

37. *The Spectator*, 8 July 1966.

38. *The Spectator*, 9 September 1966.

39. *Stone's Weekly*, 24 October 1966.

40. *Stone's Weekly*, 24 October 1966.

41. See H. Y. Schandler, *The Unmaking of a President: Lyndon Johnson and Vietnam* (Princeton University Press 1967) p. 32.

42. *Stone's Weekly*, 24 October 1966.

43. Alonzo L. Hamby, *Liberalism and its Challengers: From Roosevelt to Reagan* (Oxford University Press, 1985) p. 220.

44. *New York Times*, 22 October 1965. See also Schlesinger, *RFK & His Times*, p. 732.

45. Ted Kennedy became Chairman of the Senate Subcommittee on Refugees and Escapees in 1965, from where he launched several attacks on the Johnson administration's policy towards refugees from South Vietnam, but did not focus primarily on the war itself until October 1967, preferring to concentrate on the 'humanitarian' issues of refugee welfare. See Theo Lippman, *Senator Ted Kennedy* (Norton, New York 1976) pp. 45–73.

46. Vanden Heuvel and Gwirtzman, *On His Own*, p. 226. See also Kimball, *Bobby Kennedy and the New Politics*, p. 61, and Schlesinger, *RFK & His Times*, p. 766.

47. *Stone's Weekly*, 3 October 1966.

48. *Harper's*, October 1966.

49. Kennedy, *In His Own Words*, p. 275.

50. Kennedy, *In His Own Words*, p. 302.

51. Kennedy, *In His Own Words*, p. 302.

52. Kennedy, *In His Own Words*, p. 324.

53. Verwoerd's successor as South African Prime Minister was Balthazar Johannes Vorster. Vorster told South African journalist Donald Woods in 1968 that 'If Robert Kennedy becomes President of America, all I can say is – God help South Africa.' See Donald Woods, *Asking for Trouble* (Gollancz, London 1980) p. 199.

54. *Stone's Weekly*, 17 December 1966.

55. William Manchester, *The Death of a President* (Harper & Row, New York 1967).

56. Vanden Heuvel and Gwirtzman, *On His Own*, pp. 226–33, and Schlesinger, *RFK & His Times*, p. 766.

57. Vanden Heuvel and Gwirtzman, *On His Own*, p. 235.

58. Vanden Heuvel and Gwirtzman, *On His Own*, p. 238.

59. Vanden Heuvel and Gwirtzman, *On His Own*, p. 238.

60. Vanden Heuvel and Gwirtzman, *On His Own*, p. 254.

61. Lynd in Stein and Plimpton, *American Journey*, p. 221.
62. See Gallup, *Public Opinions, 1935–1971*, p. 32.
63. *The Spectator*, 10 March 1967.
64. *The Spectator*, 17 February 1967.
65. *New Statesman*, 10 March 1967.
66. *Stone's Weekly*, 13 March 1967.
67. See Chapter 1, note 37
68. S.1626, *Congressional Record*, 3 May 1967, p. 11524.
69. Kennedy, *Seek a Newer World*, p. 60.
70. Kennedy, *Seek a Newer World*, p. 61.
71. Kennedy, *Seek a Newer World*, p. 91.
72. Kennedy, *Seek a Newer World*, p. 91.
73. Kennedy, *Seek a Newer World*, pp. 90–3.
74. Kennedy, *Seek a Newer World*, p. 92.
75. *Congressional Record*, 10 May 1966, p. 10090.
76. Kennedy, *Seek a Newer World*, p. 97.
77. Kennedy, *Seek a Newer World*, p. 100.
78. '[Robert Kennedy] had become much more compassionate and caring ... he was a bigger, kinder, more compassionate person in 1968 than he was in 1961 ... by 1968 he was more mellow, more compassionate, a more kindly and concerned person. He was a more thoughtful, decent human being' – George McGovern, in a personal interview, March 1985. Others were more sceptical of a transformation. Former President Harry Truman said in the mid-60s that 'they say young Bobby has changed for the better ... and maybe he has, but what I can never understand and never will if I live to be a hundred is why it takes so long these days for somebody to learn the difference between right and wrong. A man who hasn't learned that by the time he's thirty is never going to learn.' See Merle Miller, *Plain Speaking: An Oral Biography of Harry S. Truman* (Gollancz, London 1974) p. 439.
79. George McGovern, quoted in Stein and Plimpton, *American Journey*, p. 249.
80. Schlesinger, *RFK & His Times*, p. 822.
81. Bureau of the Census, *Statistical Abstract of the US, Media Utilization – Multimedia Audiences* (Department of Commerce, Washington DC 1986) p. 531.
82. Vanden Heuvel and Gwirtzman, *On His Own*, p. 257.
83. Witcover, *85 Days*, p. 28.
84. Lowenstein was Co-chairman of the Conference of Concerned Democrats, an anti-war organisation looking for a candidate to challenge Johnson in the primaries, or to stand in the November election as an independent.
85. Schlesinger, *RFK & His Times*, p. 737.
86. Schlesinger, *RFK & His Times*, p. 365.
87. Johnson, unhappy that the Vietnam War was not being pursued

vigorously enough, demanded that McNamara resign. Schlesinger, *RFK & His Times*, p. 823: 'We all [in the Kennedy camp] supposed that McNamara's dismissal removed the last hope ... of government for restraint in the war – a supposition reinforced when Johnson soon announced a leading hawk, Clark Clifford, as the new Secretary of Defense.'

88. Witcover, *85 Days*, pp. 37 and 39. In early January 1968 Ted Kennedy went to Vietnam as head of the Senate subcommittee dealing in refugee problems. One of his staff, John Nolan, put the civilian casualties as four or five times higher than the official US statistics.
89. Schlesinger, *RFK & His Times*, p. 737.
90. Hodgson, *American Melodrama*, p. 489.
91. Gallup, *Public Opinion, 1935–1971*, p. 23.
92. Schlesinger, *RFK & His Times*, p. 842.
93. Witcover, *85 Days*, p. 67.
94. Witcover, *85 Days*, p. 52.
95. *Congressional Record*, 10 March 1968, p. 21048.
96. Witcover, *85 Days*, p. 106.
97. Witcover, *85 Days*, p. 100.
98. Witcover, *85 Days*, p. 102.
99. Witcover, *85 Days*, p. 104.
100. Schlesinger, *RFK & His Times*, p. 864.
101. Schlesinger, *RFK & His Times*, p. 864.
102. *New York Post*, 11 May 1968.
103. *New Republic*, 28 April 1968.
104. Witcover, *85 Days*, p. 245.
105. For full primary results, see Stanley and Niemi, *Vital Statistics on American Politics*, pp. 44–6, and Chapter 5 below.
106. Witcover, *85 Days*, p. 254.
107. Hodgson, *American Melodrama*, p. 309.
108. Hodgson, *American Melodrama*, p. 309.
109. Personal interview with McCarthy, May 1985.

5. THE PRESIDENTIAL CAMPAIGN

1. *Wall Street Journal*, 17 October 1968.
2. Schlesinger, *RFK & His Times*, p. 207.
3. According to several reports, Daley had falsified ballot returns in Illinois to give JFK a crucial victory in 1960. 'Mr President, with a bit of luck and the help of a few close friends, you're going to carry Illinois', Daley told JFK on election night. See Thomas C. Reeves, *A Question of Character* (Bloomsbury, London 1991) p. 214. Also Peter Collier and David Horowitz, *The Kennedys: An American Drama* (Warner, New York 1985) p. 245.
4. Vanden Heuvel and Gwirtzman, *On His Own*, p. 335. Daley had

promised Kennedy to postpone any endorsement until June. 'And in June he'll tell me to wait 'til August', said Kennedy.

5. Quoted in the *New Republic*, 15 October 1966.
6. *New Republic*, 15 October 1966.
7. *The Nation*, 14 November 1966.
8. Hodgson, *American Melodrama*, p. 111.
9. *Life*, March 1967.
10. Witcover, *85 Days*, p. 31.
11. Witcover, *85 Days*, p. 32.
12. Hymin, *Youth in Politics*, p. 104.
13. See Hodgson, *American Melodrama*, p. 81, for a fuller explanation of the primary system as it stood in 1968.
14. Witcover, *85 Days*, p. 32.
15. Hodgson, *American Melodrama*, p. 89.
16. Witcover, *85 Days*, p. 74.
17. Witcover, *85 Days*, p. 53.
18. See Stanley and Niemi, *Vital Statistics on American Politics*. All voting statistics are from here unless otherwise stated.
19. Witcover, *85 Days*, p. 80.
20. *The Listener*, 14 March 1968.
21. Witcover, *85 Days*, p. 87.
22. Hodgson, *American Melodrama*, p. 509.
23. Hodgson, *American Melodrama*, p. 509. In 1967, Daley won every ward in Cook County in his re-election victory.
24. *New York Times*, 3 May 1968.
25. *Wall Street Journal*, 3 April 1968.
26. Hodgson, *American Melodrama*, p. 165.
27. *New York Times*, 6 May 1968.
28. *Wall Street Journal*, 1 May 1968.
29. *New York Times*, 6 May 1968.
30. *New York Times*, 7 May 1968.
31. *New York Times*, 7 May 1968.
32. *New York Times*, 8 May 1968.
33. Stein and Plimpton, *American Journey*, p. 276.
34. *This Week*, 12 May 1968.
35. Schlesinger, *RFK & His Times*, p. 891.
36. Schlesinger, *RFK & His Times*, p. 891.
37. Newfield, *RFK: A Memoir*, p. 83.
38. David Halberstam, *The Unfinished Odyssey of Robert Kennedy* (Barrie & Jenkins, 1968) p. 122. Halberstam, although sympathetic to Robert Kennedy, had been a thorn in JFK's side. The President had suggested to the *New York Times* publisher Arthur Hays Sulzberger that Halberstam be removed from his position as correspondent from Vietnam because the stories he was filing were not sufficiently sympathetic to the administration's policy. The *New York Times* refused.

39. Witcover, *85 Days*, p. 231.
40. *New Republic*, 15 May 1992. Clinton's association with Kennedy's legacy is double-edged. In the final weeks before Clinton's presidential election victory, a man was arrested in Las Vegas after threatening to assassinate him. 'This Thursday coming up Bill Clinton is coming to town and he's going to have a big surprise just like Robert Kennedy. He's going to get what he deserves. Robert Kennedy, he was killed,' the man was quoted as threatening (*Evening Standard*, 21 October 1992).

   At the Democratic Convention in New York on 15 July, 1992, Ted Kennedy also alluded to his brother's poverty coalition. Addressing the convention immediately after the documentary film of Robert Kennedy had been shown, Ted Kennedy declared: 'Perhaps more than any other leader in memory, my brother Bobby reached across the deepest divides of American life – black activist and blue-collar, suburb and city, the young students on campus who protested the war and the young soldiers drafted to fight it ...'
41. Quoted in Vanden Heuvel and Gwirtzman, *On His Own*, p. 348.
42. Vanden Heuvel and Gwirtzman, *On His Own*, p. 348.
43. Witcover, *85 Days*, p. 180.
44. See Moldea, *Hoffa Wars*, pp. 180–220.
45. Personal interview with McCarthy, May 1985.
46. Witcover, *85 Days*, pp. 196–7: 'The Negro–blue-collar base, centred around Omaha, had come through as hoped – about 85% for Kennedy among Negroes, nearly 60% among blue-collar whites. In addition, Kennedy had swept all counties with concentrations of European ethnics – Poles, Czechs, Germans, Scandinavians.' Vanden Heuvel and Gwirtzman admit that 'the Kennedy organization originally believed the [black-white coalition] misconception and encouraged it', p. 348.
47. Witcover, *85 Days*, p. 207.
48. An organisation called the Association to Preserve Our Right to Keep and Bear Arms, Inc., campaigned against Kennedy in Roseberg, Oregon.
49. Arthur Herzog, *McCarthy for President* (Viking, New York 1969) p. 171.
50. The PFP ran Eldridge Cleaver as their nominee. He was Minister of Information for the Black Panthers, but on parole for murder at the time of the election and did not meet the minimum age requirement to be President as stipulated by the Constitution.
51. Paul Schrade was in the pantry with Robert Kennedy when the Senator was shot. Schrade was also wounded, hit by a bullet in the head.
52. Herzog, *McCarthy for President*, p. 149.
53. Hodgson, *American Melodrama*, p. 131.
54. Hodgson, *American Melodrama*, p. 344.
55. Hodgson, *American Melodrama*, p. 354.

56. From *Statistical Abstract of the US Department of Commerce*, p. 551.

57. Halberstam, *Unfinished Odyssey of RFK*, p. 203.

58. Halberstam, *Unfinished Odyssey of RFK*, p. 203.

59. Vanden Heuvel and Gwirtzman, *On His Own*, p. 379. *The Times* (6 June 1968) estimated that 90% of the 73% of registered Mexican-Americans voted for Kennedy, and that over 80% of blacks voted for him. Overall turnout in the California primary reached 3,181,970. Turnout in 1964 was 2,492,244, and in 1972 3,564,518.

60. Vanden Heuvel and Gwirtzman, *On His Own*, p. 348.

61. Halberstam, *Unfinished Odyssey of RFK*, p. 195.

62. Richard Goodwin, quoted in Stein and Plimpton, *American Journey*, p. 313.

63. Vanden Heuvel and Gwirtzman, *On His Own*, pp. 390–1.

64. Personal interview with McCarthy, May 1985.

65. Jeremy Larner, *Nobody Knows: Reflections on the McCarthy Campaign* (New York 1970) p. 189. A 'Draft Ted' [Kennedy] campaign gained momentum in the final days before the Democratic convention, before Ted announced that he would not accept the nomination.

66. *Village Voice*, July 1968. There is no way of knowing how the Wallace votes would have split had he not been a candidate, although it is likely that most would have gone to the Democrats.

67. See L. H. Gann and Peter Duignan, *The Hispanics in the US* (Westview Press, Boulder 1986) and Ronald Walters, *Black Presidential Politics in America* (State University of New York Press 1988).

68. Walters, *Black Presidential Politics*, p. 32.

69. Richard Scamman and Ben Wattenberg, *The Real Majority* (Coward, New York, 1971) p. 32.

6. THE ASSASSINATION

1. Kimball, *Bobby Kennedy and the New Politics*, p. 148.

2. Kimball, *Bobby Kennedy and the New Politics*, p. 152.

3. Personal interview with Walter Fauntroy, 3 March 1985.

4. RFK to Roger Mudd, *CBS News*, March 1968, quoted in Hodgson, *American Melodrama*, p. 312.

5. Vanden Heuvel and Gwirtzman, *On His Own*, p. 184.

6. Vanden Heuvel and Gwirtzman, *On His Own*, p. 184.

7. Stein and Plimpton, *American Journey*, p. 327.

8. Stein and Plimpton, *American Journey*, p. 327.

9. Stein and Plimpton, *American Journey*, p. 328.

10. Witcover, *85 Days*, p. 148.

11. Romain Gary in *New York Times*, 7 June 1968; John Stewart in Stein and Plimpton, *American Journey*, p. 327.

12. Louis Heren in *The Times*, 6 June 1968.

13. Unnamed magazine quoted by Heren in *The Times*, 6 June 1968.
14. Stein and Plimpton, *American Journey*, p. 371.
15. John Pilger, *Heroes* (Jonathan Cape, London 1986) p. 129.
16. *The Times*, 7 June 1968. Schrade has since led the struggle to have Los Angeles Police Department records on the assassination made public and for the murder investigation to be reopened. With other assassination experts, Shrade believes that there may have been more than one gun fired at Kennedy that night and that Sirhan may have been part of a conspiracy.
17. His right eye was open, but the other was partially closed and within seconds his wife Ethel was kneeling at his side, urging people to stand back and give him room. A few days before, in Chinatown, Los Angeles, she had nearly panicked when firecrackers had gone off near the Kennedys' car, 'yet when the real thing came along, she was in control', reported one journalist. See *The Times*, 6 June 1968.
18. *New York Times*, 6 June 1968.
19. *The Listener*, 13 June 1968.
20. Pilger, *Heroes*, p. 127.
21. *The Times*, 6 June 1968.
22. Philip Melanson, *The Robert F. Kennedy Assassination* (Shapolsky, New York 1991) p. 313.
23. Melanson, *The RFK Assassination*, p. 65.
24. Melanson, *The RFK Assassination*, p. 66.
25. The LAPD took the door frames away and later explained they had been destroyed because they were 'too big to fit into a card file …': Melanson, *The RFK Assassination*, p. 176.
26. The police, keen that the girl in the polka-dot dress be accounted for, eventually produced someone they said fitted her description to explain the sightings. She was Kennedy supporter Cathy Fulmer, they said, who had been at the Ambassador that night and who witnesses had mistakenly thought was with Sirhan. In fact Cathy Fulmer admitted to reporters that she had not been wearing a polka-dot dress at all, but a polka-dot scarf, and she had not been within 30 or 40 feet of Sirhan all night. (See *The Times* June 8 1968). Nevertheless, by producing Fulmer the police maintained they had cleared up the mystery of the girl in the polka-dot dress.

The most compelling evidence for the girl in the polka-dot dress came from Sandra Serrano, who said she not only saw the girl but spoke to her immediately after the murder. Serrano was sitting on an outside staircase when a Mexican-American man with a woman in a polka-dot dress (whom she had seen with Sirhan earlier in the evening) ran past her shouting 'We shot him! We shot him!' Serrano asked: 'Who did you shoot?' and the woman in the polka-dot dress said 'Senator Kennedy' (see British TV Channel 4's *Secret History*, 22 August 1992).

Although it might appear unlikely that an assassin would immediately blurt out a confession to a complete stranger while making a
getaway, the exchange was witnessed by other people. A middle-aged
couple, the Bernsteins, approached LAPD Sergeant Paul Schraga as
he arrived at the scene and told him what had passed between Serrano
and the girl in the dress. Schraga immediately issued an all-points
bulletin (APB) on his radio to police in the area to look out for the two
suspects – one a woman in a polka-dot dress (see Melanson p. 99).
Schraga's APB was then cancelled by a senior officer, despite his
protests, and LAPD communications tapes reveal that the police
appeared unenthusiastic about pursuing potential accomplices. 'Dis-
regard the [APB] broadcast,' says one officer at 1.41 a.m. (about 80
minutes after Kennedy was shot). 'We got Rafer Johnson and Jesse
Unruh who were right next to him [Kennedy] and they only have one
man and don't want them to get anything started on a big conspiracy.'
(see Melanson, *The RFK Assassination*, p. 99).

Although Serrano stuck by her story despite vigorous bullying from
LAPD officers to get her to change it, the Bernsteins were never
found again. Sergeant Schraga had taken down their address and
passed it to headquarters, where it was misplaced. Schraga left the
LAPD the following year and now suspects CIA involvement in the
assassination as the best explanation of why the girl in the polka-dot
dress was allowed to escape (see Channel 4's *Secret History*).

27.   *Congressional Record*, 5 June 1968, p. 16044.
28.   *Congressional Record*, 5 June 1968, p. 16044.
29.   Photograph of page of notebook reproduced in Melanson, *The RFK
      Assassination*.
30.   Melanson, *The RFK Assassination*, p. 178.
31.   *The Times*, 6 June 1968.
32.   Melanson, *The RFK Assassination*, pp. 145–9, persuasively argues that
      'Sirhan's motive did not emerge immediately and clearly. Instead it
      was an evolutionary product of his sessions with the defense team.'
33.   Although first-degree murder carried a death sentence in California in
      1968, Sirhan adamantly refused to plead insanity and appeared more
      worried about being thought crazy than being found guilty. He
      insisted that his notebook not be brought up at the trial in case people
      thought he was insane. Sirhan therefore went ahead without an insan-
      ity plea, despite having no recollection of committing the crime, and
      was duly found guilty and sentenced to death. Before he could be sent
      to the gas chamber, however, the US Supreme Court ruled that capital
      punishment was unconstitutional, and so his sentence was commuted
      to life imprisonment.

      Sirhan was due for release in 1984, but the state refused to free him.
      Subsequent parole hearings have also proved unsuccessful, but Sirhan
      has stuck with the Arab nationalist motive for the killing and at

hearings presents himself as a reformed political fanatic who is now remorseful and no longer a threat to society. Should he plead diminished mental capacity, his chances of release could be even smaller, as the board might consider him an unpredictable psychotic. See Melanson, *The RFK Assassination*, p. 120.

34. *The Listener*, 13 June 1968.
35. Melanson, *The RFK Assassination*, p. 167.
36. Melanson, *The RFK Assassination*, pp. 172–6. See also John Marks, *The Search for the Manchurian Candidate: The CIA and Mind Control* (Allen Lane, New York 1979).
37. Robert Kaiser Blair, *RFK Must Die!* (E. P. Dutton, New York 1970) p. 212.
38. Martin Dillon, *Stone Cold* (Hutchinson, London 1992) describes the assassination of a suspected Republican activist Philip Fay in Northern Ireland in the 1980s by a Loyalist paramilitary agent Albert Walker Baker. 'When Fay fell to the ground Baker crouched over him and fired three bullets into his head behind his ear, a technique used by SAS and other covert military groupings around the world' (p. 39).
39. Melanson, *The RFK Assassination*, p. 153.
40. Melanson, *The RFK Assassination*, p. 154.
41. *The Times*, 8 June 1968.
42. *The Times*, 6 June 1968.
43. *The Times*, 6 June 1968.
44. *The Times*, 11 June 1968. Sirhan, however, was not Jordanian but Palestinian.
45. *The Times*, 7 June 1968.
46. Stein and Plimpton, *American Journey*, p. 385.
47. *The Times*, 11 June 1968.
48. Schlesinger, *RFK & His Times*, p. 875.
49. Personal interview, March 1985.

CONCLUSION

1. Witcover, *85 Days*, p. 342.
2. Hayden, *Reunion*, p. 18.
3. Tip O'Neill, *Man of the House* (Bodley Head, New York 1987) p. 329. Politicians inspired by Robert Kennedy include German activist Petra Kelly. Kelly, the leader of the Green movement which swept through Germany during the 1980s, had worked in Kennedy's senate office in Washington. She was found dead in her apartment in October 1992.
4. O'Neill, *Man of the House* p. 243.
5. Peter Edelman, quoted in Witcover, *85 Days*, p. 352.
6. Kennedy, *In His Own Words*, p. 414.
7. Gary Hart, quoted in Edwin O. Guthman and C. Richard Allen (eds), *RFK Collected Speeches* (Viking, New York 1993), p. xl.

8. Mario Cuomo, quoted in Guthman and Allen, *RFK Collected Speeches*, p. xliv.
9. *New York Times*, 8 October 1994.

BIBLIOGRAPHY

1. Emerson, 'The American Scholar', a speech to Harvard students delivered in Boston in 1837, from *The Norton Anthology of American Literature* (Norton, New York 1979).
2. Salinger, *With Kennedy*, p. 222.
3. Schlesinger, *A Thousand Days*, p. 245.
4. Witcover, *85 Days*, p. 306.
5. Witcover, *85 Days*, p. 321. The word 'day' or 'days' appears in the title of a remarkable number of works by and about the Kennedys. Perhaps 'day' is chosen for its sense of immediacy and urgency. Apart from Witcover's *85 Days*, there are plenty of examples. RFK's account of the Cuban missile crisis is, of course, *13 Days*. Schlesinger's history of JFK's White House is *A Thousand Days* (while his chapter on RFK's presidential campaign in *Robert Kennedy and His Times* is called 'The Long Day Wanes'), and a collection of RFK's speeches from 1968 is titled *A New Day*. An article by Theodore White (for *Life*) on RFK's last primary is called 'A Precious Last Day', while Richard Goodwin's article is titled 'A Day in June'. Ted Kennedy's book published to coincide with his 1980 presidential campaign is *Our Day and Generation* (ed. Henry Steele Commager, Simon and Schuster, New York 1979).
6. Newfield, *RFK: A Memoir*, p. 312.
7. Fairlie, *Kennedy Promise*, p. 180.
8. David Horowitz, *From Yalta to Vietnam* (Pelican, New York 1977) p. 278.
9. Hamby, *Liberalism and its Challengers*, p. 323.
10. Townsend in Witcover, *85 Days*, p. 346.
11. Reeves, *Question of Character*, p. 210.
12. Kennedy, *In His Own Words*, p. 185.
13. Kennedy, *In His Own Words*, p. 313.

Index